THE HENRY'S FORK

THE HENRY'S FORK

by Charles E. Brooks

LYONS & BURFORD, PUBLISHERS

Map by Paul Chinelli.

Printed in the United States of America

10/9/8/7/6/5/4/3/2

Library of Congress Cataloging-in-Publication Data

Brooks, Charles E., 1921–
    The Henry's Fork.

    "Nick Lyons books."
    Bibliography: p.
    1. Trout fishing—Idaho—Henrys Fork. 2. Fly fishing—Idaho—Henrys Fork. 3. Henrys Fork (Idaho)—History. 4. Henrys Fork (Idaho)—Description and travel.   I. Title.
SH688.U6B758 1986   799.1'755   86–3055
ISBN: 0-941130-94-X

CONTENTS

A map of the Henry's Fork Watershed appears on pages xii and xiii.

ACKNOWLEDGMENTS

I HAVE HAD THE HELP OF A GREAT MANY PEOPLE IN RESEARCHING THIS book: friends, neighbors, local people, and even people unknown to me personally, who sent messages through mutual friends. Too numerous to mention individually, I am grateful and appreciative and take this method of thanking them.

Those persons and organizations who provided extensive help and assistance are identified alphabetically below.

Bobbi Andreason

Bob and Emmy Lou Burnham

Bureau of Reclamation

Hal and Rosy Cameron

Bill and Louise Enget

Dean H. Green and James Allison, authors of *Idaho's Gateway to Yellowstone; The Island Park Story*

Mike and Sheralee Lawson

Bing Lempke

Dick Manus, Bureau of Land Management

Virgil Moore, Idaho State Fish and Game Department

Martin E. "Port" Portman

Bob Roher, Idaho Fish and Game Department

Dave Rydalch, North Fork Reservoir Company

Donna Garner Spainhower

Bob Spateholtz, Idaho Fish and Game Department

Jim Vermillion

University library personnel of California State University, Sacramento and Ricks College, Rexburg, Idaho. My debt to these two organizations is great. They not only furnished me with tons of research material, but helped me to find my way through their computer system in order to locate special volumes and documents.

INTRODUCTION

THE HENRY'S FORK OF THE SNAKE RIVER IS ITS FULL, OFFICIAL NAME. IT is one of the three or four top trout streams in the contiguous forty-eight states. It is also one of the most diverse and beautiful rivers anywhere. Its roots in American history go back almost to Lewis and Clark; one of the members of that expedition, John Colter, was the first white person to visit the Henry's Fork watershed although he did not actually see the river itself.

There is a considerable body of history associated with the river, some local, some national. In researching that history, I've come to some conclusions that differ from what is commonly accepted by historians.

History is the most inexact of disciplines. The history we read is someone's opinion of what happened at some time. Much of what we know is second, third, or fifth hand. Some of it, posing as fact, is now known to be fictional. Some history has been deliberately altered by later writers to reflect either an attitude or a fact that did not exist at the time of the incident in question. Scientific evidence is constantly changing what we know of geologic and cultural history. There will never be such a thing as a history that can be taken into court and defended as totally correct.

This is *not* a source work intended for use by scholars to expand on or to educate other scholars. It is a narrative of the life and times of a great trout stream, along with everything that has affected, or is affecting, it. Therefore, footnotes are minimally used. I have added appendices both on historical matters and on insects, artificial flies, and other matters which would be of interest only to certain devotees.

The changes affecting the river today are in some way affected by changes yesterday. The river changes as it runs toward its confluence with the Snake and its history changes as time moves ever onward. There will never be a time when either river or history stands still. At least, for the sake of the human race, whose continued existence depends on six inches of top-soil and the fact that it rains, I hope not. When rivers no longer flow to the sea, both man and his history will cease to exist.

I have utilized the resources of two educational institutions in researching this book and have spent four years in both academic and physical, on-site study. I have fished the river since 1948 and have lived for twenty years just two miles over the Continental Divide from its headwaters. Over those twenty years, increasing knowledge has led to a growing affection for the river and its watershed. I have become deeply attached to both.

I have noted that I am not the only one to be thus affected by the river and its environs. A continually growing number of people, residents and visitors, have come to regard the river with fondness and respect. Some are passionate in their love and defense of the area. Not all of those are fishers.

Fishers are, by and large, the major force involved in the river directly. And those who have fished it for years and noted changes in the watershed and the river are upset by the changes. This is normal; man resists change and often refuses to recognize and accept it. Fishers are among the most ardent in this respect.

Not all of the changes are for the worse. The Idaho Fish and Game Department has long been involved in stocking rivers with hatchery catchables. Only fairly recently has it been learned, through accumulated studies, that stocking is not beneficial to a fishery, it is actually harmful. This aspect is being addressed; for the last few years Henry's Fork has been improving as a fishery. And that will continue.

There has been improvement in other areas, too—small, but important. Residents and longtime visitors, both, are aware now of the dangers of environmental degradation and are working to prevent further damage and to reduce the impact of past damages. This same thing is going on countrywide, but it is a little more intense here. The results are encouraging. Although most efforts are presently aimed at saving and protecting the great beauty of the area, it is axiomatic that protection of natural scenic beauty almost surely benefits everything and everyone.

The Henry's Fork Foundation* was recently formed to further the efforts to protect this river and its environs from spoliation. It is not strictly an organization to protect the fishery. Many of its founders live here. They neither wish to see a beautiful river become a sewer, a conduit to pipe more irrigation water away from the area, nor to see rampant, uncontrolled building destroy the scenery.

Changes for the better will be slow, and difficult to see, day-by-day. But, looking back twenty years, or even ten, I can see that things are changing mostly for the better.

In the nearly forty years I have been acquainted with Henry's Fork, I have slowly become aware that it is an extremely diverse trout stream. Its upper reaches are a pleasant mountain brook, and when I fish that area I believe it to be the most satisfying such stretch that I know.

It is a bit more challenging and difficult than the meadow brook section flowing across most of Henry's Lake Flat. Here is where I go when I am troubled or restless or fatigued, because out in this mountain girt but completely pastoral area all sense of urgency leaves one.

*The Henry's Fork Foundation Inc., can be reached at: Box 61, Island Park, ID 83429.

The marsh-swamp section at the southern edge of the Flat has a brooding primordial aspect that arouses thoughts of dinosaurs and of earth's beginnings. It is the most difficult area of all to fish because normal fly-fishing methods cannot be used.

Some of the appeal of the glides and riffles above McCrae Bridge is reduced for me because of the number of homes along the banks, the constant coming and going of tourists, and the crowded resort atmosphere. I tend to return here in September, and later, when all is quiet and one can fish quietly with his thoughts.

The fast-water canyon sections—Coffee Pot, Box, and Cardiac canyons—have always had great appeal for me: practically no one else fished them much until a few years ago. I could and did think of them as *my part of the river*. It is different now. More fishers are finding these rampaging waters filled with huge trout to be much to their liking. That's all right—I like to think that others are just coming to discover what I knew all the time.

The more popular sections of the river—Last Chance to Riverside—are pleasant and fruitful miles of perhaps the most prolific trout water anywhere. I visit them mostly after the masses leave, when Green Drake Madness is over and Pale Morning Dun is queen. Most regulars agree with me, and thus I meet many old friends along here at this time. We talk and joke and hash over old times—then we speak with wonder of the fact that the fishing is better now than it was then. It is, in fact, getting better all the time.

The broad sweeping stretches of the river flowing through agricultural acres awaken mixed emotions. As a farm boy, these kinds of waters had strong appeal, and still do. But I now know what I only suspected then: that farming practices are sometimes not good for streams.

And of late, I've come to think of the river when it was new to whites and to remember that it was beaver and *not* trout that brought the first white adventurers to this area. I think of Colter and Henry, of Wyeth and De Smet, of the Shoshone and the Nez Percé. I hurt for what was done to the Indians—and the beaver—and I wonder if we are a better people now than we were then. I think we are.

Though this book is written from the standpoint of a fly fisher with over fifty years' experience, it is also the chronicle of the river and its watershed as seen by Indians, trappers, early settlers, and present-day residents and visitors.

This river, as most others in this country, is threatened by tunnel-vision progress. To those with this narrow-minded view, a river is useless unless developed. This means to them that any water that escapes their grasp and returns to the sea is wasted. To those opposing this view, who say "God save us from developers," I say "He won't. You will have to do it yourselves, with the help of other people."

So, you will find herein some hard-nosed ideas and some suggestions, as well as much information. Wherever credit is due, I take it. I also take the blame for whatever may be incorrect. It's my book and I'm responsible for it. I'm also responsible for the river and what happens to it. So are you.

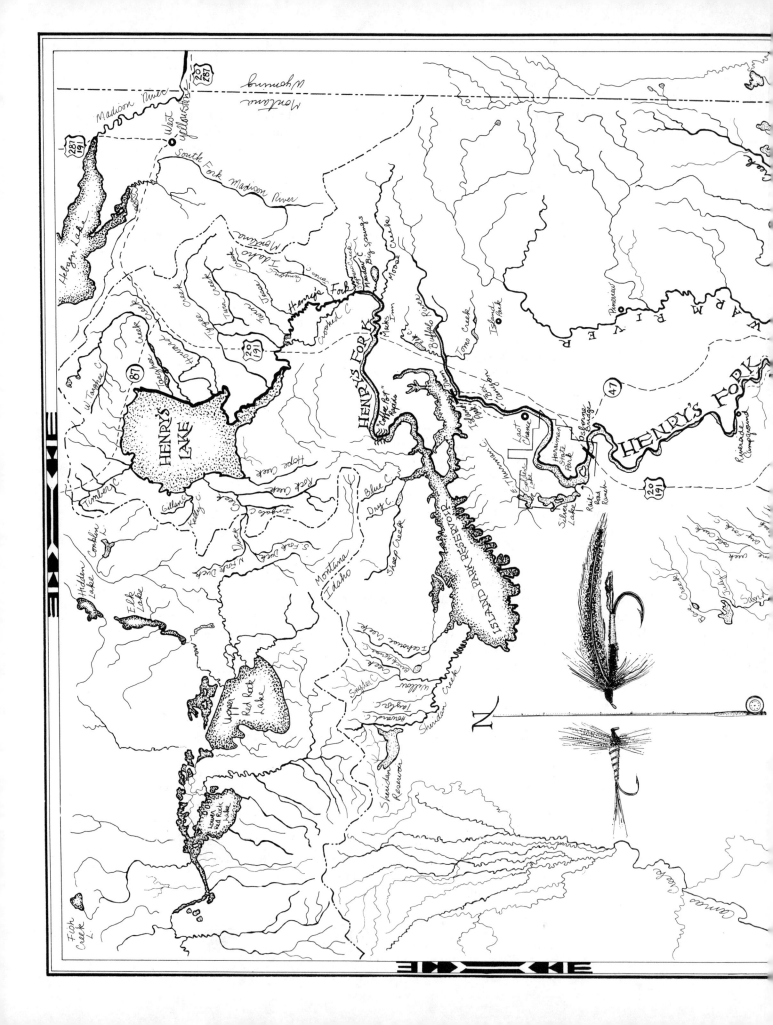

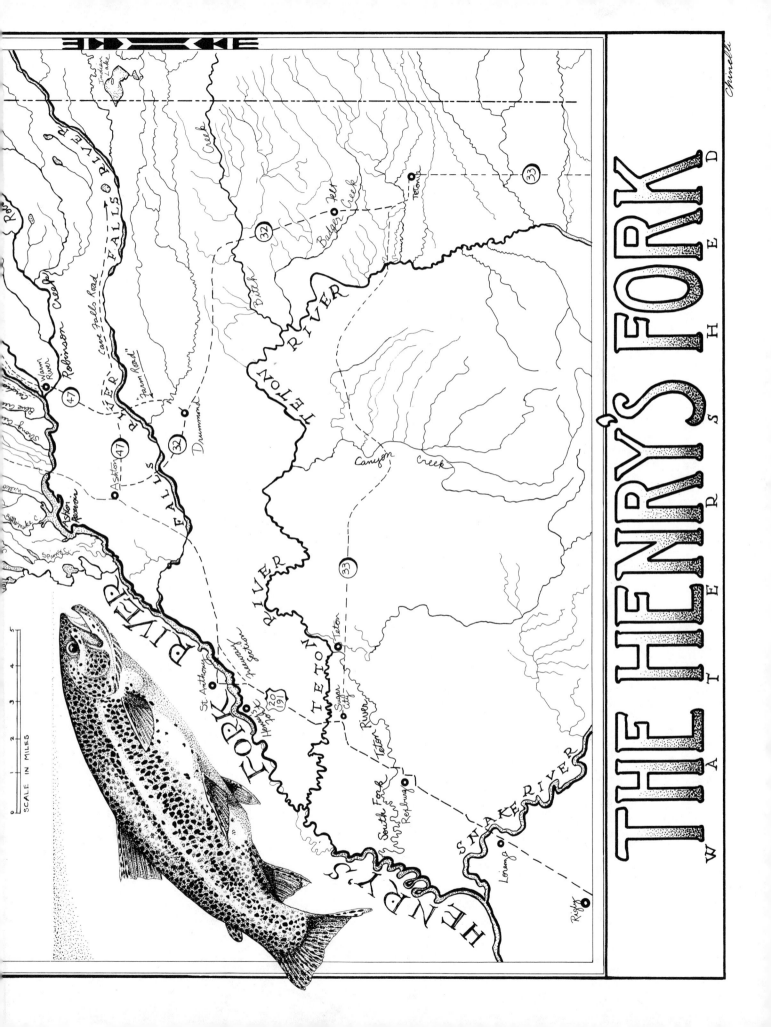

THE HENRY'S FORK

WATERSHED

ANDREW HENRY— UNLUCKY OR INCOMPETENT?

THE QUESTION OF ANDREW HENRY HAS BEEN DEBATED FOR OVER A HUN-
dred years by scholars and historians. Fishermen, however, are concerned
only with the fact that he was the first white person to discover and explore
what just may be the finest trout lake and river in the contiguous forty-eight
states.

Andrew Henry, 1775–1833, was born in Pennsylvania and moved to Missouri while a young man. In 1806 he was made a present of a grant of a lead
mine near Potosi, about eighty miles southwest of Saint Louis. This valuable
property made it possible for him to invest and become a partner in the
Missouri Fur Company in the spring of 1809. Henry's partners in this company were a band of giants in early Saint Louis history and the fur trade.
Among them were Manuel Lisa, earliest American fur trader on the upper
Missouri River; Pierre Menard and William Morrison, partners of Lisa in
that early venture; Benjamin Wilkinson, brother of James Wilkinson, Governor of Louisana Territory and intriguer with Aaron Burr; Pierre and Auguste Chouteau, who had traded and trapped to Santa Fe; Sylvestre
L'Abbadie; Reuben Lewis, brother of Merriwether Lewis; and William Clark,
not long back from the Lewis and Clark Expedition.

Henry was a tall, slender, blue-eyed man with dark hair. He was well
educated for the day and was fond of reading and of playing the violin. His
association with the Missouri Fur Company was his first such venture.

The Lisa party left Saint Louis in several groups in the spring/summer of
1809. There were about 450 men in thirteen keelboats, with some barges
and pirogues, bound up the Missouri River.

It might be well here to take some note of keelboat travel, which was the only way to move large loads on inland rivers before the coming of the steamboat. These boats, designed for moving freight and livestock, ran from thirty to eighty feet in length, were seven to ten feet wide at the deckline (thus, quite narrow), and drew three or four feet of water with about three feet of freeboard when loaded. There was usually a small cabin amidships for the keelboat captain.

Platforms inside along the gunwales, running the length of the vessel, were walkways for the keelboatmen: polers who propelled the boat upstream by planting a twenty-foot pole in the bottom, facing the stern, and walking. (Actually, the poler did not move in relation to where his pole was planted. As he walked sternward, the boat moved forward at the same speed, keeping the poler stationary.) When the stern was reached, the poler pulled up his pole and trotted forward to the front, turned, planted his pole, and walked the boat forward. Boats of seventy or eighty feet in length would have ten or more polers each side. This enormous manpower was necessary to propel a boat of twenty to thirty tons burden against a current. Thus, the Lisa group would have to be about 250–280 of these brawny hell-raisers along in 1809.

There were also about 100 trappers, 30 laborers—*engagees* to cook, clean, fetch firewood, and do other menial tasks—and a dozen or so administrators, most of them partners in the company. There were also some horses.

The limited records of the journey do not indicate if the horses were in some of the keelboats or barges or were ridden and driven along the bank. Nor do they say which of the men were in charge of which boat. Pierre Menard was known to be in one of the lead boats, and the Chouteaus were each in charge of one—but beyond this information, arrangements were vague.

The food of the keelboatmen was "fried hominy for breakfast, a slice of fat (salt) pork and biscuit for lunch, and a pot of mush with a pound of tallow for supper." I've eaten all of those for a good part of my boyhood, except the "pound of tallow." This baffles me. How was it prepared? Melted and poured over the mush like gravy? Ugh! Chopped into cubes and fried? Eaten raw, like an apple? However it was prepared, some notekeepers recorded that the food was *better* than keelboatmen usually got.

Even so, there was mutiny aboard over the food. Through very bad planning, most of the food was apparently in Lisa's boat, which left Saint Louis nearly a month after the first boats departed. By the time the first groups reached Fort Osage (near present Jefferson City) there was revolt and desertions. The trip threatened to be aborted before it was well started.

Menard and Henry were able to avert this by insisting on more food and better pay. This was typical of these two men, who were referred to by all who knew them as "honest, fair, just and compassionate." The need for this expressed accolade is found in the character of most other fur traders since cheating, chicanery, lying, and outright theft was common. (See Don Berry, *A Majority of Scoundrels*.)

Even with the intervention of Henry and Menard, there were numerous desertions. By the time the group ran almost completely out of food near present Council Bluffs, Iowa, they were too far from civilization for more to desert.

Hunters on horseback had been riding both banks, killing what game they could find, but their luck was not good. By the time the party had reached the mouth of the Platte River, near Saint Joseph, Missouri, they were being rationed to a quarter pound of meat a day and boiled corn (hominy) without salt. Since there were about 300 men in this first group, that quarter pound of meat daily added up to seventy-five pounds, or *only* about one deer a day. Still, the hunters could not do better.

The men were still rebellious. The work was murderous for the keelboat men, who would shove off from each night's encampment at daylight and pole through the day until nearly dark to the next night's camp.

These men were used to keelboating on the Ohio, or the Mississippi, relatively placid streams compared to the rambunctious Missouri. The Big Muddy,* called too thick to drink but too thin to plow, ran four to six miles an hour. This forced the boats to navigate close to shore or in slack water. *Cordelle* (rope tow), oars, and even sails were used to help the laboring boatmen. But the wind blew mostly downstream. And the work was dangerous. Overhanging trees swept the stern-facing polers overboard; most could not swim. *Sweepers* and *sawyers*—partially sunken trees bobbing in the current—came up under the boats and tore their bottoms out or turned them over. Sandbars were everywhere, grounding the boats. The *embarrass*— floating islands of logs, trees, brush, and debris, even dead buffalo—swept down on them and forced them to flee out of range. Sometimes these lodged on sandbars and built up to the point that the current on either side was too swift to run and a channel had to be chopped through the mess. This sometimes took days. The Big Muddy was a river to make strong men weep and rich men poor.

But the group doggedly persevered. Near the present South Dakota southern border, they dropped off an administrator (post manager) and some trade goods at the Arikara* (Uh-rik-uh-ruh) Village, as they did at the villages of the Sioux, Mandan, and Hidatsa (Minnetaree, also Gros Ventre, the current official name of this latter tribe).

The purpose of this was not so much to trade, since none of these tribes procured many furs, but to give them "face" to indicate that the traders considered them important and thus to placate them. Most of the time it worked.

At one of the Mandan villages they stopped, unloaded most of the boats, and built a permanent post called at first Fort Lisa, later Fort Mandan. This should not be confused with the Lewis and Clark Fort Mandan.

---

*275,000 *tons* of soil enter the Missouri River daily.

*Also called *Arikaree* and *Rees*.

There were six or eight Mandan villages strung out along the Missouri River from just south of Bismark, North Dakota, to near Williston, about fifty miles from the Montana-North Dakota border. The Mandan were agricultural: farming in the rich river-bottom land; raising corn, squash, and other crops; and living in earth lodges. They were only incidentally hunters and had been friendly with whites since 1738, when they were first visited by the French fur trader, La Verendrye. He had worked as far south as Pierre, South Dakota, and traded in the area off and on until 1743. The idea that he may have worked as far west as Yellowstone Park is now discarded. He was only in the area to trade, and at that early date there were no permanent Indian tribes in the area west of the Wyoming border to beyond the Rockies.

The post established by Lisa and company was near Stanton, North Dakota, about 140 miles southeast of Lewis and Clark's Fort Mandan, just downstream of Williston. Here most of the goods were unloaded, a stockade built, most keelboats were sent back to Saint Louis, and the party divided. Here also, they picked up the services of John Colter, the most experienced trapper and guide for the entire area north and west of Fort Mandan.

Colter, an original member of the Lewis and Clark Expedition, had left that explorers group in 1806 when it had returned to the Mandan Villages area and had joined two men who wanted to trap around the Yellowstone-Big Horn river confluence. He had a disagreement with his partners during the winter of 1806/1807 and had left them by canoe to return to Saint Louis. In July 1807, he met Manuel Lisa bound upriver to establish a trading post in the area Colter had just left. Colter had accepted employment with Lisa as a guide, and it was in this guise that he had agreed to meet with the Menard-Henry group to guide them to Fort Raymond (also known as Fort Lisa and Fort Remon) near the mouth of the Big Horn River, and later to Three Forks on the Missouri (See the John Colter chapter for further information on this most important of mountain men.) The party left Lisa's newly established Fort Mandan in two groups. Pierre Menard was in charge of the one keelboat that continued on, carrying engagees, supplies, equipment, and trade goods. Andrew Henry was in charge of the 100 or so trappers that Colter guided overland.

It is time to straighten out the relationship and positions of these two men, partners in the Missouri Fur Company and leaders of this particular brigade, historically the most influential on the fur trade.

Historians have taken differing views regarding which of the two was in charge of the brigade. The fact is, they both were, but of different aspects. Menard, often called Captain or Colonel (he was neither, but military titles were commonly given fur brigade leaders), was the chief administrator in charge of the business end: the post, the engagees, the supplies, and the day-to-day operations of the post. Henry was the field leader, who directed the operations of the trappers. In spite of the troubles which attended the operations of these two men, they were good friends and perfectly compatible. They were also fine men of unimpeachable personal integrity. But both were totally inexperienced in the kind of wilderness in which they were to operate. Also, they were the first to attempt to penetrate the stronghold of the ferocious Blackfeet. (The name of this tribe is Black*feet*. Those who call them Black*foot* Indians seem to think they were a tribe of one-legged Indians. One Indian is a Blackfeet, 100 Indians are Blackfeet.)

The two groups arrived at Fort Raymond in late October or early November 1809 and spent the winter hunting, yarning, and preparing for the spring trapping operations.

Beaver trapping was done in the spring, April-June, and in the fall, August-October. Beaver spend the winter months in their lodges, seldom venturing out, and thus are not available to trappers at this time. Then, snow, frozen beaver ponds, icy streams, and temperatures far below zero made trapping at this time absolute, pure hell—although some individual trappers did kill beaver in winter.

In March 1810, Henry and Menard with about eighty trappers and engagees set out on horseback with supply-laden packhorses for Three Forks. Colter was their guide. Near the Bozeman Pass area, between present Livingston and Bozeman, Montana, they were struck by an equinoctal blizzard, common even now in this part of the country. They holed up to ride out the blizzard and then, when it was over, moved on in the blinding sunshine that nearly always follows this spring storm. They suffered snow blindness so bad that some of the men begged to be shot and put out of their misery.

At this time, they encountered a large band of Crow Indians. This tribe is notorious for taking advantage of smaller or less well-armed groups. Yet, they presented the trappers the greatest kindness—showing them how to bathe their eyes with soothing herbal concoctions and how to make protective shields of wood utilizing narrow slits to see through—and generally took care of them until they had recovered their eyesight.

There has been much speculation about this incident because the actions of the Crow were so uncharacteristic. Some of this speculation is due to the fact that neither Henry nor Colter left any writings about themselves. (All we have is Colter's signature on an agreement with Lewis and Clark and Henry's on the agreements with his fur company partners, plus one letter from Henry to Francis Valle written while Henry was at Three Forks in 1810. This letter makes no mention of the snow blindness and later incidents.)

Leroy Hafen, perhaps the most indefatigable chronicler of mountain men, bemoans the fact that many of them couldn't or didn't write and left neither letters nor journals. Thus, says Hafen, what we know of many of the important figures of this time (1800–1845) is second, third, or fifth hand.

It has always puzzled me that otherwise competent historians are willing to speculate about things that they seem unwilling or unable to logically deduce from other known events.

It has been known for years that Colter travelled with a band of Crow Indians in the Gallatin Valley in September 1808 and that they were set upon by a band of Blackfeet. Colter was forced to defend himself from the Blackfeet—which he did with great skill, allowing the Crow to inflict a defeat on their sworn enemies—thus earning him the undying enmity of the Blackfeet and the loyalty of the Crow.

It is also known that Colter had spent the winters of 1806/07 and 1807/08 among the Crow and had dealt extensively with them. Thus it is logical to deduce that some of the Crow band who came upon the trappers in their snow blindness were those who knew and were friendly with Colter and perhaps had even fought the Blackfeet with him. The probability that this is what happened is far stronger than mere speculation and would certainly account for the uncharacteristic actions of the Crow.

Henry and Menard, with Colter and the rest of the band, moved on to Three Forks when they were able to travel, arriving there on 3 April 1810. They built a stockade and post building for sheltering supplies and the beaver pelts they expected to obtain. And they set to trapping.

They found trouble with the Blackfeet almost at once, and this continued all the time they remained at Three Forks.

On April 12th they were attacked by the Blackfeet, who killed five trappers, stole seven horses, and took the dead trapper's traps, furs, guns, and ammunition. Just a few days later, three more trappers were killed and horses and goods lost.

Colter left for Saint Louis on 22 April 1810. Some historians have alleged that he was intimidated by the Blackfeet. However, the current view is that he had contracted only to guide the Henry-Menard group to Three Forks and had intended to return after seeing them settled.

The group was under almost constant attack. Blackfeet raided every few days. Grizzlies got into their food supplies, stole beaver out of traps, charged the trappers, made off with fresh-killed beavers before they could be skinned, and generally added to the trappers' miseries.

Pierre Menard and a small group departed for Fort Raymond in early July. Here again, historians have postulated that he became discouraged with the constant grizzly-Indian troubles and because they were low on food. Later research has revealed that this was a planned withdrawal: Menard returned with the spring's catch to take over Fort Raymond and to send a report to his partners farther down the Missouri and in Saint Louis.

The Blackfeet attacks had caused the trappers to trap in small groups, rather than singly, as was the custom. But one trapper, George Drouillard (Drewyer to the trappers) felt himself too experienced to be caught out by the Blackfeet, and he said so. He had, with Colter, been one of the chief hunters for the Lewis and Clark Expedition and had spent the winter of 1808/09 trapping alone in the upper Big Horn River area. Drouillard felt that he could never be surprised by Indian raiders. He lost his life the first day he went out alone.

This is presumed to have been the clincher in Henry's deciding to leave the area. But we have no explanation of why he went up the Madison instead of returning by a route that he knew: up the Gallatin and over Bozeman Pass. One theory offered is that, due to some misjudgment, only enough powder and lead were carried to provide food, but not to fight Indians *and* procure game. Whatever the reason, Henry did go up the Madison, over what is now Raynolds Pass, past the lake and down the river that now bear his name.

On this trip, before crossing Raynolds Pass, Crow Indians stole thirty of the group's horses. Since this was the same group that the Crow had aided in their snow blindness some three to four months earlier, it strengthens the probability that it was Colter, and not Henry's group in general, to whom was extended earlier that friendly gesture.

Henry and his group traveled down the river to about five miles beyond what is now the town of Saint Anthony, Idaho. Here they constructed a "fort" which became known as Fort Henry, although it little resembled and never was a military structure, consisting of only some huts built of cottonwood logs, some two to three hundred yards from the river on a small spring creek.

Excavations by interested scholars in 1925 and 1933 at the site uncovered artifacts that confirmed that both Henry and Wilson Price Hunt had spent time here. Stones on which were carved the names of "A. Henry, J. Hoback, P. McBride, B. Jackson and L. Cather," bearing the date 1810, have been found in other areas a few miles away. Others bearing the carved names: A. Henry, J. Day, and W. Weir, also with the date 1810, were found near Menan Buttes, twenty-five miles from Fort Henry. Actual artifacts found on the fort site were a flintlock rifle barrel, an axe, a chain, a medallion, and three stones, carved: "Gov. Camp 1811—H. Wells," "Al the cook but nothing to cook," and "Ft. Henry 1811 by Cap Hunt."

The medallion is interesting because its design tells something of its date of manufacture. It was of bronze, the size of the palm of a hand, shield-shaped, with sixteen stars in an arc, under which were two American flags with sixteen stars each, and a pair of crossed cutlasses and pistols. The stars on the flags indicate that the medallion was struck *after* 1 June 1796, when Tennessee became the sixteenth state, but before 19 February 1803, when Ohio became the seventeenth. Two of the men in Henry's group were known to be from Tennessee. Hoback, McBride, Jackson, Cather, Day, and Weir, whose names were carved on the stones found, were known members of the Henry force. Thus, the site of the fort and the fact that the stones bore names of members of the group are established facts.

In spite of its location being found long ago, the site of Fort Henry was not marked until just a few years ago—and this marker was put on the road-side about 300 yards a little north of west of the actual site. When Mike Lawson and I set out to photograph the site in September 1983, we were unable to locate it with certainty. I photographed several locations that seemed likely, including a mound near a little creek that looked as though some digging had taken place there. This was the spot that Mike believed to be the fort site.

There then came one of those fortunate coincidences that seem to come along every time I research a book. The only reachable television stations from my Montana home, two miles over Targhee Pass from the Henry's Fork watershed, are in Idaho Falls. One of them, each Sunday in summer, has a five-minute segment on local history conducted by narrator Quincy Jensen. Two Sundays after Mike and I visited the area, Jensen did a segment on Fort Henry, and in his research, he had gotten hold of Dr. Merrill Beal, eminent Southeast Idaho historian, and Louis Clements, both of whom had previously located the Fort Henry site. Clements, along with the son of the property owner, who had been shown the site in the 1930s, took Jensen and his television cameras to the little mound beside the creek that Mike had identified as the probable place. The television cameraman photographed the site from the exact spot where I had stood with Mike to take my pictures.

Now we come to the most puzzling time in Henry's fur trading career and the one some historians cite as illustrating that he was incompetent. Henry and his group had left the Three Forks area in mid-July 1810. The trail distance over the route they took—up the Madison, over Raynolds Pass, past the lake and down the river to where they built the fort—is about 180 miles. Traveling on horseback, it should not have taken more than ten days to make the trip. There are no rugged areas, no steep climbs, no real difficulties anywhere along the way.

Some of the group later told other persons, including Wilson Price Hunt, that Henry and his group reached the Fort Henry area in late July. That is reasonable and consistent with known facts.

So, they arrived in mid-summer to build some shelters and spend the winter. They had a minimum of two to three months to procure food for the winter. There was known to be game in the area—deer, elk, antelope, and some buffalo. Yet, the group came near to starving and survived only by eating some of their horses. Remember the stone found at the site with the message "Al the cook but nothing to cook"? That had to be Henry's cook since the stone was found at the site of the fort and the only other group known to have visited the site was that of Hunt in 1811, and Hunt's group was well supplied with food while at Fort Henry. So, the question is: Why? Why a starving winter in the midst of good game country two or three months before the snows came?

We now get back to the theory that the group left Fort Raymond on the Bighorn without enough powder and lead to last them through the year. An implication that this may have been the case involves three of Henry's men who met Hunt in 1811. These were Hoback, Robinson, and Reznor, who advised Hunt not to try to reach the Columbia by the Lewis and Clark route, but to go back the way they had come from Fort Henry: across Wyoming to Union Pass, down the Hoback River canyon, across the main Snake River and Teton Basin (Pierre's Hole), and so to Fort Henry. Hunt took their advice and found it worthwhile. Hunt's records imply but do not say directly that the men were nearly destitute when he met them on the Missouri near current Pierre, South Dakota, in mid-summer 1811.

The men did tell Hunt that the winter of 1810/11 at Fort Henry was very cold with deep snow, and that they had eaten some of their horses to avoid starvation. But the *why* is missing from Hunt's and all other records I can find. On another note, which we will tackle later, the same thing was to happen to Hunt in the fall of 1811.

Though it may have been that Henry expected further Indian troubles and saved ammunition for a future battle, this is not borne out by other evidence. Carved stones bearing the names of members of the group, including Henry himself, were found twenty miles east of Fort Henry, others were found twenty-five miles southwest of the fort. Thus the men roamed rather widely and were not confined to the fort area for fear of Indian attack.

The limited information we have on the Shoshone and Bannock tribes indicates that the nearest any of these wintered to Fort Henry was some fifty miles to the west and that most of the groups of both tribes wintered farther west and south of that. None of the survivors of the Fort Henry group ever told anyone else of any Indian troubles while at Fort Henry. So why did this group come near to starving in a peaceful area well supplied with both large and small game? We shall probably never know.

When Henry and his group departed in the spring of 1811, there is evidence of a disagreement among them. One group left the main body and went south, heading for the *Spanish Waters* as the area of southern Utah, southern Colorado, and New Mexico was known. Hoback, Robinson, and Reznor went across Teton Basin and Teton Pass, up the Hoback Canyon, crossed the Continental Divide at Union Pass, across Wyoming and South Dakota to the Missouri River, where they encountered Hunt.

Henry, as usual, has left us in the dark about how he returned. Piecing the few available clues together, historians seem to believe that he returned up Henry's Fork, across Raynold's Pass, down the Madison to about the mouth of Beartrap Canyon, turned east over Bozeman Pass and on to the Mandan Village area, where he met and turned over forty packs of beaver (about one-tenth a normal years catch) to Lisa in September 1811.

While Henry was at Three Forks in the summer of 1810, one of Lisa's posts, at Cedar Island, in Sioux territory, burned down with the loss of about $15,000 in beaver pelts stored there for a later shipment down river. Lisa asked Henry and his remaining men to rebuild this post before they returned to Saint Louis. Henry did this, returned to Saint Louis, and got out of the fur trade for some ten years. But he had advised Lisa and others that a route to Idaho, Oregon, and the mouth of the Columbia—all called Oregon Territory then—was better reached by going across Wyoming to the Teton Basin and on west. This is the route that Hoback, Robinson, and Reznor advised Hunt to take, but we are again in the dark as to how Henry knew of it. He also is said to have suggested that a wagon route could be established up the Yellowstone, over Bozeman Pass, up the Madison, over Raynolds Pass, and on to the Columbia.

Henry had under his charge, during the period 1809-11, various groups of trappers running from fifty to as many as eighty men. In that three-year period, twenty-seven of those trappers died or were killed, although some had already left his group before their deaths. But no charge of incompetency was ever raised against him, though one Thomas James left a journal in which he called Henry "inexperienced" while acknowledging his other qualities.

In 1812, Henry became an officer in the 6th Regiment, served through the War of 1812, and was separated at the close of it as a major, a title by which he was known thereafter.

He is thought to have stayed close to his lead mine holdings near Potosi for the next few years. There are records of his activities in Sainte Genevieve County indicating that he served on juries and held minor civic posts.

In 1822, he joined with William Ashley in another fur trade adventure, and he and Ashley led back to the upper Missouri what Clarence A. Vandiveer, in *Fur Trade and Early Western Exploration,* called "the most significant group of continental explorers ever brought together." Among them were Jim Bridger, on his first trapping trip at age nineteen, Thomas Fitzpatrick (Broken Hand), Hugh Glass (*The Saga of Hugh Glass*), David Jackson (Jackson's Hole), Etienne Provost (Provo, Utah), Jedediah and Thomas Smith (Peg Leg), William and Milton Sublette, Louis Vasquez, and others, including Manuel Alvarez, who later became U.S. Consul to Mexico at Santa Fe. Nearly all of this group, though no longer with Henry, would become involved in the Battle of Pierre's Hole in 1832.

Henry, before he would join Ashley, insisted on terms for his trappers that were the most liberal and generous of the era, and which other traders were forced to meet in order to attract first-class men.

These "free" trappers were to get one-half of all the furs they trapped and were furnished traps, powder, lead, guns, and all ordinary supplies at no charge. For this they were expected to help build and defend the post and turn in the other half of their furs. The half they were allowed to keep would then be purchased at Saint Louis prices.

The expedition started up the Missouri in April 1822 in several groups. Henry's usual luck held when quite early in the trip one keelboat with a $10,000 cargo was smashed and sank. The party reached the mouth of the Yellowstone, about 2,100 miles upstream, in October, averaging about 350 miles a month or more than 10 miles a day. This was really excellent time for this trip. But before they reached the Yellowstone a group of Assinaboine Indians raided one of their camps at night and made off with thirty-five horses.

A fort was built as a base at the confluence of the Yellowstone and the Missouri. Then Henry and his group moved overland to near the mouth of the Musselshell River (on the Missouri) and built another post like Fort Henry (Saint Anthony), consisting of four log huts and a stockade. Here, Henry's group wintered.

In April 1823 Henry sent a group of eleven men toward Three Forks, along the Missouri, a distance of about 400 miles. This group was attacked by Blackfeet beyond Fort Benton, and four men were killed.

Shortly after this Henry received word that Ashley was besieged by the Arikara farther down the Missouri, over 300 miles in the opposite direction. Henry and his men rushed to the aid of Ashley, who was being aided also by an Army contingent. Although the Arikara were routed, the Henry-Ashley group lost fourteen men, and because of the ineptitude and interference of the army commander, no attempt was made to follow and destroy the intractably hostile Arikara.

This enraged the Mandan, on whom the Arikara had preyed for years, and, in anger, they fired on Henry's group, and two more men were killed. Then, on the way back overland, Hugh Glass was attacked by a grizzly and mauled so savagely that it was considered that he would soon die. His pelvis was broken, one leg also, and his back lacerated so that the pleura (membrane encasing the lungs) could be seen through holes in broken ribs. Two men were left to attend Glass until he died, thought to be only a matter of hours. One of these two was believed to have been the nineteen-year-old Jim Bridger.

Glass lingered on, lying on a blanket, being guarded by the two. He didn't regain consciousness, and after four or five days, fearing attack by the Arikara, the two men rode to rejoin Henry taking Glass' horse and rifle, but leaving the unconscious man his knife and his blanket. (Some historians do not mention the knife).

The story of Hugh's recovery and his 250-mile, seven-week crawl through barren territory swarming with angry Indians is told factually in *The Saga of Hugh Glass,* and fictionally in *Lord Grizzly*—both exciting narratives of an absolutely incredible adventure. The indomitable ex-sailor lived to go on a manhunt for the two who abandoned him.

The fall following this, Henry, after returning to the Musselshell, then transferring to the Yellowstone, got in an extremely good season, and a better one in the spring, after which he returned to Saint Louis and left the fur business for good.

He left behind knowledge of how to reach the area west of the Rockies over a shorter distance and easier travel than the Lewis and Clark route, and he left the trappers better off financially than he found them. These are the things that historians judge to be his accomplishments. But fishermen who fish Henry's Fork and Henry's Lake will remember his discovery of these long after his other deeds are forgotten, and they will keep alive his memory.

An Afternote: Some historians have mistaken Andrew Henry for two other Henrys, uncle and nephew, both named *Alexander,* and both in the fur trade, mostly in Canada. The nephew was an employee of the infamous North West Company, circa 1780–1790, and wrote a journal that was published as *New Light on the Early History of the Greater North-West* (3 vols.) in 1797. I can find no record that either of these men were ever in the fur business in the U.S. or that they were ever west of the Rocky Mountains.

2

FROM THE LAKE
TO THE SNAKE

HENRY'S LAKE LIES IN A HAIRPIN BEND OF THE CONTINENTAL DIVIDE, THE open end of the hairpin facing south. It is perhaps the finest trout lake in the contiguous forty-eight states. The Henry's Fork of the Snake River runs out of it.

There is a popular fallacy that some rivers originate from lakes. Not so—all rivers, wherever they exist, are born in the mountains. It may be that some seem to spring full blown out of the ground and to run off as a river, but the waters that feed them fell as rain or snow in mountains, sometimes many miles away as we will see later.

The mountain ranges surrounding the lake are, on the east, the Henry's Lake mountains (on the eastern slope of which I live), the Gravelly Range to the north, and the Centennial Mountains to the west, including a long spur that pushes south along the lake.

These mountains are the walls of an old volcanic caldera, said to be the largest in the world. It is about twenty by forty miles across and, strangely, is a part of a geologic feature known as the Snake River Plain.

The Snake River Plain is a 350 mile long crescent of volcanic lava flows stretching from the northeast corner of Yellowstone Lake to just beyond Twin Falls, Idaho. From Ashton Bench, about forty miles south of Henry's Lake, to the Twin Falls area, the Plain flanks the Snake River and looks more or less like a plain. But the section from the Bench through the caldera and on to beyond Yellowstone Lake is some thousands of feet higher than the rest of Snake River Plain, and it is broken and laced with mountain ranges.

The reason is, that for about the past million years, the area from Ashton Bench to Yellowstone Lake has been rising a few millimeters a year and the rest of the plain has been sinking a few millimeters a year. The difference has amounted to only about a quarter inch a year, which doesn't sound like much. But over a million years, that difference is more than 20,000 feet. Glacial and other types of erosion around the lake have reduced the dif-

Henry's Lake and the Centennial Mountains on a calm day.

ferences to less than 10,000 feet, but it is that difference which gives the river its character and quality.

The region in which the lake lies, and where the river begins, is known as the Island Park Caldera. Some geologists believe this area was still volcanically active only 2,000 years ago—much more recently than the rest of the Snake River Plain, although the lava in both areas is basalt.

Shortly after the volcanoes became quiescent, glaciers appeared in the mountains and pushed out onto the area known as Henry's Lake Flat. These glaciers were of short duration. Their quick melting caused them to slide south, gouging out the lake bed and pushing a large mound of debris ahead. This debris reached the Mesa Falls area, and it was one of the factors creating the falls. The river bed was also moved by the glacier but not so much as it was in previous eras when lava filled the river and forced it to create a new channel some miles to the east.

The entire Snake River Plain, from beyond Yellowstone Lake to the region of King Hill, Idaho, is composed of lava, 2,000–3,000 feet thick, lying on top of much thicker sedimentary rock which is impervious to water. Old river channels lie beneath this lava and on the sedimentary rock. This is an important geologic condition, and a strange one.

How strange? There are over thirty streams, some of them good-sized rivers, that originate in the mountain ranges on the north edge of the Snake River Plain. But for 250 miles of Snake River run, the only river or stream that enters the main river *from the north* is the Henry's Fork. The rest of these, including fine large rivers such as Little Lost River, Big Lost River, Birch Creek, and Cottonwood and Camas Creeks, run out of the mountains onto the plain and disappear.

Where does this immense amount of water—more than one million acre-feet per year, over three hundred twenty billion gallons—go? Some of it emerges from the Hagerman area called Thousand Springs, a few miles from Twin Falls. And 480,000 gallons a day, about 175 million gallons a year, comes up at Big Springs and runs into Henry's Fork twelve miles from the outlet at the lake, more than tripling the river's size. This section of Idaho has more large springs than any other known area, and this contributes mightily to the quality of trout streams in the area.

Seven or eight streams, many of them spring fed, emerge from the mountains and help form the lake. I say *help* because there are large springs in the lake itself and these are beneficial in summer, keeping the lake cool, and in winter, keeping some water open and preventing winter kill of trout.

These streams—mainly Targhee, Howard, Hatchery, Timber, Hope, Duck, Gillan, and Kelly creeks—are all located on private land. They are spawning streams for trout from the lake, and this poses problems which have affected the fishery. We will cover this in detail later.

The lake itself is about 2½ miles wide and four miles long, with its long axis lying north-south. It is a shallow lake that *averaged* only five feet deep before a dam in the mid-1920s raised the level.

The outlet is on the south end of the lake and the river runs across the center of Henry's Lake Flat. The mountains encircle the lake, close by, on three sides. Scores of small creeks run across the flat and into the river. Scores of springs emerge from a few feet to a few hundred yards from the river and also run into it. But the fishermen, noting all this water running into the river, will also notice that it does not seem to get much, if any, larger.

Where does this water go? Over its 120 mile length, Henry's Fork *loses* 700,000 acre-feet—over 200 *billion* gallons—of water yearly into the Snake River Plain aquifer. Water flowing over cracks and fissures in the river bed goes down into the aquifer to appear later many miles away, or to remain deep in the porous lava underlying the plain. There are over 100 *cubic miles* of water held in the lavas of the Snake River Plain.

Because of the immense amount of water running onto Henry's Lake Flat, the meadows, which are extensive, are marshy and boggy most of the summer. There are willows along the stream at the outlet to a mile downstream, and also at the southern edge of Henry's Lake Flat. By and large, the river here is a meadow stream.

Just beyond the edge of the Flat, the river enters the dense lodgepole pine forest which caused trappers of the 1820–40 era to call the Island Park area "The Piny Woods." Then it turns sharply right, back to the west, and is immediately joined by the 480,000-gallon daily flow of Big Springs Outlet, which more than triples its size.

From here, down past the resort area of Mack's Inn, past the Flat Rock Club, and on to the head of Coffee Pot Rapids, the river runs west and is a large mountain trout stream of deep runs, pools, and long, bedrock-bottomed riffles.

At Coffee Pot Rapids, the river resumes its southerly flow through a short, deep canyon (called by some, Cardiac Canyon, although the true Cardiac Canyon is miles downstream). Then there is a short, placid run under McCrea's Bridge and into Island Park Reservoir.

Island Park Reservoir is unique in that its long axis, some ten miles long, lies *across* the flow of the river, which emerges below the dam and into Box Canyon, one of the best, if not *the* best, fast-water trout-fishing areas in the lower forty-eight states. Trout of eighteen pounds have been caught here, and fish of eight to ten pounds, most every year.

The Box, as it is affectionately called by us locals, is only about 2½ miles long, but it is a splendid large-trout fishery. Below it are the resort residential areas of Box Canyon and Henry's Fork villages, with splendid long runs of moderately deep water. Then comes the important commercial village of Last Chance with accommodations and splendid fly shops, plus the two-mile stretch of Last Chance Run leading into Railroad Ranch (Harriman State Park). This is the most heavily fished area of the river (Last Chance Run) and rightly so. There is no other such trout fishery in the nation so prolific and of such quality, so accessible. Its regulars, and they are legion, tend to be a little possessive and haughty about their water. But they will make room for a stranger, and if he appears to need help, will render it willingly. They who fish here are ladies and gentlemen in the best sense.

Harriman State Park is synonomous with Railroad Ranch to the fly fisher. There is almost five miles of the finest fly fishing water anywhere, with everything a trout needs to make it happy and prosperous. There is an abundance of cover provided by the floating and submerged weeds and more species of insects than any place I know. But these things, so beneficial to the trout, make it difficult for the fisherman. The fish are provided a banquet almost daily, and it takes a good and knowledgeable fly fisher to succeed here.

Although the water leading down to and under the Highway 191 bridge (Osborne Bridge) is part of Harriman State Park, it is not generally considered *Ranch Water* by the regulars who fish it. It is somewhat easier to fish than the water in the heart of the Ranch, but the fish are somewhat smaller.

Beyond the bridge, around a couple of big curves, the river flows broad, smooth, and easily waded or floated. Two miles further on it traverses the little subdivision of Pinehaven, which started out as a fishing club. The water here—a medium-deep, bottom-channeled run, well-weeded—is a truly excellent piece of water, the last of its kind for miles.

At the lower end of Pinehaven, the river begins to trot, and its bed begins to be filled with stones and large boulders. At Riverside, two miles downstream, the trot has become a restrained gallop which takes it all the way to Sheep Falls, seven miles of river run downstream.

Pitching over the bedrock breakover that is Sheep Falls, and racing down a long, rock-bluff-flanked chute, the river roars into the canyon which stretches twelve miles to the confluence with Warm River. Just which part of this canyon is the *real* Cardiac Canyon is a matter of opinion. Having been down into and climbed out of the canyon several places in those twelve miles, I can assure you that anyplace along its length will do just fine if a heart attack is what you're looking for.

Warm River and its major tributary, Robinson Creek, enter the main river at a point where it undergoes a major character change. It leaves the canyon and cuts along the southeastern edge of Ashton Bench, which is the edge of Island Park Caldera, and emerges onto the floor of an immense broad basin. Through this basin runs two more of the Henry's Fork's major tributaries, Falls and Teton rivers—both excellent trout streams. Henry's Fork is now a very large flatland trout stream: bigger, warmer, and more silt laden as it cuts through farmland.

The river runs generally westward along the Bench edge for seven or eight miles, then turns south into Ashton Reservoir, a three-mile-long lake for generating electric power. It is thus operated differently and has different effects on the river than Henry's Lake Dam and Island Park Dam, both of which are purely irrigation dams.

Coming out from beneath Ashton Dam the river is much cooler, and for the next several miles it is a really excellent large trout stream, although it now begins to have more species and more coarse fish than above the dam. It is a little over six miles of river run to the confluence with Falls River. This tributary is warmer and more turbid than the main river at this point, but there still exists several miles of good trout fishing and some very large trout are taken. A fifteen-pound brown came out of this section in 1982. Good trout fishing extends twenty or so miles further downstream to well below Saint Anthony and Old Fort Henry.

Trout become scarce from the mouth of the Teton River's north branch, twenty miles from where Henry's Fork joins the main Snake. The Teton enters Henry's Fork as two branches, the south branch coming in nine or ten miles downstream of the north branch.

For the thirty or so miles of river run downstream of Saint Anthony, the Henry's Fork is very much a low-gradient, braided, delta-type stream, with scores of side channels, islands, sloughs and blind cutoffs, and marshy areas. It is further degraded by weirs, diversion wing dams, canals leaving and entering, and the runoff from irrigated farms. It is less a trout stream, here, than a source of water supply. It supports an excellent coarse fishery that is probably underutilized. It enters the Snake River through several ever-changing channels at the base of Menan Buttes. In 120 miles of river run it has dropped 1,672 feet at an average rate of 13.9 feet per mile and has changed from a high mountain trout stream to a river of commerce, subdued and changed to support a changing civilization.

Its character and quality have also changed as well as its appearance. The finest mountain trout stream in the country is now just a tributary to the main Snake River, which itself is the largest tributary of the Columbia.

Our trip has been swift and for the purpose of getting a quick overall look from Henry's Lake down. When we go hence and return thither in following chapters, you will be able to orient the area under discussion with the stream as a whole. Also, we must look at people and places, for they are important to the river—what it has been, what it will be.

3

ON THE FLAT

HENRY'S LAKE FLAT IS THE HEART OF THE ISLAND PARK CALDERA. ON the flat lies Henry's Lake, and the outlet of the lake is the headwaters of the Henry's Fork River. You will now and then find this stream referred to as the "North Fork of the Snake." This is the result of settlers in the area constantly trying to change the names of areas into which they move. But the name Henry's Fork was long established before any settlers arrived.

The lake is shaped like a shallow bowl. Before it was dammed in the 1920s it averaged only five feet deep. The dam raised the level of the lake sixteen feet but increased the average depth only to twelve feet. The reason is that the rising water pushed out onto the flat and created large areas of very shallow water.

It is perhaps the finest trout fishing lake in the contiguous forty-eight states. One says "perhaps" because these things cannot be measured like a piece of string.

The trout originally in the lake were Snake River cutthroat. Rainbow trout got into the lake, probably around 1900, from George Rea's private hatchery. The rainbow and the cutthroat are close cousins, and their interbreeding resulted in the famous Henry's Lake hybrid, now considered the lake's prime anglers' fish, although there are those that favor the large brook trout found in the lake.

The *exact* origin of these brookies is under dispute. In all probability they escaped from Rea's hatchery, as did the rainbows. But whether it was Rea who established them, or A. S. Trude, who took over Rea's holdings when the latter went bankrupt in 1902, is not known precisely.

Rea homesteaded the Shotgun Valley area in 1878 and established a commercial trout (rainbow) hatchery on a spring creek near his house in 1893–94.* The waters of this creek—and some of the trout—eventually found their way into the Henry's Fork. In a letter to a friend and lawyer, James Hawley, dated June 1897, Rea speaks of hatching 5,000 *brook trout* eggs in his hatchery. Since the dams on Rea's rearing ponds were not breached until sometime after this, it is probable that his was the original brook trout stock into the river and, eventually, in the lake.

*Joe Sherwood had a rainbow hatchery on the lake in 1891–92.

18

South Arm of Henry's Lake showing State Campground.

According to Dave Rydalch, current manager of the dam on Henry's Lake for the North Fork Reservoir Company, during the 1931–32 drought years the dam gate was left open to feed irrigation water to farmers downstream and the brook trout showed up in the lake for the first time shortly thereafter. The lake is a rich, extremely well-nourished lake with an enormous insect population, and the brookies flourished. A seven-pound-four-ounce brookie was taken from the lake on a damsel nymph pattern in the 1950s; many of five pounds and over have been caught since then. Rainbows of eighteen to twenty-two pounds were caught from the lake in the 1940s and 1950s on flies—so it wasn't only the brookies that did well. Since the mid-1960s it is the rainbow-cutthroat hybrid that is capturing much of the attention.

The Idaho Fish and Game Department first started emphasizing the breeding and stocking of the hybrids in 1950. They had occurred randomly due to natural crossbreeding before that, and their qualities for the angler are such that they became the favorite of fish and game biologists. The biologists have been caught in a bind with demands from fishermen wanting more and bigger hybrids, and the fact that there must be an undiluted gene pool of pure cutthroats in order to insure continuation of the program. They have struggled, but by hard work and devotion above and beyond plain duty, they are winning the battle to maintain both a pure gene pool and a quality hybrid fishery.

I must here devote a few words to the young fisheries biologists of today. They are coming to their jobs with better education than their predecessors and a far more complete understanding of all the ramifications of their actions. Couple this with an almost universal desire to produce a quality fishery while protecting the ecosystem and the trout, and they are, quite simply, undoing most of the past damage and giving the public top value for each dollar spent. They are the fisherman's hope—and almost a guarantee—that trout fishing for sport will not only survive but will get better year by year. My hat is off to them.

Henry's Lake is about four by six miles depending on water levels, its long axis northwest-southeast, from the mouth of Timber Creek to the dam at the outlet. Its greatest depth, about twenty-six feet, is about two miles southeast of Staley Springs. It lies in its shallow basin just out from three ranges of moutains forming the Continental Divide.

On the east are the high, rounded peaks of the Henry's Lake Mountains. I have lived for twenty years on the east slope of this range, two miles from the headwaters of Targhee Creek, one of the source streams of Henry's Lake. Just north of the lake, a gentle sloping spur pushes westward becoming the wide, low pass that is named after Captain W. F. Raynolds, who crossed it on an exploring expedition in late June 1859. Jim Bridger was his guide.

The spur connects the Henry's Lake Mountains with the south end of the Gravelly Range which runs northward flanking the Madison River. The west edge of the *Gravellies,* as they are known locally, ends at picturesque Red Rock Pass. The western rim of Red Rock Pass is the east edge of another north-south range, the majestic Centennial Range. All these mountains are part of the rim of the ancient Island Park Caldera. All of these ranges are above 8,000 feet and the Centennial and Henry's Lake ranges have peaks approaching 11,000 feet. The abundant snow on their flanks feeds Henry's Lake.

Henry's Lake is shaped like a rectangle with a rounded top (north edge) and a pigtail at the bottom (the outlet). The lake elevation is 6,470 feet at high pool.

Sawtell Peak, named for Gilman Sawtell, the first settler in the Flat, lacks a foot of being 10,000 feet high. It is the southern tip of the Centennial Range, jutting abruptly above the flat, visible from all directions for miles. There is an Federal Aviation Administration (FAA) air traffic control radar station on its peak.

Almost everyone, including people born in the area, thinks that Sawtell Peak is west of Henry's Lake. In fact, it is exactly even with the western edge of the lake, and four miles *south* of the dam. I bring this up, because Sawtell Peak is a landmark reference point used in giving directions, especially in the case of anglers. This has led to some confusion. No one has ever actually gotten lost but people planning vacations or fishing trips with map and compass find the peak is not where they have been told that it is, which means most everything else seems out of place also.

Sawtell was the first settler in the area, but he was far from being the first white. Andrew Henry and about eighty others traversed the area in 1810. Trappers were around the mouth of the river from 1818 to the 1840s, but I can find no record of them being on the Flat before 1826, and then only crossing to get to trapping areas at Three Forks or in Yellowstone Park. Father De Smet was here in 1840 with 1,600 Salish (Flathead) Indians and left a stone carved "July 23, 1840 De Smet."

Although trappers crossed the area frequently between 1826 and 1842, they did not directly cross the Flat itself, but only skimmed the edges. Coming from Pierre's Hole (Teton Basin) they traveled across the southeast edge and went either to the Yellowstone Park area via Rea's Pass, through which the old Union Pacific Railroad tracks ran to West Yellowstone, or they trekked along the foot of the Henry's Lake Mountains and went north through Raynolds Pass to Three Forks. These routes were more direct than crossing the Flat itself, and the footing was better because much of the center of the Flat is boggy.

After 1834, when Fort Hall was built on the Snake, upstream from present Pocatello, Idaho, trappers going to Yellowstone crossed the "Piny Woods" (the present Mack's Inn-Last Chance area) and over Rea's Pass. If going to Three Forks, they crossed Camas Meadows, skirted around the base of Sawtell Peak, and over Raynolds Pass.

None of the records of the day that I could find make more than a passing reference to the lake or flat. It obviously was not important in the scheme of things in that era. Neither trappers nor Indians were much interested in fishing. They were primarily red meat eaters.

Sawtell homesteaded the area now known as Staley's Springs in 1868 but did not file homestead patents until years later. He raised produce and some meat animals, obtained fish from the lake, and sold these products to the gold mining camps at Alder Gulch and Virginia City in Montana. Later he caught fish through the ice in winter and shipped them via the Utah and Northern Railroad to Butte and Ogden, packed in ice from the lake.

How much fish? In the 1890s Joe Sherwood who had settled on the east shore of the lake on a homestead, still in possession of his heirs, estimated that some 90,000 pounds of fish a winter were harvested from the lake and sold. Sherwood built the first hatchery in the area when the state of Idaho declared the selling of wild trout illegal. He built a store and a sawmill, established the first post office, called Lake, and built and patented the world's first snowmobile. In 1907 he received U.S. Patent No. 844,963 for a "powered snow sled" or "tractor-sleigh." A replica and a picture of the original may be seen today in the Sherwood Museum, in the old store-post office building at the Lake.

A man named Dick Rock settled on the Flat in the 1880s. Rock, known as

Rocky Mountain Dick, caught and trained wild animals. A female moose named Nellie Bly was used by him as a carriage horse, and it was Rock's claim that, in scores of races with other carriage drivers, and even in sulky races, Nellie was never beaten. Rock was alleged by some to have been brutal to his animals, and, in 1903, he was gored to death by a buffalo he had raised from a calf. His ranch was then purchased as a stage station, the last stage stop before the one in Yellowstone Park at Riverside, just inside the Park West boundary. This was replaced by West Yellowstone when the railroad reached there in 1909.

Settlers came rapidly to the area in the 1890s. The Engets, Ed Staley (who took over Sawtell's place), the Garners, Sherwoods, and many others came to stay. Their descendants still own much of the original property, and the grandchildren and great-grandchildren of the original settlers still live here or nearby.

My dear friend Donna Garner Spainhower is postmaster at West Yellowstone. Bill and Louise Enget, brother and sister, are the third generation of Engets on the greatly expanded original Enget homestead where a very popular local tradition has grown up. Each August Bill and Louise host a huge barbecue on the saddle of Two Top Mountain, in the Henry's Lake Range.

Since much of the land on the Flat is still in the hands of the descendants of original settlers, the people have a somewhat different attitude here than farmers and ranchers farther down the river. Having seen what *progress* has done there, the Flat people have become much more concerned with protecting the environment and the natural beauty that surrounds them. These differences were strongly brought to light in the summer of 1983.

The Targhee National Forest surrounds Henry's Lake Flat and much of the area farther down. Sheep and cattle permits for grazing are leased in the area, and much of the area is the range of the grizzly bear, an endangered species. Because of this, certain areas of Targhee National Forest are Situation One bear habitat. This rating means that in conflict between the rights of bear and the rights of man, man must give way.

When a grizzly sow and her cubs threatened and later killed some sheep in the mountains on the east of the Flat, there was a gathering of ranchers and Forest Service people to deal with the situation. The meeting was televised. Bill Enget and his neighbors were moderate, with Enget stating that the grizzly was a part of the West, had been there before man, and must be accommodated. But ranchers whose home areas were farther away and who were leasing Situation One grazing land took a different view, some saying "the only good bear is a dead bear," bringing back an attitude that most of us thought existed only in the past.

The matter was resolved in favor of the bear; those protesting were offered in exchange grazing permits in other, non-Situation One areas.

However, this was not my first experience with the protective attitude of the Flat people toward their beloved land and lake.

In the summer of 1981 two young fisheries biologists stationed at Henry's Lake came to see me. These were Bob Rohrer and Bob Spateholtz. Over the past fifteen years, the quality of fishing in the lake had deteriorated. Limits had been adjusted, but they were only partially effective in slowing the decline since overfishing was not the primary cause. Drought was.

Henry's Lake is mostly snow fed. Snow depths of ten or more feet are reached on the Flat, but in the mountains, depths of 200–300 inches is normal. But in the 1976–1980 period, and in the 1967–69 period as well, much less than half the normal snow had fallen. Cutthroat and rainbow are spring spawners and in six or seven of the last fifteen years there had been too little water in the tributary streams for successful spawning. This had been greatly aggravated by drawing off of irrigation water from the streams at spawning time.

The two Bobs knew that I had been involved with stream conservation for many years and that an organization that I belonged to had been largely responsible for getting attention that had resulted in restoring the fishery in Montana's Madison River. People around Henry's Lake, residents and long-time summer residents, had approached the two biologists to find out what could be done at Henry's Lake. Their visit to me was to get me to address a group of concerned people about how to form an organization to save the fishery quality at Henry's Lake.

Before we talk about that meeting, and its results, we need to talk about what quality we are discussing. From the 1940s, when fishing pressure began increasing on Henry's Lake, to the mid-1970s, the quality of fishing was quite simply the best anywhere. As an example, a doctor who taught medicine at a southern California medical school had been a summer resident on Henry's Lake for over twenty-five years. In a two page article in the magazine section of the Sunday *Los Angeles Times,* the doctor said that in each of those years he had caught *over* 100 trout per summer that weighed more than five pounds each, as well as thousands in the two-to-five-pound class.* The doctor was well known around the lake and no one doubted his claim for a minute—or found it unusual. That's how it was—then. This was the quality that an organization was to be formed to restore.

I went over on a Sunday evening to Wild Rose Ranch, a lodge on the lake, to address what I thought would be about forty people. But well over a hundred showed. There were far too many to crowd into the room where I spoke; they stood in the doorway, in the hallway, and on the lawn outside, or hung through the open windows.

In simplest terms what I told them was this. First, form an organization for the sole purpose of restoring the fishery, permit no dissention on that subject, and if any member wished to insist on discussing other conservation projects, hand him back his membership money and bid him farewell. Second, be sure that one of the earliest members is a lawyer who will volunteer time because if opponents arise to attack you, their first step will be to declare what you are doing is illegal or that you are not a legally formed organization. The next person to entice should be an accountant because if the charge of illegality fails, the next thing opponents will do is say that your

---

*Most of these fish were released alive and well.

money comes from tainted sources or is spent in a suspicious manner. Third, set goals with a priority for each. Pursue those goals with the single-minded intensity of a fireman saving people from a burning building—take one at a time and do not look up or back until that one is safely on the ground and out of danger. Then go after the next.

Over 100 people joined what was to become The Henry's Lake Foundation that night and over $3,000 was raised. In the next meeting a charter was voted and goals set.

In July 1983 I attended a meeting of the Foundation. President John O'Neall told the members that the Foundation had purchased and donated research equipment that was needed by biologists at the lake but which the Idaho Fish and Game budget did not allow. Fencing for spawning streams was being installed, with the approval of ranchers involved, to keep cattle away from spawning streams; that screens for irrigation ditches had been purchased and were being installed, to keep spawners and fry from going to their death in irrigation water (some springs there was a ninety percent loss of fry into irrigation ditches).

He also noted that the next goal was a big one: to raise over $60,000 to drill wells for irrigation purposes on land now being irrigated from spawning streams, to install pumps, and to pay the cost of running those pumps. All the ranchers involved, he said, had not only agreed to donate their water rights in those streams to the Idaho Fish and Game Department if this were done, but some had donated money toward the project. All had told him the quality of the lake fishery was important to the local economy, and they wished to see it restored.

The above demonstrates not only what can be done by a determined, single-minded group, but also the willingness of the local people to cooperate and lend a hand. As one who has been involved in such organizations for over forty years, I can tell you that this is not often the case. As of now, the future of Henry's Lake and its fishery is, in my opinion, in the best possible hands—that of a people who love it and will work and fight to protect it, an informed Fish and Game Department that recognizes the value of the fishery, and landowners who feel the same way. In emphasizing the fishery, I wish to point out that the Department of Fish, Wildlife, and Parks of Montana has long espoused the idea that a livable environment for trout means a quality environment for man.

While The Henry's Lake Foundation was going about its good works, Bob Rohrer and Bob Spateholtz were going about theirs, that of doing all within their power and purview to enhance the fishery. Spateholtz, as a project for his master's degree in fishery biology, had undertaken to restore the brook trout fishery to its former state of excellence. He had learned that Dwight Webster, Cornell University's eminent trout authority, had been hatching strains of fast-growing brook trout. Spateholtz, in 1980, obtained from Cornell the eggs of the Assinica strain for planting in Henry's Lake, and, in 1981, the eggs of the Temiscamie strain.* These were hatched out in the lake

*These two Quebec native strains are the fastest growing known.

hatchery that Idaho had purchased from Joe Sherwood in the 1930s, after having leased it from him in 1924.

The fingerlings were fin clipped for identification and released into the lake. In 1983, netting turned up brookies of the two strains that were sixteen inches long and more than two pounds in weight.

According to Idaho's Fish and Game Department, the trout native to Henry's Fork and Lake, were Yellowstone cutthroat, *Salmo clarki boverie.* Since these are not quite the same fish as the cutthroat below Shoshone Falls in the Snake River and west of there, the assumption is that they came to be in the river during the period millions of years ago when Yellowstone Lake emptied into the Lewis River and thence to the Snake.

Also native to Henry's Fork and Lake are sculpins, dace, suckers, and Rocky Mountain Whitefish, *Prosopium williamsoni.* Introduced fish in the river are brook, rainbow, and brown trout and, into some areas, redside shiner and chub. (The latter two probably escaped from the minnow buckets of bait fishermen.) Currently, fish in the lake are rainbow, brook, cutthroat, and rainbow-cutthroat hybrid trout and sculpin and redside shiners.

The major insects in the lake are damselfly, *Hyalella* and *Gammarus* genera of scud (freshwater shrimp), caddis, midge, and *Daphnia.* There are also leeches. The two shrimp form thirty-five percent of the fishes diet over the season, but the damselfly, nymph and emerging adult, form about fifty to sixty percent of the trout's intake during the emergence (hatch) of that insect. This commences around the first of July and lasts about three weeks. It is this period most fishermen on short vacation aim for.

The fishing method is unvarying. One locates in a boat along a channel in the weeds that grow in impenetrable masses on the lake bottom. The cast is down or up the channel so that one's line and lure may be retrieved *in* the clear area among the weeds. Then one retrieves with what Nick Lyons calls "a slow, haunting rhythm." The depth at which one fishes varies with the stage of maturity of the damselfly nymph. As they approach adulthood, the nymphs work higher in the water and migrate toward a surface object— weeds, logs, shoreline, etc.—on which to cling while transforming into the flying adult. The most prevalent damsel nymph in the lake is green, a medium-shade, and is about one inch long at maturity. Good patterns are found locally; Dave Engerbretson's marabou damsel is good, and a green Wooly Worm pattern in the right size works well at peak emergence.

When the damsel nymphs are up very close to the surface or are working shoreward in very shallow water, things can become very difficult. The trout are up there, too, and in the shallows or up close to the surface, they become as wary and as spooky as bonefish on the flats. One uses a floating line and a long leader, and you stalk. Along shore that means moving slower than molasses in January, being careful not to make ripples or to stumble. In a boat, no rattling or banging of oars, gear, feet—or anything. You either make no sound or you get no fish. It's that tough.

In the time when the damselfly is not emerging, the shrimp are the day-in, day-out meat and potatoes of the trout's diet. However, the leech may be more productive for the angler; it requires less skill to fish than do the shrimp imitations. It is also much larger and more easily seen from a distance by the trout. Brown, olive green, and black leech patterns are used, and even a Wooly Bugger of those colors works well. The best retrieve seems to be a steady, fairly rapid stripping motion. This imitates the undulating wiggle of the natural better than the slower hand retrieve that some use.

Although it can be fished from shore, the lake is much better fished from a boat. A large boat is not required, one sees everything from float tubes to cabin cruisers. No matter what one uses, *do not* remain on the lake if the wind comes up. Get off as quickly as possible. Remaining for "just one more cast" can cost you your life.

Henry's Lake is subject to sudden and violent convection winds. It lies cupped in the curve of very high mountains that are snow-covered much of the year. These are cooler that the Flat, which soaks up the full force of the sun. The warm air rises; the colder air rushes down the mountains and assaults the lake at speeds up to fifty miles per hour. The shallows are lashed to a froth and whitecaps three feet high run over deeper water. Each year there are several capsizings and every few years one or more deaths by drowning. The Fish and Game people and local residents have signs warning of the dangers but fishermen tend to ignore them, to their peril.

The cavalry came to Henry's Lake in 1877 when General O. O. Howard pursued the Nez Percé through the area and in 1878 for a "battle" with the Bannock in the so-called Bannock War, caused by the U.S. Government's confining the Shoshone and Bannock tribes to a small reservation, then literally starving them to death. The battle, however, was averted.

At present the Flat is the home of ranchers who have dwelled there most of their lives, and a large number of permanent summer residents. The winters in the area are so fierce that only the most determined spend them on the Flat.

The temperature may drop to fifty degrees below zero Fahrenheit some winters and forty below is not uncommon. Snow will lie seven to ten feet deep. This will be true of the surrounding country, but what makes the Flat more inhospitable and dangerous are winds. Because of the cold, the snow is dry, the moisture frozen out of it and when the winds come, the snow blows, creating what in the West is called a ground blizzard. This often occurs when the weather is otherwise perfectly clear.

The river, from the outlet of the lake to nearly its junction with the outflow of Big Springs—twelve miles of river run—is a small, winding trout stream. The first mile or so from the dam outlet is willow-lined and mostly riffle water, with occasional deeper spots under the willows at the bends. Once it crosses under the 191–20 highway bridge, it becomes rather quickly a winding meadow stream, mosty shallow but with occasional riffles and now and then a fine deep pool.

Cattle and sheep have grazed the Flat for a hundred years. They still do, and have broken down the banks of the stream in many areas, causing extensive silting of the stream bed that has ruined many of the spawning stretches by silting in the gravel. Because of the vast area of flat, deep-soiled land surrounding the stream and because of the dam at the lake controlling the waterflow, the stream on the Flat is not subject to flooding which would clean out the riffles of silt.

Insect populations are mostly small and of few species due to these factors. Holding areas are mostly confined to the deeper pools and areas under the banks. However the vast meadows produce hosts of land-borne insects: crickets, beetles, horseflies, blackflies, soldier flies, grasshoppers and grass moths which supplement the trouts' diet. There are not many fish per square yard of bottom, but those that are there are in excellent condition.

Evidence of the rich nature of the Flat is constantly before one. Herds of antelope come and go. Flocks of geese compete with sheep and cattle for the lush meadow grass. Stilts, curlews, snipe, sandpipers, killdeers, herons, blackbirds, cowbirds, marsh hawks, ravens, seagulls, phalaropes, and other marsh area inhabitants abound. The sandhill cranes, four feet tall, loud and vociferous, stride across the meadows in phalanxes like Romans of old, gleaning the terrestrial insects that make up most of their diet.

The flowers, in spring and early summer, cover acres blue, yellow, and white, in such masses that they turn vast sections into a floral display to dazzle the most blasé. With the tall mountains so near at hand in the clear air that one feels that a tossed stone would hit them, there is still a wonderful feeling of airy openness combined with a pastoral beauty that is literally perfect. The fisherman who is also a nature lover will find much to distract and please him.

The fishing will be spotty, the normal run of stream will contain few, mostly small fish. Those in the deep pools often require that you get down to them with dragon or damselfly nymph. Hopper, cricket, beetle, or moth pat-

You won't see this bull elk on Henry's Lake Flat in hunting season.

Antelope and cows have shared Henry's Lake Flat
for a hundred springs.

terns drifted along undercut banks where the water is deep, colored with the
dusky bloom of purple grapes, will produce showy rises and, usually, good
fish of a pound upwards. I've seen cutts of three pounds and brookies of two
here in these pastoral waters, and they are firm, beautiful fish in excellent
condition.

Mobs of sandhill cranes along Henry's Fork on the Flat. A regular
spring occurrence.

A deeper stretch of Henry's Lake Outlet. A two-pound brookie
came out of the notch in the upper right.

There is twelve miles of this small, winding, mostly smooth-surfaced water before the outlet joins the Big Springs, which triples the flow. The river, which has been running just a little east of south, hits the Big Springs Outflow running west, about 1½ miles from where Big Springs rises. Just before the confluence of the two streams, the verdant pasture land gives way to a tangled, boggy area of dense willows which Idahoans refer to as *moose swamp* and we in Montana call *beaver bogs*. Both moose and beaver are here, the latter posing more of a threat than the former. Here, the lordly moose seems to regard the intruding fisherman with sublime contempt. On the other hand, the beaver, perhaps gaining revenge for what man did many years ago, lays traps with masterful cunning into which the angler obligingly falls. I know—I've fallen into them countless times, and one such sent me off to the hospital for a month. So, beware the beaver.

In the fall, rainbows and kokanee (landlocked sockeye) salmon run from Island Park Reservoir up as far as two miles above the confluence of the two streams to spawn. Both *can* be caught on brightly colored steelhead flies, but it is not easy. The salmon will go about two and one-half to four pounds; the trout, a bit larger. If the salmon have not passed the peak of condition, they are delicious smoked. Some coho (silver) salmon have been stocked but the run is not yet large.

The rainbow run is not nearly as widespread and heavy as it was twenty-five years ago, and there are far fewer fish in current runs. Biologists are aware of this but differ on the causes. Some believe that the decline began when rotenone was used on Island Park Reservoir in 1959 to eliminate an overpopulation of chub. Huge rainbow trout were killed by the housands in that fiasco, but there is no hard evidence linking that to the decline of the rainbow run. Some trout did survive and, in twenty-five years, would have restocked the reservoir, and it appears that they have. However, frequent, almost continuous stockings of other races of rainbow trout into the reservoir have taken place and this is perhaps the reason. The original stock of fall spawners has been diluted by inbreeding with other strains. This seems the most likely theory.

And so, we come to the edge of the Flat, leaving the stream here to move onto the larger river in the area known as Island Park Village.

4

A VILLAGE WITH PRETENSIONS

ISLAND PARK VILLAGE BEGAN AS A STAGE REST STOP IN THE LATE 1800s. Natural clearings in heavily forested areas are known in the West as parks. There were several along Henry's Fork between Ashton and Henry's Lake Flat. Doc's Park, Elk Park, and Island Park were some of them. The latter got its name from the fact that it was bounded by water on nearly all sides. On the north was Buffalo River; to the east, Split Creek and Little Warm River; on the south, Tom's Creek; and the Henry's Fork is to the west—enclosing a clearing nearly four square miles in size.

The original Island Park stage stop location was moved southeast a little when the railroad came through in 1909, but it retained the earlier name. A post office called Island Park was established there, but subsequently the whole affair—post office, lodge, village name, etc.—moved to the site of present Pond's Lodge when the highway came through in 1916. Over the years, as an easy term of reference, other areas became included in the Island Park area by custom and usage. As of now, the Village stretches almost thirty miles along U.S. Highway 191–20* from Sunset Lodge at the foot of Targhee Pass to Pinehaven, below Railroad Ranch. Generally included are Shotgun Valley, Last Chance, Pond's Lodge, Flat Rock, Mack's Inn, Big Springs, and Henry's Lake and Flat, as well as the places mentioned above. So, if one directs you to *Island Park* it behooves you to know just where you are being sent. I raise this point because in 1983 while getting photographs for this book, I encountered a couple from Twin Falls. They had reservations for Island Park, but had been informed at Pinehaven, Last Chance, Mack's Inn, and Island Park Lodge that, yes this was Island Park, and, no, their reservations were not for here. It turned out to be Big Springs but only after a half-day of searching for the true Island Park.

*During the writing of this book, this highway was renumbered as just 20. But road maps prior to 1985 will carry the old 191–20 designation.

The whole area is resort oriented, with summer homes, as well as motels, lodges, trailer parks, state parks, campgrounds, tackle shops, gas stations, restaurants and cafes scattered throughout. There are even time-share condominiums and a golf course. And trout fishing is the major drawing feature, with the fact that it's on a major route to and from Yellowstone Park accounting for the next largest number of visitors. There are a number of fishing clubs located along the stream. Some, founded about 1900, have become summer home areas and are no longer clubs.

The earliest of the surviving clubs is the Flat Rock Club, downstream a mile or so from Mack's Inn, on the opposite bank. It has a limited, exclusive membership (no children under eighteen allowed) and was founded in 1902. The North Fork Club is about a mile upstream from Mack's, also on the opposite bank. It has a more liberal family membership policy. It was founded a few years later than Flat Rock.

In 1926 Alexander MacDonald, a Los Angeles attorney, along with some others who wanted wives and kids to accompany them, split off from the Flat Rock group and formed the Coffee Pot Club at the foot of Lower Coffee Pot rapids. MacDonald is the author of two excellent books on fly fishing in the area. (See Bibliography). These clubs are important from the standpoint that their members were influential men who led the conservation movement in the area.

The first of these was A. S. Trude, famous Chicago attorney. Trude was not a club member but took over George Rea's holdings about 1900 and turned the place into a ranch where he hosted important fly fishers of the era. It was at Trude's Algenia Ranch (named for Mrs. Trude) that, in 1901, Carter Harrison, five-time mayor of Chicago, invented the Trude fly. Harrison preferred large flies for his fishing—number 4s—whereas Trude and his friends preferred smaller flies of size 8 or 10. Trude kidded Harrison about his *monstrosities,* so, as a joke, Harrison took a musky hook—used yarn from a fireplace rug, fox squirrel tail for a wing, and some red hair from a dog—made up a fly and, over drinks, presented it to Trude. However, Trude had the last laugh. The fly looked so good to him that he tied up some—as did Harrison on number 4 hooks—and, in the words of one guest, caught "a wagon load of trout" on it.

The original Trude was—and is—tied with a red yarn body, silver tinsel rib, fox squirrel tail wing *behind the hackle,* and Rhode Island Red rooster hackle. It was tied on a regular-length hook and the body was somewhat fat. It is still used like that but a more popular version in the area uses a red silk body, silver tinsel rib, long fox squirrel tail wing behind the red-brown hackle, and a long-shank hook. It was developed in 1936 by Vint Johnson who opened that year the first tackle shop in West Yellowstone. It's called Vint's Special and is a very good pattern for rainbow and cutthroat.

Trude's descendants still own what of Algenia Ranch in Shotgun Valley is not covered by Island Park Reservoir, and these people still preserve his tradition of conservation of land and water. Trude is credited with the saving of Big Springs from spoliation and exploitation.

The Trude was the earliest fly developed in the area but there is another which gained greater fame as a more useful fly, although it originated elsewhere.

In 1938 or 1939, Harry Darbee in conjunction with Percy Jennings developed a fly with clipped deer hair body, rather fat, and divided wings of Barred Rock, variously hackled. Darbee called it Beaverkill Bastard. But Mary Dimock, daughter of noted fly fisher A. W. Dimock, and a friend of Jennings' daughter, protested the name. The fly had character, she argued, and should have a name with character, so she called it Rat-Faced McDougal. The name stuck.

In 1939 Alexander MacDonald and a friend were fishing the Rising River-Hat Creek area of northern California. This friend was using the new Rat-Faced McDougal and slaughtering the trout. But the trout took their toll of his flies. So, he attempted to replenish his supply at night in the cabin. He was unable to do a good job on the clipped deer hair body and resorted to folding the deer hair over in the manner of Jack Horner's Horner Bug.

The next year this fellow accompanied MacDonald up to the Coffee Pot Club and, in a single day, took two trout of over five pounds each on this bug-fly. This gave the fly instant fame in the area and a new name: Goofus Bug. Some insist it is just the old Horner Bug. It isn't. Horner's Bug originally had no wings and just grizzly hackle. This new bug had deer hair divided wings and the mixed brown and grizzly hackle of the original Rat-Faced McDougal. It is a hybrid Rat-Faced/Horner Bug.

Pat and Sig Barnes, in their fly shop in West Yellowstone, became the first commercial tiers of this pattern, which became a very big seller for them. It migrated over the Tetons into Jackson's Hole where it became known as Humpy, the Wonder Fly. This fly today is the number seven best-selling fly in the West Yellowstone-Henry's Fork area and ranks even higher in Jackson's Hole. It is one of the very best fast-water dry flies and also one of the best general (non-imitative) patterns.

Where the Henry's Fork, coming down from the lake, meets the Outflow of Big Springs is a deep, dark hole, locally called "The Bathtub." Ray Bergman, in the 1930s, wrote of seeing a tremendous rise of small brook trout here and of trying to catch six of these for supper. The fish refused all his offerings until he resorted to a size-18 Blue Dun wet fly. Bergman was a fine fly fisherman and writer whose works were influential in sending me down the same path. But he cared little for entomology and made no effort to identify what natural fly those brookies were taking.

This area has silt bottoms—deep, miry mud which makes it difficult to wade, even where the water is shallow enough to do so. The silty bottom produces mostly small insects, midges and blackflies predominating, as well as very small mayflies. When the fish are feeding on them, nothing larger than size 18 will do the job—and smaller is better. The fishing here is further complicated by the fact that the Idaho Fish and Game Department regularly stocks the section of river from McCrae Bridge, just above Island Park

Reservoir, to Mack's Inn with hatchery-catchable rainbows. This is apparently done to accommodate the flocks of tourists and children who lack the skill to catch wild trout.

A moment to cover an omission. The Outflow of Big Springs to where it joins the main stream is permanently closed to fishing. This protected stretch, about a mile and a half of the most gorgeous trout water you will ever see, is a holding and spawning area for giant rainbows. Howard Back, a professor of natural history, in his book, *The Waters of Yellowstone with Rod and Fly,* called this stretch ideal trout water, the equal of the world famous Test in his native England.

Big Springs emerges at a near-constant 52 degrees Fahrenheit, thus indicating a source not far underground since deep wells (500–1,500 feet) in the area are a constant 45. There has been much speculation about where the 480 million gallons of daily flow of Big Springs comes from. Some believe it is the updwelling of the Big and the Little Lost rivers which sink into the ground and disappear some 100 miles to the southwest. But the elevation of Big Springs is higher than that of Lost Rivers Sink. However, many creeks to the north of Big Springs run off the mountains and disappear into the ground at higher elevations than Big Springs.

There are summer homes all along the banks, and a store-restaurant at Big Springs itself.* A road bridge crosses the Outflow about 200 feet from where the Springs comes out of the hillside. People hang over its railings to toss popcorn and bread, purchased at the store, to the huge fish that hang in

*This burned down in 1984.

The Johnny Sack Cabin, an Historical Site now, at the head of Big Springs.

Big Springs Outflow—
beautiful trout water
closed to fishing as a
prime spawning area.

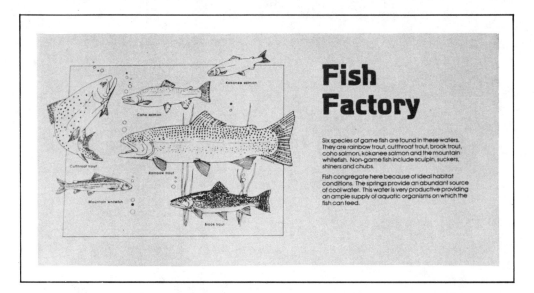

Fish Factory

Six species of game fish are found in these waters. They are rainbow trout, cutthroat trout, brook trout, coho salmon, kokanee salmon and the mountain whitefish. Non-game fish include sculpin, suckers, shiners and chubs.

Fish congregate here because of ideal habitat conditions. The springs provide an abundant source of cool water. This water is very productive providing an ample supply of aquatic organisms on which the fish can feed.

This sign at Big Springs tells the story. One can park near this sign and gaze down on trout running six to eight pounds. You may not fish for them but you can feed them.

water so clear that they seem suspended in air. Go and try it yourself, you'll enjoy it and kids love it.

The stretch from the confluence of the Outflow and the main river down to Mack's Inn is flanked by private property. One must be careful not to trespass, but the thoughtful and courteous angler will seldom be refused permission to cross private property to get to the river. Usually, one needs only to ask.

What makes it worthwhile is a good pod of large resident fish among the hatchery catchables. To catch the larger of these requires a good amount of skill, and thus is a greater challenge.

Around Mack's Inn itself, the tourists and casual lure flingers make it all but impossible to fish. Mack's is the oldest and most patronized of the resort areas along Henry's Fork. It was founded by W. H. Mack (Doc) who immigrated to the U.S. from Germany at age twelve. This enterprising man worked as a cook and baker's apprentice, became skilled at those trades, and later trained and became an optometrist. His first Inn was built at Trude Siding on the Union Pacific Railroad in 1909. This was where most fishermen of the day left the train to fish and vacation. Later, in 1916, the location was changed to its present one alongside the river and highway. It is the center of activity on the upper river.

From Mack's Inn downstream the river changes. Much of the bottom is bedrock thinly overlaid with gravel and volcanic rocks. This section has so long been stocked with hatchery-catchable fish that it has seriously affected the numbers of, and reproduction by, wild trout. Potholes and weedbeds furnish good holding area in this stretch.

The first stocking of trout *anywhere* in the U.S. was about 1883 in New York. It was less than fifteen years later that hatcheries (private) were operating on Henry's Fork and Henry's Lake. The Idaho Fish and Game Depart-

The late Robert Wuthrich, Island Park's beloved photographer-in-residence. Robert was also famous for his carved wooden bear plaques and toys.

ment took over these hatcheries by leasing, then purchasing, in the 1920s and as nearly as I can find out, have continuously stocked hatchery-catchables in the Island Park Reservoir and the river upstream since then. (Island Park dam was built in the mid-1930s, but stocking of the river began earlier than that).

This stretch is the most pleasant of trout streams to fish. It seems to be a series of long, smooth-surfaced glides with a broken lava rock bottom that

Looking up to Henry's Fork from the Mack's Inn bridge. Lovely water much disturbed by recreational floating and pedal boats.

Downstream from Mack's Inn toward the Flat Rock Club water—the beginning
of a long stretch of water of even depth and mostly bedrock bottom.

affords pleasant wading. These glides are seldom more than thirty inches
deep and are separated by short riffles. Both types of water are a delight to
fish. Even the smallest of dry flies is easily seen on the smooth surface of the
glides, and size 14 or larger will be visible in the riffles. The weeds in this
area seldom come to the surface and, thus, do not interfere with the float of
a dry fly.

The fish are mostly pan size in the ordinary run of stream but there are
resident fish of good size in better holding areas that one can find here and
there. Then, in spring, there will be a holdover of run-up fish, some of
which are quite sizable. The fall run of a few big rainbows, some coho, and
large numbers of kokanee salmon can be profitably fished with bright steelhead patterns. However, caddis patterns, dry or wet, are the best producers
most of the time.

As this part of the river approaches the Upper Coffee Pot Rapids, about
four river miles from the bridge at Mack's Inn, it narrows and the current
picks up speed. The broken surface and more current barriers provide se-

curity and holding places for larger fish, and they are there, although not plentiful. The rapids dash down into the steep-walled, mile-long canyon that is called "Cardiac Canyon" by some. It is a pale imitation of the real Cardiac Canyon, but it is difficult to get into and out of. The fishing is spotty. The fast pocket water will produce fish of a pound or so, and the deep canyon pools with huge boulders thrusting above the surface has rainbows up to eight pounds and perhaps larger. They are not often caught. The angling, here, is with big streamers and spinning lures. One cannot wade these deep pools, and fishing from the bank is difficult.

Out of the canyon at Lower Coffee Pot Rapids is more pocket water. Then the stream gradually deepens as it heads down, under McCrea Bridge and on into the upper end of Island Park Reservoir. The depth of the reservoir has a definite effect on this stretch of river. As the level of the lake fluctuates, so does the fishing from below Lower Coffee Pot on down to the lake proper. At times it is very good and for sizable fish.

The reservoir lies athwart the axis of the river, spreading west up Ice-house Creek and east up Crow Creek. Except for the lack of current, the lake, which bends and twists, narrows and broadens, often looks like a river and many areas can be fished as though it were one.

Regular lake fishing methods—trolling, casting, and bait fishing deep— all produce fish but with no method proving consistently superior. Morning and evening fly hatches allow the fly fisherman to get in his licks. But the serious fly fisher spend most of his time on the river below the dam, where there are twenty, or so, miles of perhaps the best trout stream water in the world.

The dam is located about a half-mile upstream of the mouth of Buffalo River and a half-mile west of Pond's Lodge, which hosts the Island Park Post Office.

The lodge was originally four or five miles southeast of its present location, but it moved beside the highway where it crosses the Buffalo when auto traffic began to preempt the train. However, that was not the major reason

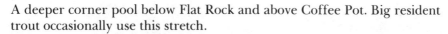

A deeper corner pool below Flat Rock and above Coffee Pot. Big resident trout occasionally use this stretch.

A pair of anglers try their
luck at a corner pool.
Can you spot them?

A series of bedrock breakovers in a stretch above
Coffee Pot Campground.

for the move. The original site had been founded to take advantage of the railroad-tie-making operation that centered at Island Park siding. From about 1917 until the early 1930s, tie cutting was a major industry in the area. At its peak there were 1,500 *tie hacks,* as they were called, located at Trude, Guild, Big Spring, and Island Park sidings.

These people converted the dense lodgepole forest into railroad ties by hand, with two-man crosscut saws, chopping axes, and broad axes. I did a lot of this between 1930 and 1933 in the Missouri Ozarks. The lodgepole was much easier to make into ties than were our Missouri oaks. The western tie was flattened on only two sides, the other two being peeled with a straightened out hoe called a *spudder.* Sawmills gradually took over tie making, both in my Ozark home area and here at Island Park. Earthquakes and fires eventually forced the mills out of the latter area. The Stoddard mill relocated to Saint Anthony after the 1959 earthquake that dammed the Madison River. It was still in operation the last time I was by that area on the old road.

As the tie making industry faded, the tourist industry increased and is now the major economic factor in the area. Today's visitor will see scores of pickup trucks, cars with trailers, and regular logging trucks each day, hauling polewood out of this section of Targhee National Forest. This is not your conventional logging operation. For the past fifteen years the pine bark beetle has infected the northern Rockies, killing most mature pine trees. To reduce what would be an enormous fire hazard, the Forest Service has allowed firewood cutting, free for personal use, and with a small fee for commercial purposes. One will see many devastated areas with the red-brown needle trees still standing; others are almost completely cleared of standing dead timber.

This harvest is a mixed blessing. It makes use of timber that would otherwise go to waste but there is a paradox here. Evergreen forests, *dense* evergreen forests, are literally timbered deserts. Practically no other plants can grow among the acidic carpet of dead needles on the forest floor, even if the dense shade would allow such growth. No large animals can live in such a forest *unless* there are extensive clearings. There is no food for them. Only porcupines, pine squirrels, and chipmunks—among mammals—live in dense evergreen forests, and gray and Steller's jays are about the only birds that will be found in the heart of such forests.

Evergreen trees take up minerals from the soil. If these trees die or are harvested for timber, these minerals are not returned to the soil. In such dense forests, only a few of the trees that die can fall to the ground, and in the arid West, it takes fifty years for one that reaches the ground to rot. Fire, once thought to be disastrous, is now known to be beneficial if allowed to burn *under control*. Burning restores not only the minerals in the wood to the soil, but produces others by converting wood fiber to ash, a fine soil enricher. Also, there will be clearings, sun can get in, an entire community of new plants can grow, animals and birds move in, and just about everything is improved. Nature needs soil, sun, and rain to provide for its creatures; a forest fire restores the balance that a dense forest does not have.

Upper Coffee Pot Campground. Few anglers cross over and fish from the other side as this one did. It improves one's chances.

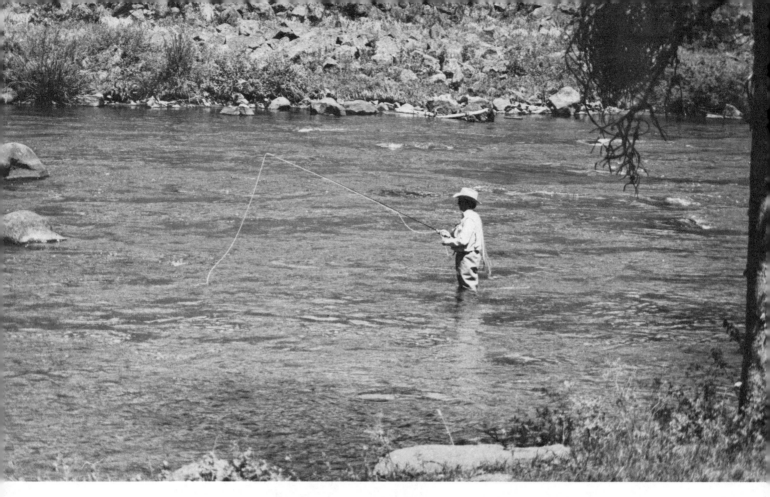

Here, just above the head of Coffee Pot Rapids, I observed this angler fishing dry fly directly downstream. He was catching fish.

So, why doesn't the Forest Service just wait for a fire to do its work? In such a dense forest of *mostly* dead trees, the fire could not be controlled. It would be a holocaust so hot that essential minerals might be destroyed. And it could cause a fire storm wind that would create a monster that would sweep everything before it. The Targhee National Forest people are pursuing the most prudent and most beneficial course under the conditions that face them.

From Island Park Dam at the head of Box Canyon to the mouth is three miles of the best fast-water trout fishing anywhere. It and some miles of water below Island Park Dam are restricted to artificial lures and flies, with barbless hooks. This rule is strictly enforced. It is simply loaded with rainbows of every size up to and over 20 pounds. This stretch is also loaded with insects, including five species of stoneflies, such as the giant *Pteronarcys californica,* or salmonfly. The name *salmonfly,* by which this large insect is known throughout the West, is due to the color of the belly of the mature adult. There is a strip of dusky salmon orange on the underside of the thorax and abdomen, broader in some, narrower in others. The sides and back are dusky greyish brown or greyish black, as are the legs. Some have a little crimson strip across the back of the head.

These large boulders signal the approach to Coffee Pot Rapids.
Some fine trout are taken here by knowledgeable anglers.

All these insects will vary somewhat in the amount and intensity of the orange on their bellies, but *none* are the brilliant orange all over the body that one sees in many commercial salmonfly patterns.

I was shocked to find, while researching about Island Park Dam, that until recently the dam was shut down completely during the winter, drying up the river below down to the point where Buffalo River joins Henry's Fork. This was done by the Bureau of Reclamation, which built the dam, although the water rights—for irrigation—belong to the Fremont-Madison Irrigation District, under the auspices of the State of Idaho.

The above illustrates a statement by a famed conservationist, that when a dam is built, there is nowhere in the official chain of command of government and private organizations controlling the dam and using the water, anyone or any organization looking after the needs of fish and wildlife.

Montana has recently—about six or seven years ago—passed laws requiring that an amount of water sufficient for the needs of fish and wildlife must be at all times released from any non-private dam. The law has been upheld by the courts, but no such law exists in Idaho or most other states.

Recently, using the nesting of the trumpeter swan—an endangered species—as a lever, the Idaho Fish and Game Department was able to get the

The head of Upper Coffee Pot Rapids. Fine pocket-water fishing.

Bureau of Reclamation to release sufficient water during the winter so that the nests of the swans, built at very low flows too close to the river, would not be swept away when spring runoff forced the release of much larger amounts of water. As of now, a specified amount of water must be released during the winter to avoid spring destruction of trumpeter swan nests. So far, the farmers have not taken the matter to court, but a low precipitation winter could change all that. In most cases of this nature, the courts have voted with the endangered species, but that too could change. As the great Lee Wulff once said, "Each victory is temporary, each defeat is permanent."

One can enter Box Canyon at the road just north of Pond's Lodge, turning off Highway 191–20. There seems to be an ongoing effort in Idaho to have this highway renumbered to just 20, and current road maps reflect this. But it has always been known before as 191–20, and 191 is the longtime and current number of this same U.S. highway in Montana. The road turning off a half mile or so north of Pond's runs west to the reservoir where it dead-ends into a road running around the east side of the reservoir. One turns left and follows this road almost to the dam, where an indistinct road turns off left past the little housing area of dam personnel and goes to the river and a boat launching site.

The half-mile or so of river upstream to the dam and downstream to the mouth of Buffalo River, coming in on the left, is excellent water, less swift and turbulent—and with fewer big boulders—than the rest of Box Canyon. There are nearly always a few anglers in this stretch of river.

Another road turns off Highway 20 just south of the highway bridge over the Buffalo and runs parallel to the Buffalo to near where that river enters Henry's Fork. Then a set of ruts turns left and runs parallel to Box Canyon all the way to near the mouth of the canyon where this "road" strikes an un-numbered road of occasionally broken blacktop. This goes on into Last Chance, passing, as it does, Box Canyon and Henry's Fork Villages, little clusters of summer homes along the river. These villages are private; you must have permission to cross them to the river.

Where to turn off and park anywhere along Box Canyon is strictly by hunch. The entry into and down the canyon wall is about equally difficult anywhere. It is only a hundred or so vertical feet down into the canyon but, although there are numerous fishermen's paths down the wall, none are easy

The tail of Upper Coffee Pot Rapids spilling into the head of the Canyon. Very good fishing but not easy.

Island Park Reservoir looking toward Sawtell Peak (right background)
and the Centennial Mountains.

going down or coming back. But, believe me, it's worth the effort if you love
fast-water fishing for large trout as I do.

The fishing is difficult, more so when there is a major release of water
from the dam. The walls of the canyon press onto the banks of the river
most everywhere. Where they are back some few feet, the space is filled with
trees, shrubs, bushes, and vines which form an almost solid wall. Finding a
spot where one can wade out clear of the bank always presents a problem.

Then, the bottom complicates matters further. It is rubble-boulder, one
of the most productive bottom types for both trout and insects. But on this
bottom of stones piled on stones are boulders, here and there, from the size
of a basketball to as big as a sofa. The larger ones you can see—it is those less
than three feet in diameter that cause the problem.

As you are wading and fishing, you will step or turn and your outthrust
forward foot will strike one of these boulders and you will trip. Or your foot
will glance off the round slick surface with the speed of light, and you will
hurl headlong into the stream.

Light conditions are murderous. The shadows play havoc with your attempts to pierce the clear depths to spot these booby traps. So, wade carefully, fishing *only* when you have both feet wedged solidly on the bottom.
When you wade, probe ahead with your wading staff or feel carefully with
that front foot. The instant you relax from doing this, one of those boulders,
obeying Murphy's Law, will appear out of nowhere and dump you into the
icy water.

What makes all this trouble worthwhile? Every year trout of over six
pounds are taken, every two or three years trout of eight or ten pounds. And
every six to eight years, one larger than fifteen pounds will fall prey to a
visiting angler. There are larger ones. In 1982 an angler took one of ten and
one of eighteen pounds in less than a week from the tumbling icy waters of

The tailrace of Island Park Dam shooting into the head of Box Canyon.
The beginning of three miles of the best fast-water
trout fishing anywhere.

Box Canyon. The fish and game agent, on viewing the latter trout, was not impressed. "There's a larger one there, in that same spot," he said. "We shocked that stretch earlier this year, and there's a twenty-four pounder still there."

What makes these trout so large in this three-mile stretch? Well, there are loads of insects, including millions of the largest stonefly nymphs, nearly two inches long just before emerging as flying adults. The large trout forage on whitefish as well as on smaller members of their own kind. And now, I find, there are huge crayfish here. I had known since the late 1940s that there were big crayfish in the river below Mesa Falls. But I didn't think they would be in the much colder waters of the Box. A friend who knows the Box like the palm of his hand says he has found them there. His integrity in such matters is unimpeachable. So, they are there.

That there is an enormous food supply available to the trout is unarguable. The fish themselves are the greatest proof of this.

The major inhabitant of Box and Cardiac canyons—all fast water on Henry's Fork. The nymph of the "salmon fly"—*Pteronarcys californica.* My version—Montana Stone Nymph—of an artificial.

In 1978, Mike Lawson caught a 22½ inch rainbow in Box Canyon that weighed 7½ pounds. In most rivers that fish would have weighed three or four. I have seen ten pounders here barely twenty-six inches long. All the very large trout here are relatively young fish for their size. They have the small heads, deep bodies, and thick backs of healthy young fish. But these Box Canyon biggies carry things a step further. All those over five pounds that I have seen are grossly fat fish, deep and thick, with the belly of a sumo wrestler. And they are as strong as they are large. What makes it possible for the fly fisher to land them on his relatively frail tackle is that they are homebodies. They are not runners, and the truly huge ones not leapers. They fight an enormously strong fight but in a limited area.

The water is varied, although all of it is more or less swift. But there are deeper spots, eddies, and broader areas that are shallower, and the bottom structure changes. This is a lava bed area, and there are small bottom areas of lava bedrock. The growth on the banks at times approaches a tropical jungle in lush, green growth, backed always by the big firs and spruces, which replace lodgepole pine in damp areas hereabouts.

A float through the canyon—and there are many who do this—is enchanting. I floated through it the first time in the fall of 1983 to get pictures. Hal Cameron was at the oars of the big, white-water rubber raft. Hal and

The Buffalo River, a lovely small trout stream that runs into Henry's Fork near Pond's Lodge. Forest Service campground on the left bank. There's some great fishing for large trout where the Buffalo enters the Henry's Fork.

This choppy-water stretch just below the mouth of the Buffalo River
has produced rainbows of fourteen pounds.

Rosie have the first summer cabin at the edge of Forest Service land at the
very mouth of the Box, near where that twenty-four pounder lives. We saw
many fishers through the canyon, none human. Three or four were bald
eagles, several were ospreys, a couple were great blue herons, and a half-
dozen were kingfishers. And one was a mink. There could be no better testa-
ment to the quality of the water or its wildness.

Here the river in Box Canyon shows its teeth. Don't be afraid—
there are fifteen-pounders here. Best reached by floating.

The beginning of the end of Box Canyon—and three miles
of the finest fast-trout water anywhere.

Once out of the canyon, the river broadens and shallows, becoming more
even in bottom and in current flow. It curves leftward (on streams, left and
right are defined facing downstream) around the villages of Box Canyon and
Henry's Fork, the lovely summer cabin areas of lovely people. The people
who live here do so because they love the area and they translate that love
into strong protective effort to keep the river and its environs unspoiled.
This is not selfishness; I've never encountered anyone who was dog-in-the-
manger about it. If you, by your bearing, attitude, and good manners, assure
them that *you* pose no threat to these things, they will welcome you. But fish
hogs, vandals, louts, and despoilers get short shrift from them. Hurray for
that.

Where the river straightens out to run parallel to Highway 20 is the commercial village of Last Chance. Here is located Will Godfrey's and Mike and
Sheralee Lawson's fly shops. In these two places one will find in Jim Ver-
milion, former manager of Godfrey's place, and in Mike Lawson more accumulated knowledge about this river than in any other single place. And if

you are lucky, you may come across the resident leprechaun of Henry's Fork, the enthusiastic and voluble Bing Lempke who knows about the stream's insect life and who is learning more all the time. He also ties exquisite dry flies to imitate the prevalent hatch and he uses them with superlative skill. (My debt to him will be found in Appendix B, as will information about those important insects and their imitations).

As with all fly fishers, these three have somewhat different opinions as to what is the best fly to use and the best time to be on the stream. As with any of us nuts who are long-time fly fishers and fly tyers, these are more personal preferences than a differing of knowledge and experience.

Jim believes that the best time for the *average* fly fisher is the month between 25 June and 25 July. The best fly, both for this period and for most of the summer, is Pale Morning Dun. This artificial is designed to simulate three species of *Ephemeroptera: Ephemerella inermis, E. infrequens* and *E. lacustris.* Although anglers argue volubly about which species is which, entomologists say that *they* cannot tell the difference between them without a strong magnifying glass. Since trout do not carry magnifying glasses, and really don't care what fly has which name, I go with the trout and lump these together as Pale Morning Duns. (This lovely name—which roused the envy of Ernie Schwiebert, who in his superb book *Nymphs,* wished he had thought of it himself—was coined by Carl Richards and Doug Swisher in their equally fine work *Selective Trout.* I would suggest that the serious fly fisher have both of these, not only for Henry's Fork, but for nationwide use. They're unbeatable at present, though each in a different way.)

Jim believes that for larger trout, and for the more skilled fly fisher, that a hopper pattern from 1 July onward—especially in September, when aquatic hatches lag a bit—is the better choice. Jim's choice of this ungainly fly as requiring more skill to use than a hatch-matching dry will raise a few brows. But Jim knows, as do some of the rest of us who fish Henry's Fork regularly, that the larger trout on this river are a different breed of cat than

The mouth of the Box—and the home of giant trout. There's a twenty-four pound rainbow living here and in 1982 an eighteen-pounder was caught here.

Local Ron Dye with a big trout and a small grin. My grin would
have been bigger—*much* bigger. From the mouth of the Box.
(Photo courtesy of Kathy McKay).

the run-of-the-mill hatch feeders. They're a stalking proposition, and one
must possess more knowledge of their habits, holds, and lies than is required
for trout feeding on the prevalent hatch who betray themselves by their re-
petitive rise forms.

Mike Lawson states things a little differently. He believes, with Jim, that
25 June to 25 July is the time of most activity and thinks also that the relatively inexperienced fly fisher has his best opportunity then—and that Pale
Morning Dun is the best fly at that time. But for the *average* fly fishers, Mike
believes that the best times are the first two weeks of July and the last two
weeks of September. He bases this on several things. First, the hordes of fly
fishers who arrive in June for Green Drake Madness are gone. One can
choose his water and spend more time on it. The number and frequency of
hatches has slowed. The fish do not have the water covered with hatching
naturals and thus have become more opportunistic. Thus, there is less need

for an imitative fly and more opportunity for a variety of general dries, nymphs, hoppers, and terrestrials. But for the larger trout, Mike likes October and the deeply-sunken, dead-drifting, big black stonefly nymph. He remembers one day when several fish of four to seven pounds came to this method and how amazed some visiting anglers were at the number of large trout coming to this nymph.

Both Jim and Mike work their shops and guide during the season. But the ebullient Bing Lempke is retired and he "lives" on the river almost year around. His choice of times and flies is based on being there just about every day.

The average fisherman, he thinks, does well during the Green Drake-Brown Drake period, mid-June to mid-July. The Pale Morning Dun is a more consistent producer more of the time. But the best and most productive flies season long are the Blue Duns and Blue Winged Olives. Success with *Callibaetis* (Speckled Spinner) is spotty. And of course, like all of us in the West, fish the hopper regularly in its season.

I do most of my fishing later in the season. During Green Drake time I do fish a few days. I have better success with two versions of my Ida May nymph than with the dry fly. I believe the reason is that there is more activity during the prehatch with this natural, *Drunella* (formerly *Ephemerella*) *grandis,*

The head of Last Chance Run, which reaches from here to Railroad Ranch.
One of the most prolific pieces of trout water on earth.
Trout are plentiful and large—twelve pounds and up.

Green Drake Madness Time at Last Chance Run.

than there is during the time when the dun is actually on the water. I start in the morning, using my original Ida May sunk deep and dead drifting. As the morning draws on, the prehatch activity begins increasing and I switch to an emerger Ida May—which floats in or just under the surface. This fly, the greatest commercial success of any of my patterns, was developed on this stream in the mid-1950s. I had seined the nymph from the Last Chance stretch. At the time I didn't know the scientific name and called it Idaho Mayfly nymph, shortened later to Ida May. I believe it to be the best artificial nymph available for this area.

A little sidelight here. In his book *On Becoming a Fly Fisherman,* Alexander MacDonald expresses wonder that this insect, so abundant in Henry's Fork, doesn't exist across the Continental Divide to the east. It does; I've found it in several streams in Yellowstone Park. Professor Roemhild in his booklet, *Aquatic Insects of Yellowstone,* implies this but does not implicitly state it.

I agree with Mike Lawson that more larger trout may be taken later in the season in areas where the big stonefly nymphs live by the millions. This nymph is in the water either three or four years, depending on location, year-round water temperature, the amount of calcium bicarbonate in the water, and perhaps other factors. They outweigh *all* other insects in the stream. Their size and numbers make them the most common item of the trout's diet, and this is especially true when other insects have emerged and are gone for the season. Thus in Coffee Pot Rapids and the canyon between upper and lower rapids, in Box Canyon and in all the fast water from just above Riverside to below Ashton, the big black nymph is the prime producer of large trout in the fall and is very good any time of year.

Green Drake Madness Time, usually the last ten days of June, brings a host of fly fishers to the river at Last Chance and to the entire stretch from the mouth of Box Canyon to below Railroad Ranch (Harriman State Park). The weather is early spring like, meaning you can't depend on it—or as Mark Twain once said—"if you don't like it, just wait a few minutes." I've seen everything from bright, warm sunshine to eight inches of snow with temperatures below zero. Most often it seems to be cloudy, blustery, and showery—and always changeable.

At this time, most every day during the hatch (emergence of flying adults) there will be 200 to 300 fishermen between Box Canyon and Osborne Bridge. They fish in perfect harmony, each following his or her hunches as to where to be, which way to cast, and whether to use a Green Drake or a Pale Morning Dun, which also emerges, just to confuse things. Then toward the tail of the Green Drake hatch, to make things really easy for the trout and tough on the angler, along comes Brown Drake *(Ephemera simulans)*. But a jolly time is had by all.

We locals may mess around a bit during this two to three weeks of concentrated madness, but mostly we prefer to come along a little later when we can have a quarter- or even a half-mile of stream to ourselves to help shield our inadequacies from others. But any time is a lovely time on the Last Chance Village section of Henry's Fork.

The area is rich in history. During the beaver trade years, 1810–40, it played host to hundreds of trappers. However, though I have found occasional mention of "plenty beaver" on Henry's Fork, I cannot find one single mention that anyone ever actually trapped this section. Nearly everything I have been able to find in published works indicates that this area was generally bypassed by trappers on their way somewhere else.

In August 1877, the Nez Percé, fleeing government oppression, and fresh from the butchery of their wives and children at the Big Hole Ambush, crossed Camas Meadows on their flight to Canada. They camped the night of 18 August at the juncture of Camas and Spring Creeks, and on 19 August camped on Sheridan Creek, which runs into a section of Henry's Fork now under Island Park Reservoir. General O. O. Howard and his pursuing troops were just one day behind, and camped, on the 19th exactly where the Nez Percé had camped the night before. At this time the two groups were less than twenty miles apart.

The Indian leaders (Joseph was only *one* of several Nez Percé leaders, others were Lean Elk, Looking Glass, and Ollikut) decided that, in order to slow up Howard's pursuit, it was necessary to steal some of his horses and, especially, his pack mules. They executed an early morning raid of daring skill and escaped with three horses and about 200 mules.

The troops quickly mounted and gave chase, and caught the Indians about halfway between the two camps. Here the Indians ambushed the cavalry, causing them to fort up in a mound of lava rock, where they were held by some Nez Percé while others made off with the captured animals. The troops lost one man killed and eight wounded, three of whom later died. No Nez Percé were killed in the raid.

Howard was forced to make a trip to Virginia City, Montana, about seventy miles away, to obtain fresh pack animals, causing a delay of several days in the pursuit.

The final capture of the Nez Percé was brought about, not by the tactical skills of General Howard and Colonel Nelson Miles, nor by the superior

Centennial Mountains, Henry's Fork Village, and Last Chance Run—
and, of course, a few fishermen.

fighting qualities of their troops, but by the telegraph. While at Virginia City,
and later at Bozeman, Howard wired ahead and troops from eastern Montana under Colonels Sturgis and Miles moved to cut off the Nez Percé. Fleeing from attack on front and rear, the exhausted Indians were surrounded
and subdued, to the shame of all whites anywhere in this nation. Our Army
had robbed, hounded, and murdered as fine a people as ever lived in America.

The Henry's Lake Flat area had been settled earlier than any other part
of southeast Idaho, but settlement along the rest of the river trailed far behind. Rexburg, Saint Anthony, and nearby villages were not founded until
1879 and later. In the 1890s a stage line began from Saint Anthony to Yellowstone Park, with stops at Niess Inn, Osborne, Railroad Ranch (not known
by that name then), Ripley's (Last Chance), and Udens. Charles Ripley's
homestead and stage stop is now Last Chance, Railroad Ranch is Harriman
State Park, and Osborne's name survives in the bridge across the river between Last Chance and Pinehaven.

Although the villages in the area have grown steadily, they have grown
slowly, so that no great environmental changes have occurred. The area
around Mack's Inn, which has the largest population and the most summer
visitors, developed sewage problems in the 1970s due to the excessive
number of septic tanks. But in the period 1980–82 the local people got together and built a large modern sewage plant, which, with about eighty percent of the area's homes already hooked up, has alleviated most of the
problem.

Now, it is Last Chance that is having sewage problems, and, at present,
even experts are stymied over what to do about it. What stumps the experts
is that underlying the entire Pond's Lodge-Last Chance area is a bed of very

This pair played this five to six-pound rainbow for over an hour before losing it. Note the slight bend of the rod.

porous lava which makes it extremely difficult, if not impossible, to establish a leach line drain field that will not leach effluent into the underlying aquifer, thence into wells and springs, and eventually the river. The problem is beginning to assume serious proportions, and with no answer in sight. The people are willing, even anxious, to do the right thing, only no one knows what that is.

Another threat looming over the Last Chance area—and some others along the river—is that of drilling for oil and geothermal heat sources. Oil drilling permits have already been granted in several areas along the river, which would even allow drilling slantwise under the river. At present there appears not to be sufficient prospects for economic gain. It is that and not moral or legal concerns that have so far prevented such drilling.

Geothermal resources do exist, but when the administrators of Targhee National Forest attempted to file a draft Environmental Impact Statement and hold hearings on the subject, a storm of criticism arose over the way Targhee National Forest attempted to handle the matter. The result was that public outcry forced Targhee National Forest to hold a hearing in West Yellowstone, and information produced at that hearing eventually resulted in the decision by the Secretary of the Interior deciding geothermal drilling permits would not be granted in the Island Park area until it could be shown conclusively that such drilling would not cause damage to the environment and, especially, would not affect the thermal features in Yellowstone Park.

The threat still exists, and if the economic situation becomes favorable for such oil and geothermal development to be done, another attempt will be made to subvert the desires of those who wish to protect the area from spoliation and environmental degradation. We must be ever alert to see that this does not happen because no one is watching.

This drift on Last Chance Run is a favorite holding spot for large trout;
I've seen three of over five pounds taken here.

Over the past few years, the biologists of the Idaho Fish and Game Department have made great advances in the management of the fishery in the area; the quality is better now than ten years ago. Stocking of catchables between Ashton and Island Park Dam has been stopped; the area contains only wild trout among game fish.

Both catchable trout and fry are stocked in Island Park Reservoir; studies have shown that survival rate of stocked trout in lakes makes this practical. Coho and kokanee salmon are also stocked in the reservoir. Also, the tributary Buffalo River is stocked with catchable trout in the campground stretch. This river, for reasons not known, cannot seem to sustain a large wild trout population. But Henry's Fork from Island Park Dam to below Lower Mesa Falls, can and does sustain one of the finest populations of wild rainbow trout in the country, and present management procedures will assure that this will continue. There is probably not a better twenty-mile stretch of wild trout water anywhere in the world.

The end of Last Chance Run. The mass of parked cars are at the
upper boundary of Railroad Ranch.

5

RAILROAD RANCH (HARRIMAN STATE PARK)

IN THE 1890S FIVE MEN FORMED THE ISLAND PARK LAND AND CATTLE Company and began to purchase land along both sides of Henry's Fork in the area south and west of the mouth of Box Canyon. Some of the men were also owners of the Oregon Short Line Railroad, so the ranch was named Railroad Ranch. These men were unable to get some of the homesteads on the east bank of the river in the Last Chance area but continued getting land southwestward until 1903, when a change in views halted the expansion.

In 1907, Edward Henry Harriman began acquiring the Oregon Short Line, and by 1908 he also owned Railroad Ranch, along with Solomon Guggenheim, head of American Smelter. Both men were major stockholders of, and had controlling interest in, the Union Pacific Railroad. In the process of gaining the Oregon Short Line, the two also obtained the Saint Anthony Railroad which owned the line from Idaho Falls to West Yellowstone, through Island Park.

In 1908, the two added the Bob Osborne ranch which lay mostly to the south of present Osborne Bridge. This substantially completed what is now Railroad Ranch. It was to be operated as a working cattle ranch. Harriman died suddenly in 1909, his majority portion passing to his heirs. He never saw the property.

The Harriman sons, W. Averill—former governor of New York and Federal cabinet officer—and Roland, continued to operate the ranch. Though Averill's interests were largely elsewhere, he visited the ranch frequently. But it was Roland who came to love the place, and who managed it until his death.

61

Solomon Guggenheim died in 1949. His share of the property was bought by Charles S. Jones, president of Richfield Oil Company (later Atlantic Richfield, now Arco). After Jones' death, the Harrimans obtained total ownership.

In 1961, they began to arrange a transfer of the property to the State of Idaho, working carefully to see that nothing was left to chance, and insisting on strong, permanent covenants to protect the environment and the wildlife.

These latter were the legacy of Roland Harriman, who throughout, lived up to an injunction he said that he received from his father, "whatever you touch, leave it better for your having touched it."

Roland was a fly fisher, and fly fishers everywhere owe this fine gentle man an eternal debt of gratitude for his peerless stewardship of what is perhaps the finest five miles of trout water anywhere.

The property (plus some other large tracts elsewhere in Idaho, *and* in Montana) was given over to the Idaho Parks and Recreation Department, a state organization with an excellent reputation for taking good care of all properties in its jurisdiction.

The total gift by the Harrimans was 14,564 acres, more than 22 square miles, in several parcels. Railroad Ranch itself, in Harriman State Park, comprises 4,330 acres, almost seven square miles. Nearly 900 additional acres adjacent, to the southeast, is being held by the Idaho Park Foundation and can be added if usage dictates.

Among the covenants dictated by Roland was that fishing could not begin each season until after the waterfowl had completed their nesting. This was to protect the rare, beautiful trumpeter swan which nests and spends both summer and winter here. The Henry's Fork is loaded with an abundance of waterfowl food, and it does not freeze in winter due to the enormous number of springs along its course. There are also bald eagle, osprey, herons, and numbers of ducks and geese that call the Ranch water home. It is not known if Roland was responsible for the fly-fishing-only status on Ranch

One of the covenants accompanying the gift of Railroad Ranch to the State of Idaho included protection for these trumpeter swans.

Signs like this mark fishing access points within Harriman State Park
(Railroad Ranch). They explain the multi-use purpose of the Park.

water. Among animals, black bear, mule deer, elk, moose, and antelope may
be seen, and if one is quiet and observes well, mink and otter, beaver, coyote,
skunk, and porcupine are also evident. Pine squirrel, chipmunk, ground
squirrel, and vole are all highly visible, and a quantity of small bird life as
well.

Flowers in spring, especially along the river, turn large areas into masses
of color, and many species occur in small clumps throughout the sagebrush
meadows and along the edge of the timber. Both fisherman and nature lover
will find Harriman Park a quiet, lovely blessing to enjoy.

The official opening of the Park was 17 July 1982. Grace and I were
there; it is a particularly easy date for us to remember, it was our thirty-sixth
wedding anniversary. Several thousand people were nice enough to come
along to help us enjoy it.

The Idaho Parks and Recreation Department has done a first-class job of
making just about everything in the Park available to the public while at the
same time taking all necessary steps to protect the environment from all but
superficial damage.

One of the odd things that has happened since the Parks Department
opened the Ranch to the public is that fishing pressure has declined. Formerly, access to the Ranch water was down the river 2½ miles to the center,
up the river from Osborne Bridge the same distance, or a mile walk in from
the gate on the highway at about the center of the Ranch. Now, there are
two excellent fisherman's access points, one in the center, and one toward
the lower end of the Ranch that one may drive to. But fewer persons fish the
Ranch water than before. No one seems to know why. I fished perhaps a
dozen days there in 1982–83 and visited four or five times to take pictures
for this book, and the water, except on two occasions, was nearly deserted.
The pictures which accompany this chapter will clearly show that fishing
pressure on this superb piece of trout water is very light.

It is, and always has been, difficult water to fish with success, but lack of fish has not, within my memory, going back to about 1948, been a reason. There are hordes of small fish which can present problems by getting between the angler and his larger quarry, and which have to be dealt with before one can approach the larger trout without spooking them. Then, there are insect hatches that literally blanket the water, making it almost impossible to determine the taking fly. I've seen days where three species of mayfly, five of caddis, and three of stonefly were emerging, ovipositing, or spent and dying, and they were joined by midge, blackfly, damselfly, and cranefly, so that, at times, eight or more different insects were on the water at a time. There are hatches (emergence) of single species such as *Pseudocloeon edmundsi* (Tiny Blue-Winged Olive, size 22–24) that simply cover the water like a layer of pollen. Here one has the problem of the trout finding his imitation among the millions of naturals on the water.

This is why the local experts prefer to fish the Ranch when only a sparse hatch, or even no hatch, is on. The hordes of smaller trout will be quiescent and one can prospect for the larger ones without too much interference. Hopper time can be a joy on this piece of water, flanked almost throughout by sagebrush and grass meadows, haunts of millions of hoppers. And there are times when even coarser lures produce action from really large trout.

I have used deer hair mice for years for large trout, and introduced them to friends who would accept the fact that trout ate such things. A friend, Bob Holmes, who fishes Henry's Fork about six weeks a year, once hooked a rainbow estimated at eight pounds on the Ranch, using a deer hair mouse I had given him. Bob is prone to using very fine leaders and this time his leader proved unequal to the task.

Those who fish the Ranch water, even the regulars, probably don't go quite as large as a mouse in their choice of lure, but they all know that when no hatch is on and the fish are being difficult, something out of the ordinary is required to bring up the larger trout that abound in this stretch. Non-regulars, those who are just on a fishing vacation, sometimes opt for large numbers of smaller fish, and they usually go with smaller flies—and hope.

The upper end of the Ranch water is a continuation of Last Chance Run, the long, relatively smooth-surfaced stretch reaching from Henry's Fork Village through Last Chance and about a half mile into the Ranch. This type water has great appeal, it is of fairly even depth, although there are deeper spots, the bottom provides good footing and the fish feed—and thus show themselves—more often than elsewhere.

From the little bridge across the river near the center of the Ranch, or actually, somewhat above there, the river subtly changes. It becomes deeper, the bottom is occasionally silt as the current slows, and islands appear here and there, making channels which are fun to explore. They are also often the best places because one may approach his quarry more closely. The area is a vast meadow.

The river widens and shallows, there are more islands, cutoffs, side channels, a most diversified piece of trout water.

Near the center of the Ranch from one of the several islands.
The Ranch, though more accessible since becoming a state park, is less fished.
It's a puzzler.

In July, August, and even September, the taking fly is often one of the terrestrials. The grasshopper, of course, is best known and most imitated. But there are others equally important, and on occasion, more so. There are more ants and anthills through this stretch—the Ranch center—than any-place I know, and at times flying ants blanket the water. Edward Hewitt once said that when there are lots of ants on and in the water it is useless to imitate anything else because trout prefer them above all else. Hewitt ate some ants to find the reason for this. He discovered they had a sharp taste—they contain high levels of formic acid—and concluded this was what the trout liked. For whatever reason, when around, they are preferred trout food, and they abound on the Ranch.

There are also large numbers of various small beetles here and, toward the lower center—near the ranch buildings—many large crickets. A good ant pattern in black or red—size 16—a selection of beetles, also size 16, and some black cricket patterns in sizes 14 and 12 will almost insure good fishing if used with care and intelligence. This is one of the secrets that some of the locals depend on when things are tough. But don't reject the mouse, either. This ungainly floater is absolutely the best bet to produce a sizeable trout anytime and especially at dawn and dusk. Try it, you'll like it.

The deep pools below the little bridge at the center of the ranch contains very large fish but one must pursue them with care. There is still a strong current through the pools, and the bottoms are tricky.

Green Drake Time on the Ranch. You'll seldom see this many fishermen
here any other time.

There is a warning here. The water in the central Ranch area is often
over five feet deep, in places it approaches ten. There is always a *bloom* of
suspended material in the water; one cannot see very far into the dusky
depths. Wading is very tricky. Also, the shallows and even medium depths
sometimes have a foot or two of silt. If you stand too long in one place, you'll
find yourself anchored halfway to your knees and will have a devil of a time
breaking loose.

Also, these deep, dark still waters have glassy surfaces and any defection
on your part will spook the trout. You must not only wade carefully, but you
must cast well and make no unnecessary movements. As an English fly fisher
once said "this is kittle fishing, no work for a novice or a bungler." It is much
like fishing a secluded pocket of a lake, except the ever-present current is
always there to add to your other troubles.

The scene is pastoral and peaceful, a calm, winding stream in a large
meadow, with mountains looming, high and far away. The little clump of
neat buildings does not disturb the feeling of isolation that one may feel even
with other anglers in sight.

As the river leaves the sight of the ranch buildings, it narrows, picks up
speed, and enters the lodgepole forest which it traverses for a half a mile. It

This is Millionaires' Row—the Harriman, Jones, and Guggenheim cabins. Some are now open to public viewing.

then splits around a very large island, along with some smaller ones. Just below the large island is a fisherman's access point with parking lot and an explanatory bulletin board. Just upstream, on the west side of the large island is a bay-like curve which is really good fishing for trout of twelve or so inches. There is some good water on the west channel also. Below—downstream again—is a strong riffle of varying depth that reaches to Osborne Bridge and the highway. You are theoretically still in the *Park* but you have left *the Ranch*.

Toward the lower end of the Ranch but still a half mile of great water to the lower access point.

6

OSBORNE BRIDGE
TO RIVERSIDE

ABOUT A MILE EAST OF OSBORNE BRIDGE, A ROAD, THE OLD HIGHWAY, now called Mesa Falls Scenic Drive, turns off from the current, or new, highway and runs along back from the east side of the river for some thirty miles. The two meet in the town of Ashton.

Turning off both roads are others, some *wood* roads, some *fishermen's* roads. What is the difference? The wood roads have signs and are numbered: Wood road 16 leaves the Mesa Falls Road about three miles from the junction of the two highways and comes to the river about halfway between Osborne Bridge and Pinehaven.

These wood roads are somewhat like a padded bra—they lead you to believe something that is not true. Where they leave the main road—old or new—they have the appearance of a maintained good road. Around the first bend that illusion vanishes like Friday's paycheck. They become a set of ruts much like fishermen's roads. And the closer either of these gets to the river, the worse they become, and the more they branch off to right and left. But they do provide passage, if somewhat perilous passage, to many spots that would otherwise require a long hike to reach. At some spots, Highway 20, the current highway, is sometimes five miles from the river. Mesa Falls Road is never more than three miles, airline, from the river.

All these roads come to an abrupt end at the edge of Cardiac Canyon. Some end before reaching the canyon rim, while others just wander off and disappear. Better have good U.S. Geological Survey-quadrangle maps when you tackle any of them, also a shovel, a full tank of gas, and lots of determination. Because only a few have enough of the latter, there are very fine fishing spots along this stretch of river that see only one or two anglers a year.

I've purposely taken you a little farther afield here than the heading of this chapter covers. There is a strong tendency to explore this area by road

Looking upstream to Harriman State Park from Osborne Bridge. This is the last boat-launching spot *before* Cardiac Canyon.

and one should be prepared or at least know how conditions are before doing so.

There are about three roads coming in from each side in the Osborne Bridge-Riverside stretch, and by using them, one can reach most spots along the river from both sides. Only the roads to Riverside Campground and through Pinehaven are in good condition.

The water undergoes a rather steady change in current speed and bottom type. Near and just below Osborne Bridge are long riffles, mostly gliding, but occasionally broken surfaced. There is about three miles of this kind of water, although some short stretches have depth enough to be called runs. Whatever it is called, it is very nice water to fish. However, in my experience, the larger fish are most always found in the deeper water.

Float trips from the bridge to the campground are regularly done. This is five to six miles by river, and to cover it in one float day requires skipping some of the less productive water. I would prefer preselecting about five spots, in conference with my guide, and hurrying through the rest so I could spend more time on those five. Because fishermen are all strongly individualistic, no two will choose the same five spots, and thus the river would be well covered.

One of my favorite places is that mile of water lying up and downstream of Pinehaven itself. Pinehaven is a lovely little subdivision about two miles by highway or three by river from Osborne Bridge. If one enters it near the gas station and pottery shop, signs saying "Private Property" will immediately be seen. This is a legal subdivision; the land is private but the roads—not the driveways—are public.

This riffle leading to Osborne Bridge is the first for many miles.
Excellent fishing, dry or wet.

I like to park near the boat dock and prospect from there. The depth of the river here will vary according to the amount of water being released from Island Park Dam, and this is true from that dam downstream to past Warm River or even to Ashton Reservoir. Sometimes, in the middle of the best fishing you've ever seen, the river will start to raise swiftly, perhaps two feet in as many hours. Water weeds and other debris ripped loose from the bottom or swept from the bank will cover the water, playing havoc with line and leader. What is really exasperating is that the stirring up of things puts the fish fully on the feed, but wrecks one's chances of doing anything about it. Fortunately, this is not a daily occurrence, though it is a regular one.

The Pinehaven area is choice water. The bottom is mostly lava bedrock with a partial overlay of gravel and rocks. There are *nice* weedbeds—nice in that they are scattered and seldom reach the surface. They provide haven for insects and for trout. There are numerous potholes in the lava bottom, shallow enough to cause the wading angler no problem, but deep enough to hold trout of twenty or more inches and four pounds.

The current speed is just about right to give enough movement to the fly so that drag can be immediately seen and corrected. There are fewer species of insects here than in the Ranch water but there are enough to keep the trout feeding often and in excellent condition.

In spite of this choice piece of water being easily reached by land or sea, it is not much fished. In perhaps thirty visits to the area, I've seen only three anglers fishing it. The floaters who pass through, several a day most days, do not seem to fish it, either. I don't know why, but I like it. It gives me a choice location mostly to myself and friends.

Below Pinehaven the river breaks into a trot but seldom a gallop. There is some good workable fast water that is productive to nymphs or large *shotgun* dry flies. I would rather stop and fish this water by wading because one passes rather swiftly through it by boat and many good spots will be missed. I do not much care for float fishing even though I was raised on the oldest float fishing stream in the nation. I prefer, instead, to float through less productive stretches and stop to cover well those spots that require closer attention than can be given them by a passing boat. But to each his own.

The water is not all fast below Pinehaven to Riverside; it is, in fact, quite varied. There are some excellent gliding stretches—short, but very worthwhile to give a good working over with the dry fly. Also, there are fine pocket water stretches throughout which also can be fished well with a big, high-floating dry—Royal Wulff, Goofus Bug, Renegade, or the like. Fish in these fast water pockets like something large enough to be seen and attractive enough to bring them out from their tight, boulder-protected lies. This is exciting fishing when the trout are coming well, and the strong currents will make even a pounder seem larger. These are active fish—not running far, but jumping and dashing, changing direction, keeping one alert so as not to lose them.

The big stonefly nymph is perhaps the best day-in, day-out fly to use, but

This fine stretch of water looking upstream from the lovely Pinehaven subdivision is seldom fished either by floaters coming through or by people who live here. It's very good water.

The boat dock at Pinehaven. I took a twenty-four-inch rainbow just across the river. Yet no one fishes here.

in all truth, it is more difficult to fish from a drifting boat than while wading. If surface activity is slow, the caddis wets in size 8 or 10 with grey, green, or brown bodies will usually be effective. Of course, in season, the hopper pattern is good, but not so much here as elsewhere.

The Tetons are more than 40 airline miles from where this picture was taken at Osborne Bridge. The bridge in the picture is an old cattle crossing.

This is the last smooth-water stretch for over twenty miles. The head of
Cardiac Canyon is just downstream.

For those who do not care for the boating method, there are roads that
approach the river from both sides, as mentioned earlier. By using these
judiciously, and with some walking, the entire Osborne Bridge-Riverside
stretch can be covered thoroughly and well, more so than by boating. It's a

The last boat takeout point before Cardiac Canyon, just above
Riverside Campground.

The water at Riverside Campground. Excellent fishing, with dry, wet and nymph.

little more work, but also more rewarding. However, it is not for the pool-flitting, rock-hopping, cover-five-miles-a-day type of angler. One must go in and be content to cover a mile or so of water in a day's fishing. That should be enough for the hardest working and most thorough. One can do this and have almost complete solitude, save for an occasional passing boat. These passages are swift and disturb the water but little. Take a lunch—perhaps a pleasant libation—take a friend and have a ball. The Osborne Bridge to Riverside water is, in my opinion, the best such stretch in all Henry's Fork for varied water, solitude at a small physical price, good fishing, and an over-all fine outing. Give it a try.

7

THROUGH
THE CANYON

ALTHOUGH THE LOCALS FEEL THAT CARDIAC CANYON (FISHERMEN'S name, not official) does not begin until just downstream of Sheep Falls, a careful look at the U.S. Geological Survey quadrangle maps will show that its head is just upstream of Riverside and that its mouth is at the confluence with Warm River, a distance of nineteen river miles. Its greatest depth is about 700 feet, halfway between Lower Mesa Falls and the mouth of the canyon.

This is the least-fished stretch of the entire river. There are two reasons. One is the difficulty of getting into and out of the canyon itself. The other is that it is entirely fast-water fishing: there are no quiet waters at all in this nineteen-mile stretch. The portion of the river from Ashton Reservoir to Island Park Dam, including this canyon stretch, is managed as wild trout water, no stocking of rainbows. Recently the Idaho Fish and Game Department has attempted to introduce brown trout below Lower Mesa Falls. Once these are established, stocking will cease.

Currently two men are attempting to obtain permits to build small hydropower projects in the canyon. There are four such projects being contemplated, between Riverside and the confluence of Warm River. Virgil Moore, fish and game biologist for the region says the state is opposed to the projects because they would harm the fishery. Spokesmen for the Targhee National Forest also have iterated that organization's opposition to the project. The plans of the National Forest foresee a conflict with the desire to maintain the natural character of the canyon, to maintain scenic values, and to somewhat limit further access roads. Long-range forestry management plans are in the works for possible inclusion in the National Wild and Scenic Rivers System. I believe there would be widespread support for this latter plan, but I would expect vigorous local opposition from farmers in the lower watershed.

Cardiac Canyon starts upstream of here, but this is what most anglers think of as its head. Good pocket-water fishing with nymph or streamer.

One sees more ospreys and bald eagles here than anywhere along the river. I have seen as many as seven bald eagles in the air at one time, and three or more ospreys circling above the river at a time are a common sight. The Targhee National Forest has recommended this area, from Riverside to below Warm River, along with five others, to the Secretary of Interior for inclusion as critical essential habitat for the endangered bald eagle. The Secretary of the Interior is charged with determining whether or not these areas are critical to survival of the eagle—and in all other similar cases involving an endangered species.

The other five areas designated as essential bald eagle habitat by Targhee National Forest are Harriman State Park, Box Canyon, Coffee Pot Rapids Canyon, the area around Big Springs, and the outlet of Henry's Lake. As of now, the Secretary of the Interior has made no determination regarding these areas, but Targhee National Forest is managing them as though such determination has been made and will continue to do so until the issue is finally resolved.

Perhaps the best system of fishing the nearly undisturbed canyon water is that developed by three young men I met in the canyon between Riverside and Sheep Falls. Actually, though there were three of them, I only met two. I was down along the river taking color photographs for a possible dust jacket and had just run out of film when I heard voices and rocks rolling. I looked up to see an upside down canoe moving downward slanting along the canyon wall. The low bushes that grow thickly in the area blocked my view of the men's lower bodies and their heads and shoulders were inside the upturned canoe.

They eventually achieved the bank near where I was, deposited the canoe in the water, tied it to a bush and began rigging up to fish. They were wearing only swimming trunks and wading shoes with felt soles. In the canoe, lashed under the thwarts, was their gear, fishing tackle, and *lifejackets.* They were happy to explain their system—of which they were justly proud—as they got ready to cast off and fish.

Each day they would drive into the canyon rim along one of the wood or fishermen's roads, to the spot where they wished to begin their float. Two of them would carry the canoe, with their duffle, down into the canyon to the river and begin a float. Meanwhile the third member would drive the car back to Mesa Falls Road, or the highway, depending on which side of the river they had entered, and drive down to the next road leading to the river, which he would take to the canyon rim. There, also in swim trunks, wading shoes, and life jacket, he would fish whatever water he could reach. His two companions would know where the take-out point was when they encountered their companion in the stream.

They were in the ninth day of a fifteen-day fishing excursion. Today would be their last float on the seven-mile stretch above Sheep Falls. Their companion would be waiting at the point where the power line crossed the river. They rotated the driving chore each day so that each fellow got to float two days and to drive to the take-out point one. It was a neat arrangement.

They said they had caught no big fish over two pounds, but no small ones, either. In nine days of covering the water below Riverside they'd seen only one other angler. They considered their trip, so far, a complete success. They were after isolation and fast-water fishing, and they had found it.

What about the work, the labor of getting the canoe into and out of the canyon? Nothing to it, they said. It took about an hour to work the canoe switchback fashion down the canyon wall to the water, most times, and about the same to get back out at the end of their trip. Sometimes, at very steep places, they lowered the canoe down—or pulled it up—with the long nylon rope that they tied up with when they stopped to wade and fish. All in all, it took a little time and required some thought, but for them it was the best possible kind of a fishing trip. At their age—mid-twenties—I would have agreed.

In most areas where the roads come in, one can work up or down the river a half-mile or so after getting to it, by wading or moving along the bank. Much depends on the water level, and that often depends on releases from Island Park Dam. There are some places where the canyon wall is so steep and so close, and the water so deep, that one is limited to a few hundred feet of fishing room.

I've had best success with the big stonefly nymph or the showy large

OPPOSITE PAGE: This deep run holds
the largest trout I've seen below
Harriman State Park.
It's tough to get to, tough to fish.

dries—Royal Wulff, Trude, Renegade, or Hair Wing Variant. Some of the
few fishermen I met had had some success with streamers also. The Black
Ghost was mentioned more than once as were large yellow bucktails. It
would seem that a fly which could be readily seen was the best taker, re-
gardless of pattern.

Below Sheep Falls, more a violent white-water chute than a falls, there are
long stretches of white water not so violent as the falls—therefore fishable,

This is Sheep Falls. Not fishable here, but there's a deep run
just below that's splendid.

OPPOSITE PAGE: Now we're in
Cardiac Canyon—fast-water fishing
for the stouthearted angler.

but seldom wadeable. There are four miles of such water between Sheep and Upper Mesa Falls. The young men I talked to said it could be easily coverd in a day. But they planned three such floats, partly so that all three would have two days each on the water, but mainly so they could stop and fish more spots. Then, they said, they would spend three more days fishing the seven miles from Lower Mesa Falls to the bridge across the river just beyond the confluence of Warm River. That would conclude their vacation, and the best fishing trip they'd ever had.

Although the area from Lower Mesa Falls down to Warm River is in the deepest part of the canyon, the river only drops 230 feet in that seven miles, about thirty-three feet per mile. That would be a rather steep fall if it were regular, but it is not. There are several cascades and rapids in this stretch where the gradient is much steeper than average. Also there are long stretches of somewhat slower flow. Though the river and canyon are never more than one-half mile from the Mesa Falls Scenic Drive, there are no roads off the Drive to the canyon downstream of the lower falls. Nor do any of the roads off Highway 191 go as far as the canyon. This piece of water is the most isolated of any on the entire river.

The reason seems to be the steepness of the canyon here, and its depth, from 300 to 700 feet. Apparently the only way to fish this piece of water is to float it, and that is being done mostly on an individual basis. It would be difficult to impossible to get a regular drift boat into the river here. There is a road, off the Mesa Falls Road, that goes to the top of Upper Falls, where there is a turn-around and parking area. An old frame house, formerly used by Boy Scouts and other youth groups, is here. It appears abandoned. The road continues downstream to the top of Lower Falls, about a mile. This road is passable most of the season.

Although I see anglers fishing the mile and a quarter of very fast water between Upper and Lower falls, I do not advise it. If you lose your footing, you might not regain it in time. As a ranger in Yosemite National Park, on two occasions I helped recover bodies of people swept over the falls. It was a depressing sight. One was a fisherman.

The only anglers I've encountered on the stretch between Lower Falls and the confluence of Warm River were rafters, young people. They would work their deflated raft and other gear down to the river below Lower Falls, using ropes. Then they'd inflate their raft, load up, and push off. The ones I talked to said there were only two rather dangerous spots, rapids and cascades, both within the first three miles below the foot of Lower Falls.

They were enthusiastic about the fishing, but admitted they'd caught no lunkers. They had caught large numbers of rainbows up to 2½ pounds, and a few of the recently stocked browns of a pound or so.

Some of these drifters take two days to make the float, stopping overnight in the heart of the canyon. They take food and sleeping bags and use their life jackets as pillows. I was pleased to see that all the young floaters I found on the river between Riverside and Warm River were equipped with life jackets—good ones. There are old floaters and bold floaters, but no old-bold floaters, as we used to say in the Air Force about pilots.

The lower canyon floaters favored streamer flies while moving—muddlers, sculpin, Spruce, and various marabou patterns. While stopped they were about equally divided between the big stonefly nymphs and large, showy dry flys. The consensus seemed to be that the nymph produced larger, but fewer, fish. All were agreed on one point—strong, short leaders for dry or nymph. Nothing longer than six feet or finer than 2X, and most favored 1X for the nymph.

Though I was rather surprised at the use of streamers over the dry fly while drifting, it does makes good sense. When you hook a fish here, you are moving generally at three or four miles an hour, and you cannot stop a raft safely to fight a fish. A dry-fly hook might straighten or the leader break while fighting a fish that remained in the area where he was hooked. But with big streamer hooks and stronger leaders, this didn't happen. If you had to replace a fly because the hook straightened or the leader broke, you lost a half mile of fishing. All very sound.

If you decide to float this section, take all precautions—and leave word with someone as to where you are floating. You wouldn't want to have to walk out of this canyon if your raft was destroyed or got away. At least *I* wouldn't. If someone knows you are in the canyon and you don't show up on time, about the only way they can rescue you is down the river in a raft. So, let's be careful out there.

8

WARM RIVER TO FALLS RIVER

THE SIXTEEN MILES OF RIVER BETWEEN THE CONFLUENCES OF WARM River and Falls River show the greatest change of anywhere the length of the Henry's Fork. It changes from a bold mountain trout stream to a farmland river: broader, deeper, slower, and more turbid. The change in the country around reflects itself in the river.

Warm River is a major tributary to Henry's Fork, almost equaling the volume of the main stream at their confluence. It rises only thirteen miles due east of Last Chance and runs almost parallel to the main river. The Henry's Fork edges eastward and meets Warm River near the edge of the Island Park Caldera, six miles northeast of Ashton. The Union Pacific Railroad to West Yellowstone runs along Warm River for most of the river's length, and from 1909 to the 1930s this was how fishermen got to this stream. In those days, campgrounds alongside the several railroad sidings played host to many fishermen. With the coming of the automobile there was a steady decline of fishing Warm River, and now hardly anyone fishes this stream above the Pineview siding where Hatchery Butte Road from off Mesa Falls Drive comes to the river.

There are dozens of dirt roads winding in and out all the way up to the Buffalo River Ranger Station but they are not well mapped, and it is easy to get lost in this area. Whether or not the fishing is worth the risk is up to the individual.

There is a nice campground two miles upstream from the confluence, and by staying here, one has access to Henry's Fork, Warm River, or Robinson Creek, a lovely little trout stream which enters Warm River between this campground and the confluence of the main rivers. This area is officially Warm River from an old railroad station located here. But it's better known now as Three Rivers. There is a small resort there, beautifully located, where Orvis once maintained a fly-fishing school. I don't know if they still do, but this is a choice location for the angler who likes variety in his fishing.

83

Henry's Fork left, Warm River entering from the right. Some large browns
are expected here in the late 1980s.

Within twenty-five miles, mostly over fair to good roads, is Railroad
Ranch, Last Chance, and Box Canyon; the stretch from Osborne Bridge to
Riverside, and even Cardiac Canyon, can be covered by use of side roads.

Warm River is reached for about the first three miles upstream by entering the canyon from Mesa Falls Drive or from the gravel road beyond the
campground. Robinson Creek is near at hand and, with its major tributary,
Fish Creek, furnishes very pleasant fishing for mostly pan fish. And the
Henry's Fork all the way to Ashton lies between a fair gravel-dirt road on the
right and Mesa Falls Drive on the left, going downstream.

The section of Henry's Fork at the confluence with Warm River and just
above and below has been stocked with brown trout recently. There is evidence that this section is beginning to produce good fishing. This not a
hatchery-catchable program, but one to establish a wild brown trout population in a section of river that appears eminently suitable for this species.

In the Idaho Fish and Game Department's 1981–1985 fishery report,
there is a section devoted to this area. In it the Department admits to knowing little about it. There have been no creel surveys or other investigative
procedures and no stream shocking or other census measures. The report
implies that this will be changed.

The Fish and Game people believe this stretch to be largely a subsistence
fishery, by the local farm and generally rural population. They also suspect
that creel limits are regularly violated. However, it is made clear that these
assumptions are not based on hard evidence.

The stocking of brown trout was due in part to local conservation groups
not only pushing to have it done but also supplying funds and labor to do
the job. Partly, the browns were stocked because they are a premier fly-fishing fish and partly because the local groups and the Fish and Game people
believe they are better able to survive in a subsistence fishery environment
than are rainbows.

If so, there should be some really fine brown trout showing up here in a few years. The river is more fertile here because of the input of runoff from agriculture. It is more stable in temperature than the section just above due to the flow from Warm River, which is not warm. On a given hot summer day the Warm River will be about two degrees cooler than Henry's Fork near where they come together. The name comes from the fact that Warm River is almost entirely spring fed above Robinson Creek, and some of the springs are warm. It does not, I'm told, freeze in winter. So, it is stable in temperature—but not warm.

There are some enormous whitefish currently in the Henry's Fork below the confluence of Warm River and, possibly, all the way to Ashton Reservoir. This bodes well for the browns—my experience is that in rivers where both dwell, big whitefish also means big browns.

The geology of the Henry's Fork here is most interesting. The river runs across Island Park Caldera, and here, encountering the edge, it turns aside and runs several miles just inside the Caldera and almost parallel to the rim, finally breaking through not far upstream from where it passes under the highway bridge. There is a dirt-gravel road along the right bank all the way from Warm River to Highway 191–20, and this is how most fishermen reach the river. On the left bank, Mesa Falls Drive is held back from proximity to the river by the Caldera wall. Getting to the river from this road involves, generally, a considerable walk, and a climb over and down the inside of the Caldera rim. Since there are many places where one can wade across, the latter approach is not much used.

Warm River below the Campground. The gravel road makes the stream accessible for a mile or so.

Near Three Rivers resort area on Warm River—Robinson Creek.
Lovely place to vacation and fish.

Near the confluence of Warm River, Henry's Fork is a broad, rubble-bottomed stream. It has good insect populations, and variety. In summer, terrestrials form a good portion of the fish's diet. It is not too difficult of approach, though it is too deep and powerful to wade across. It widens and shallows somewhat a half mile or so downstream and becomes more easily fishable.

There are large numbers of small trout (eight to twelve inches) all along this stretch, but larger trout are relatively scarce. It is this condition that leads Fish and Game biologists to believe that it is a subsistence fishery, with most larger trout being kept. Even so, a trout of larger than three pounds is always a distinct possibility. Several of this size, some browns, were caught in this stretch in 1983.

The river varies considerably in width and depth as it moves on toward Ashton Reservoir. By fishing the wider, shallower water *near* where it suddenly deepens the fly fisher can occasionally pick up a very nice fish. In the deeper stretches, using the big black stonefly nymphs and a Hi-D line, the chances of raising a large fish are increased.

Some floating is done on this stretch but local guides and outfitters have not promoted it. I believe they will as soon as the browns become well established. It is really a fine piece of trout water, perhaps the most suitable for float fishing of the entire river from the standpoint of right current speed and ease of travel. Since one can cover more water by floating, it increases

Excellent dry-fly fishing here on the lower Warm River
—which is not warm.

one's chances of finding more large fish. Also, it gets one into places difficult to reach on foot and which are not much fished.

In late May and early June, the salmon fly hatch is on and the river here is heavily fished, since this is the first stretch of the river where this insect shows in large numbers. Many good fish are taken by the fly fisher at this time.

The section from the highway bridge to, and into, Ashton Reservoir, is mostly a boat-fishing proposition. It is more heavily fished by the local population than is the stretch above the bridge. It is somewhat degraded and silted by the intensive farming here, but it is still a very good trout stream. It becomes a little warm for good fishing at the end of a long hot summer, but up to mid- or late July it is well worth your time.

Also, late fall—mid-September through October, or even later, is an excellent time to fish this water. There will be fewer local fishers chunking bait, simply because that practice is not too effective this time of year.

On the other hand, there will be excellent mayfly and caddis hatches, including some species not found on the upper river.

All in all, this is a very good piece of trout water, approached and fished at the proper time and with the proper method. The big stonefly nymph works all season, and there are consistent hatches of mayflies and caddis. And there are some large trout that have not yet been caught. A 24½-pound brown, from an old stocking, was caught here in 1982.

Ashton Reservoir is a power supply lake—thus different than the other impoundments on Henry's Fork. It's release is more erratic and unpredictable. But the water flowing from under the dam is about fifteen degrees cooler than that entering the reservoir. That makes the next seven miles, down to the mouth of Falls River, much more suitable for trout, and they are here. They will average about a pound, but there are larger ones. And the fishing is quite good, especially so early and late in the season.

There are a number of roads coming to or crossing the river in this seven-mile stretch. Some of the roads running down along the river are private, and since the stream is flanked by farms on both sides, one wants to be careful not to trespass. I've never been refused permission to use any of the roads, after making clear to the farmers that I would close all gates and not make ruts off the road. These are friendly people but you must respect their rights and treat their property with respect.

I've never seen boats on this stretch: launching and taking out might be a problem, but a canoe certainly would bring one over some very fine fishing. This stretch could be fished just nicely in a long summer's day, and this is how I would do it if I were a visitor. The best entry place is from the road that goes straight west through Ashton, intersecting the highway at the west edge of town, then running arrow straight 2½ miles to cross the river. Actually, this road is an extension of Mesa Falls Drive. There is a mile or so of good fishing water upstream of the bridge, but sometimes this water is too cold for good fishing. Use your thermometer. If it reads below 55° F., forget that upstream stretch.

I have not fished the water downstream during the salmon fly hatch (early to mid-May), but I've seined the gravel-rubble bottom, and the big nymphs are there in numbers. I suspect that if one could hit this hatch just right, he could have really excellent fishing. I would guess that my friend, Bing Lempke, would know the time of this hatch right to the minute. He knows about all the other hatches on this river, too, including some that no one else knows about.

The Henry's Fork strikes the Island Park Caldera wall here
and turns west. The fishing here will improve and become very good
within a few years.

Henry's Fork above Ashton Dam. A 24½-pound brown came out of
this stretch in 1982.

Although surrounded by farm land, the river is less turbid than above
Ashton Dam, the land is flatter and there is less erosion and less runoff of
fertilizing materials. It's a fine piece of trout water with many trout and large
trout.

Here, too, we begin to get into an ever-increasing number of irrigation
canals that lace through the area from this point to the river's mouth. However, there is only one diversion dam on this stretch, and it does not appear
as domesticated as the section between Falls and Teton rivers, or between
Teton River and the mouth of Henry's Fork. The domestication of the river
is gradual; it is still a very good-looking trout stream for these seven miles.

This area has only been settled since 1900 or thereabouts. Settling began
near the mouth of Henry's Fork about 1880 and settlers spread slowly upstream. Ashton began as the rural hamlet of Vernon in 1900. In 1906, the
Saint Anthony Railroad Company built a railroad from that town to Vernon,
which was renamed Ashton. The rairoad worked its way on through Island
Park and reached West Yellowstone in June 1909.

The Saint Anthony Railroad was purchased about 1907 or 1908 by the
Oregon Short Line Railroad, the owners of which had started Railroad
Ranch. Then E. H. Harriman and the Union Pacific took over the Oregon
Short Line and the Ranch.

The first settlers in Henry's Fork watershed were Mormons from Utah,
and they had, in many cases, helped build the irrigation system there. They
immediately began to work on irrigation projects in their new home area.

Actually, the first white to settle in the Henry's Fork watershed was Richard "Beaver Dick" Leigh, English by birth. Leigh settled first in Teton Basin
(Pierre's Hole) in 1860. He married Jenny, daughter of Chief Washakie of
the Wind River Shoshone. Jenny and their four children died of smallpox
while the children were still small. Leigh spent years praising the Henry's
Fork area to all who would listen, even writing letters to Denver newspapers.
He guided, in 1870, the Hayden party, fresh from surveying the area that
was to become Yellowstone Park, to Henry's Lake and the Island Park area.
Leigh Lake in Grand Teton National Park is named for Beaver Dick. Jenny
Lake in the same park was named for his wife.

Leigh settled at the confluence of the Teton and Henry's Fork after Jen-

Here, just above St. Anthony, the Henry's Fork is a lovely,
pastoral river that holds very large trout.

nie's death. He married again, a Bannock Indian woman named Susan Tad-
pole, and raised another family. He died in 1899. There is a state monument
and picnic area near his old homestead that is named for Beaver Dick Leigh.
The letters he left behind are rich in praise for the beauty and life qualities
of the area where he settled, married, raised a family, and died. The visitor
to the area, especially Teton Basin, will be just as impressed with its beauty as
was Beaver Dick.

In St. Anthony the Fork is still a fine trout stream. Shaun Lawson
caught a seven-pound trout just here before he was six years old.

9

FALLS AND TETON RIVERS

In any other area of our country, the Falls River and the Teton River would be highly regarded trout streams. It is the shadow of the greatness of Henry's Fork that prevent them from being so regarded here.

Falls River rises in south-central Yellowstone Park and runs generally southwest to enter Henry's Fork about five miles from Ashton. It crosses under Highway 191–20 about two miles before entering Henry's Fork. For most of its length, it is no more than a mile or two from some of the dozens of roads, mostly gravel, that lace through the countryside.

Because the Falls River is born on the southern edge of the Central Plateau of the Park, an area composed of rhyolite lava which is very porous, it starts out as a largely spring-fed river. Only a few miles from its source, it is joined by the mineral-rich flow of the Bechler River, a fine cutthroat stream which, until only recently, was heavily overfished. Before Falls River comes out of the Park near Cave Falls campground, it has already dropped over a series of faults and fractures that cause the falls that gives the river its name. There is a road running east from Ashton that turns off State Highway 47 and goes all the way to Cave Falls campground on the upper river. It is called, appropriately enough, Cave Falls Road. Other roads turn off it and down to the right, or north, bank of the river. On the south, or left bank, another road turns off State Highway 32 and parallels the river for some distance.

This is Reclamation Road, and other roads and jeep trails turn off from it to the south bank of Falls River. This stream, then, is much more approachable for most of its length than is Warm River, and its canyons are not as severe.

Near where Falls River enters Henry's Fork, its bottom is bedrock, basalt lava, with enormous potholes, which at times hold enormous trout. Like all tributaries of Henry's Fork that have sections that lie mainly in the flatter areas of Snake River Plain, this stream is not well shaded and will often, in summer, be too warm for the best trout fishing. Like the others also, it is degraded by the take-out and return of irrigation water, and these factors keep it from being the quality fishery it could be. But, as stated earlier, in any other part of our country, the river would be much more highly regarded than it is here.

State Highway 32 crosses Falls River between Ashton and Drummond. Here one sees what a truly lovely trout stream it is, and remains, for most of the rest of its sixty-odd mile length. The Idaho Fish and Game people have little information on the stream; they are only just beginning to inventory their trout fisheries in southeast Idaho. I suspect that, like Warm River at its mouth, and Henry's Fork there and on to the main Snake, Falls River is mostly fished by the local population with bait. But I do not believe it to be overfished. My inquiries turned up literally no interest in the river *as a fishery* among local people. As an irrigation source, yes, there is strong local interest and concern. The farmers in this area feel that there is never enough water in their streams.

The farther one gets toward the headwaters of Falls River, the more one is struck with its appearance. It is what most of us think of as a typical mountain-foothill trout stream. Not until it gets within a few miles of Cave Falls campground does it become difficult of access and pick up the mountain trout stream aspect that Warm River does five miles from its mouth.

So little is known about this stream between Cave Falls campground and its mouth that I've been unable to find *any* mention of it in outdoor magazines or fishing books. Nor does anyone I know have any knowledge of its insect life. The few times that I have been along its different stretches, I've seen either mayflies or caddis in the air along the stream and in sufficient numbers to indicate a good insect population. I'd have to postulate that there are stoneflies in its upper reaches since I know of no freestone mountain stream in this area that does not have them. But all in all, this stream has not received the attention of fly fishers that it should.

Falls River has rainbows in its lower reaches and cutthroats in its headwaters. There may be some browns in its last mile or so. I've seen enormous trout there but the river is somewhat discolored and I could not tell if the heavy-bodied trout I saw were browns or rainbows.

One factor that has caused the upper Falls River, in the Park, not to be fished overmuch was the fact that the tributary Bechler held much larger cutthroat. The Park Administration found out in the late 1970s what all of us fishermen already knew: that the Bechler was being consistently poached and that regulations for that stream were being violated. This has resulted in new regulations and constant patrol by rangers and the Bechler is slowly coming back as a quality fishery. Also, more attention is being paid to upper Falls River, taking some pressure off of the Bechler.

Falls River where it leaves the foothills and starts across the flat below the Porcupine Ranger Station.
This is about the lower limit of large stoneflies in the stream.

Two of the best reaches of Falls River are the crossings off Cave Falls Road and off Mesa Falls Scenic Drive. This latter turns south off Mesa Falls Drive just five miles due east of Ashton, where the drive curves sharply northward. It is just one mile from this curve to the river crossing, and a couple of miles of good fishing lie up-and-downstream of the bridge. It is riffle and run water with only an occasional pool. A floating line is all that's needed, and a selection of dries and soft-hackle wets with green, yellow, and brown bodies will give one some nice fishing, especially of an evening.

Farther along upstream, a road turns off Cave Falls Road just a mile and a half west of Porcupine Ranger Station, runs about a mile straight south, then curves left and right, and crosses the river. Here again one is afforded a mile or so of nice fishing water both up-and-downstream of the bridge.

Thus, these three crossings give access to about six miles of river in a twelve-mile stretch from the State Highway 32 bridge upstream to the Porcupine Ranger Station crossing. Downstream of the Highway 32 bridge is the Highway 191–20 bridge, which gives access both up and down, and another farm road crosses the river halfway between this latter bridge and the confluence of Henry's Fork.

This is all private land and the stream is not navigable, but if one is careful and can remain in the stream, most of the farmers will allow one to fish across their property. It is difficult to find who owns the property so that one may ask permission since there are large farms with some residential spots that are not farms. Thus the people in the house or houses nearest to where one wants to fish probably do not own the property along the river. All I can say is that I've never heard of anyone being arrested or bothered for trespassing in these areas, and in all truth, except as a source of irrigation water, the farmers show little interest in the stream.

The Teton River is by any standard a fine trout stream, and one that is going to improve because it is now receiving closer attention from the Idaho Fish and Game Department *and* from fishermen across the country.

It rises in the foothills of the Teton Mountains a few miles southeast of Victor, Idaho. It is already a fair-sized trout stream there because the spring-fed tributary creeks at its headwater are fair sized themselves. It runs parallel to the foot of the Tetons almost due north to its intersection with Biche (French for doe) Creek. The American trappers corrupted this to *Bitch Creek*, and local early settlers changed it to the North Fork of the Teton. You may find either of these names on your maps. The U.S. Geological Survey uses *Bitch Creek*.

The Teton crosses State Highway 32 about three miles west of Victor and is easy of approach here. This is the floor of the Teton Basin, also known as Pierre's Hole, and is perhaps one of the most beautiful scenic areas in the entire world. It is now farm and cattle country and is so wonderfully pastoral that one feels completely separated from the urgencies of the harsh modern world.

In spite of the mountains towering like the Swiss Alps just to the east, this area reminds one of English farmsteads, and the river heightens this impres-

The Teton River above State Highway 33; for the next thirty
miles the river is much like this in appearance.

sion for it looks much like the Dove of Walton and Cotton. It is a good trout
stream already, and it gets better as it flows on north past Driggs, Tetonia,
and Felt. These are very small towns; the entire population of Teton County,
which holds most of the length of the river, is only under 3,000.

There are about thirty-five miles of river between the bridge over State
32 and the juncture with Bitch Creek. It is mostly meadow stream, with deep
channels and undercut banks, often lined with willows. Already the runoff
from farm lands is causing turbidity, the river lacks the crystal clarity we
generally associate with trout streams. But it is rich in insect life and full of
fine trout.

Because all the land surrounding the stream is private, most fishing is
float fishing. I know of no outfitter* who regularly does this; most floating is
by fishermen who have come to know the stream by floating in their own
cartop boat or canoe. The river is thus very lightly fished.

There are not enough roads approaching the river between Victor and
Tetonia; thus floating is the best way to cover the water. Beyond Tetonia one
enters the Teton Canyon through which the river flows for the next twenty-
two miles. This canyon contains Felt Dam, about two miles upstream of the
mouth of Bitch Creek, and Linderman Dam, about ten miles farther downstream. It also was the location of the ill-conceived Teton Dam, near the
mouth of the Canyon, which washed out before it was completely filled up.

This was perhaps the most controversial dam ever built in the West. It
was authorized by Congress in 1964 but protests and suits delayed start of

*There were, in 1984, one or two outfitters in Driggs using small motor boats to work the
Teton River in the vicinity.

The upper Teton River in Pierre's Hole (Teton Basin);
the Teton Mountains are in background.

construction until 1972. Much of the protest was not about environmental reasons, although the opponents were mostly environmental groups such as the Sierra Club, but was over safety reasons. Opponents protested and presented evidence by geologists to show that a dam could not safely be built where it was planned—and ultimately built. One of the protesting geologists who later joined the legal moves against the dam had originally been engaged by the government in the planning and early construction stages.

The district judge of the court where the suit came to trial was a local, and this trial has become a precedent for the barring of local judges from sitting on a suit of national as well as local importance. This judge *apparently* was strongly biased in favor of the farmer-rancher coalition wanting the dam and ignored or threw out evidence by geologists, several of them who testified that the dam would not and could not be safe if built where planned.

The dam was completed, except for minor finishing and cosmetic work, late in 1975. Exceptionally heavy fall and winter precipitation, with very heavy snows, followed by heavy spring rains caused an extremely fast runoff so that the dam filled far more rapidly than had been expected. But such rapid filling *should not* have been a problem for a properly-sited and built dam.

The dam, of earth and rock, was 305 feet high, 1,700 feet thick at the base, and spanned the river near the mouth of the canyon. On Saturday, 5 June 1976, about 8:30 A.M., a worker doing some inspection of equipment noticed that the dam was leaking. His first attempts to warn of this were ignored. Partly, this was due to trouble in finding someone in charge on a weekend. By the time that someone in charge was notified, the dam was past saving. In fact, it could not have been saved had huge construction crews been right there on the site at the moment the leak was discovered.

At 11:52 A.M., 5 June 1976, Teton Dam crumbled. It had been undermined by water seeping through the porous lava bedrock on which it was built. It was this condition known to *all* geologists either working on the dam or opposing its construction, that had generated most of the opposition to its being built where it was.

I was watching a baseball game on television that Saturday morning, from an Idaho Falls* television station. When the first warnings were printed across the base of the television screen, they merely said the dam was leaking. Then the printed warnings quickly said it was reported that the dam had failed. Very shortly that became confirmed and the warnings began calling it a disaster and telling everyone in the path of the raging waters to flee to higher ground.

It was a disaster. The wall of water poured out of the mouth of the canyon, raced downstream across relatively flat, mostly farm land, crushing, destroying, and sweeping away everything in its path. It ripped through the towns of Wilford, Sugar City, Salem, Hibbard, Rexburg, Burton, and Menan. It split around Menan Buttes and flooded Roberts. The waters broke down levees, ripped out canal banks, washed away millions of tons of topsoil, deposited gravel over farm land, and took out bridges. Nine people died, their deaths either directly or indirectly caused by the flood. Property damage exceeded a billion dollars. Much of the area below the dam still looks like a wasteland.

Yet, farmers and ranchers in the area have commenced a vigorous move to get the government to rebuild the dam. All of the many farmers I talked to stated positively that the dam *would* be rebuilt. And over half of them wanted it rebuilt *exactly on the same site.* Not all of them were so vehement about this as one I talked to at a filling station in Teton.

This man stated, and I quote, "All the water in that river belongs to us (the farmers) and we will do what we damn please with it. That dam will be rebuilt exactly where it was before."

One would think this to be sheer lunacy, yet when I contacted the official in charge of the Bureau of Reclamation at Twin Falls, which was responsble for the original dam, he replied succinctly that "if there is sufficient demand, the dam will be rebuilt."

One can empathize with farmers. They live constantly on the thin edge of climatological disaster. Two or three too wet or too dry years can destroy them. Thus, one can see and understand their desire to make nature more tractable and their attempts to control it in the light of their survival. But to want a dam built back exactly on the spot where the previous one failed, on a spot which has been proven to be unequivocally unsafe, seems to be more a suicide complex than a desire to survive.

---

*Idaho Falls, on the Snake River, is about sixty airline miles from the dam site.

The river below the dam has been drastically changed by the flood waters. Great holes have been gouged out, banks destroyed or caved in, silt and gravel pushed into piles and ridges, the course of the river changed in spots. But recovery of life in the river has commenced and fish and insects are returning. The river here is now warmer than it was so coarse fish up from lower Henry's Fork are now dominant. But there are still trout there and some are quite large.

This river, before the disaster (and still), had a peculiarity I had not seen on any other. It forked *downstream;* that is, it split into two forks near the little village of Teton, and never rejoined, running into Henry's Fork as two separate branches nine miles apart at their mouths. These are referred to, on maps, and otherwise as North Fork, Teton River, and South Fork, Teton River. This can cause confusion; Bitch Creek is referred to on some maps as the North Fork of the Teton River.

The forty-odd miles of stream from the vicinity of Victor to the head of Teton Canyon is still excellent water. Although most of the trout one catches

The Teton downstream from Driggs, Idaho. This is an excellent trout stream that will get even better.

are under fifteen inches, rainbows (or hybrids) of up to six pounds are occasionally landed, and cutthroats of three, also. Brook trout are mostly confined to the section between Victor and Driggs, and on up to the headwaters.

There are more than sixty tributary creeks feeding into the river between its headwater springs and the head of Teton Canyon. Most are too small to be really fishworthy, and many of them are totally dewatered for irrigation during the summer months. But some are worthwhile if one is of an exploring nature. Almost none of them are fished, and the farmers and ranchers are indifferent to fishermen so that there is little possibility of being called for trespassing. Most of the land is not posted.

Silting due to farm activities and, to some extent, overgrazing, has occurred in various sections of the river; others are clean gravel. This allows a variety of mayfly and caddis types upstream of the canyon, which itself is loaded with stonefly and caddis types. One can have excellent fishing during the salmon fly hatch in the canyon in June, and the nymphs of *Pteronarcys* produce well there all season.

The Teton is a rich river; loaded with minerals beneficial to insects and trout. Southeast Idaho produces most of this nation's phosphate, which is converted into fertilizer. The Teton River is, in effect, a natural fertilizer factory.

There are some fishermen who claim that the river is better fishing in the canyon than in the meadow section. One must remember that personal taste plays a big part in the use of the word, *better*. Certainly the canyon water is very good fast-water fishing: the two dams help to keep the water cooler in summer, and this stretch is so little fished that one may have five miles of good trout stream to himself any day. So, beyond question it is good to very good trout water. But fishing it calls for qualities of strength and determination not needed in the quieter meadow sections.

I have a strong affinity for this type of water: boulder-strewn fast water, holding trout and stonefly nymphs. But my recent infirmities have made me unable to fish it as hard as I once did. It is water which can delight the strong wader and challenge his strength, as well as producing fine trout to the weighted nymph and sunken line technique. But it is not for everyone.

One can reach the canyon via farm roads turning off State Highway 32 and off the farm road between Saint Anthony and Lamont on the north side. On the south, State Highway 33 parallels the river from U.S. 20 almost to Tetonia, and there are several roads east of Newdale that go to the canyon rim. I've heard rumors of boats being floated through the canyon, but whether this is done by outfitters or on an individual basis I don't know.

There are fly shops in Driggs and in Rexburg which can provide information on the river as well as which flies to use. On a river as little fished and as little known as this one, it would pay well to seek out local information—and to have good maps. I recommend U.S. Geological Survey quadrangle maps for all fishing purposes. Some fly shops carry these of local rivers for sale to their customers.

Bitch Creek is a good trout stream with two distinct personalities. From

Bitch Creek at the head of Bitch Creek Canyon. I've
never seen or talked to anyone who fished downstream of here.

its juncture with the Teton, upstream for seven or eight miles, it is a boulder-
strewn, fast-water trout stream in a canyon only a bit less severe than that of
the river itself. But upstream of the point where State Highway 32 crosses
between Lamont and Felt, it becomes a lovely foothill creek that is a succes-
sion of riffles and runs that are delightful to fish. Bitch Creek heads up on
the western slopes of the Teton Mountains and fishing upstream from the
highway bridge, these towering peaks are most always in sight close ahead,
affording one of the most spectacular views seen from any trout stream in
the world.

Trout in Bitch Creek seldom exceed fifteen inches but are literally never
fished for, and more pleasant fishing than this is hard to imagine. Downstream of the bridge is, of course, an entirely different matter. Here, solitude, the challenge of strong water and the narrowness of the canyon make
the fishing a contest of strength between fisher and stream. American trappers, who traveled along streams in unknown territory to keep from getting
lost, assumed that the French *Biche* meant the same thing in that language as
their epithet did in English, because, they said, "She sure is a bitch of a creek
to travel on."

The Teton Basin is rich in history of the region. Though most of that
history dates from the fur trade days of 1820, there was a significant bit of
history recorded there some twelve years earlier. We'll take a long look at
that, and later events, in the next chapter.

OPPOSITE: Upper Bitch Creek in early September. A fine little trout stream
of riffles and runs.

10

JOHN COLTER AND PIERRE'S HOLE

JOHN COLTER WAS THE FIRST, AND THE MOST IMPORTANT, OF THE MOUN-tain men. Everything that followed in Rocky Mountain fur trade and in exploration of the area was based on what Colter had done, learned, and passed on. One can say of later, more-famous trappers what one historian said of John C. Freemont, that by the time they arrived on the scene, there were others to take them by the hand and lead them every step of the way. But there were none to lead Colter.

Jim Bridger and Kit Carson were not yet born when Colter joined the Lewis and Clark Expedition in October 1803. He accompanied that group west to the Pacific coast and back as far as the Mandan Village area, near present Williston, North Dakota. There, in August 1806, he was released from his contract so that he could join two other men who had come up the Missouri River on a trapping venture.

These two, Forrest Hancock (or Handcock) and Joseph Dixon, had heard other members of the Lewis and Clark group praise Colter as the best woodsman among them. There are numerous mentions of this in the Expedition's journals, commenting on Colter as "a most reliable" hunter and woodsman. He is one of few in the Expedition that was mentioned by name by President Thomas Jefferson.

Dixon and Hancock were relatively inexperienced woodsmen; they knew nothing of the area beyond where they encountered Lewis and Clark. But they were shrewd enough to spot Colter as perhaps the most valuable member of the party for their purposes.

Colter's turning back into the wilderness after three years of extreme hardship with Lewis and Clark caused Nicholas Biddle, editor of Lewis and Clark's *Report* of the expedition, to comment that there must be something wrong with a man who would thus turn his back on civilization. It was apparently this uncalled-for comment by the illustrious Biddle that caused Colter's exploits to be treated cavalierly and shabbily by some future historians.

Colter led his two companions back up the Missouri to the Yellowstone and up that river to the mouth of the Bighorn, where they camped for the fall and winter. Neither Colter nor his companions left any written record of their sojourn; what we know about it is second hand, mostly from trappers and traders who got it in conversation from Colter. One piece of information, however, came from the stepson of one of Colter's partners, who, more than fifty years later, took a reporter to the confluence of the Yellowstone and Bighorn and pointed out an area where, he said, his stepfather had told him the three men had spent the winter of 1806/07.

Another piece of second-hand information has it that Colter ranged into Sunlight Basin during that winter. What would he be doing in a place more than 150 miles by trail from the mouth of the Bighorn? There are several possibilities. The trio would have been finished with their camp building and fall trapping by at least mid-December. They could not commence trapping again until the spring thaw—mid-March at the earliest. Thus, they had about three months of idle time on their hands.

Colter was known to be restless; it was a salient feature of his character. That he would do some exploring during the winter was characteristic. But why so far? And why Sunlight Basin? To shed light on that we have to consider a number of factors; historians so far have been reluctant to do this.

First, Colter, after three years in the wilderness, was in need of new clothing. This is a known fact. Yet, when Colter met Manuel Lisa in July 1807 on the Missouri River near the Platte, he was wearing "a decent set of buckskins." Where did he get them?

Colter had already met Crow Indians along the Yellowstone while with the Lewis and Clark Expedition. He was known to have some familiarity with their language. He was already experienced enough in sign language to deal with Indians reasonably well. And the mouth of the Bighorn was in the heart of the Crow winter range.

I can find no record in the nearly one hundred books I have read on mountain men, trappers, and fur traders of *any* of them making their own clothing *except* in dire emergencies. They usually made only moccasins until they could find a group or camp of Indians where they could trade for clothing.

However, if Colter was looking for a group of Crow wintering in the area, there was no reason to go so far afield. Several small groups wintered along Pryor Creek, less than a third of the distance to Sunlight Basin.

Some histories, most fiction, and all movies I have seen about Plains Indians have presented them as living in tribes. They did not. All Plains Indians, of whatever tribe, traveled and lived in small family groups or clans, usually of from twelve to forty persons. Some very few groups might number less than twelve, or more than two hundred, but this was a rare situation.

This small family group is typical of *all* nomads: Arabs, Mongols, desert aborigines, or whatever. The reason is that a larger group could not exist off the land without constantly traveling. A tribe of one to three thousand people would clean the land like a cloud of locusts. Only by breaking up into small groups and scattering over a wide area could nomads exist.

Wintering Indian clans were usually smaller than summer groups. Plains Indians wintered on small creeks where that creek came out of a gully or shallow canyon onto the valley of a larger stream. These areas provided most or all of what the group needed to survive the winter. The gully or canyon mouth provided some shelter from storms. The creek provided water. There would be a grove of "sweet cottonwood," as the trappers called aspen, to provide food for horses and wood for cooking fires. Some grass was usually available nearby if the snow did not get too deep, and there was usually some game around to supplement the winter diet of jerky and pemmican. Without all of these present, a group could not survive the winter, and there seldom was such an area that would support a large group.

This is the kind of Indian village that Colter would have found when looking to trade for some clothing. And he needn't have gone into Sunlight Basin to find it, though Crow groups wintered near the mouth of Sunlight Creek well into the 1880s.

So, what was he doing so far away from his camp, at least ten days travel in winter, and possibly more? Though historians have speculated about this, none has offered a theory. I have one based on knowledge of the area, the kind of person Colter was, and some collateral circumstantial evidence.

The Shoshone River (I have never been able to find the derivation of that name) was known to the Crow as "the river that runs by the stinking water." This river rises in the mountains on the east of Yellowstone Park and runs generally east to present Cody, Wyoming, then northeast to enter the Bighorn near Lovell, Wyoming. It is, at Cody, about 140 airline miles from the mouth of the Bighorn.

Near the site of Cody, along the river, are a series of hot springs, tar springs, and boiling pots of strong smelling water—hence the Crow name. Trappers shortened that to Stinking Water, by which it was known until well after the beaver trade expired about 1840.

Sunlight Basin lies about thirty or forty airline miles northwest of these thermal features.

If Colter heard the Indian name for the river, as he must have, there is little question that he would have been impelled to investigate. It would not have been in character for him not to. This constant quest for knowledge of the country around him was what made Colter the greatest explorer of his time.

Had he gone looking for the "stinking water" in the dead of winter, he could have, more easily than not, wound up in Sunlight Basin.

In mid- or late winter, the most feasible route, from the mouth of the Bighorn, was not up that river, with its steep, rugged, almost impassable canyon. It would have been up the broad valley of the Yellowstone to Clark's Fork, thence up the narrower but still passable valley of that river to O'Hara Creek, and up O'Hara Creek to a low pass at its headwaters. From there, he could look down directly into the valley of the Shoshone, close to where Cody now is.

But if he missed O'Hara Creek, then just a few miles farther up Clark's

Fork was Sunlight Creek, also coming from the south, as did O'Hara Creek. The Crow wintering there would have been able to tell him that the land features he was seeking were only about two days travel (in winter) to the southeast. But we do not know if he made the trip. We do know that he was in Sunlight Basin, and all things considered, he would have known of the thermal features along the Shoshone.

Of what importance is this? Persons writing about Colter, unable to find any reason for this trip, have decided it was frivolous—and based on this evaluation and Biddle's later pronouncement—have more or less discounted some of his discoveries, including Pierre's Hole and the thermal features in Yellowstone Park. Some writers have treated the trip on which Colter made the above discoveries as a more or less meaningless stroll.

During the winter of 1806/07, Colter and his two companions had a falling-out.* No one knows what brought it on. A good possibility is that Colter's trip to Sunlight Basin was the proximate cause. Neither Hancock nor Dixon knew sign language or Crow language. Colter, then, was their buffer with these Indians. When he left them alone among the Indians, they may have viewed their position as dangerous and Colter's trip as a desertion. In any event, they parted next spring, and except for the stepson earlier mentioned, nothing further is heard of Hancock or Dixon.

Colter went down the Yellowstone and then the Missouri in a homemade canoe. He met Manuel Lisa, bound upstream on a trapping-trading venture, near the juncture of the Missouri and Platte in July 1807. With Lisa were George Drouillard ("Drewyer" to the trappers), John Potts and Peter Wiser—all members of the Lewis and Clark Expedition and, thus, well known to Colter.

Lisa persuaded Colter to return with him to the mouth of the Bighorn. Since Lisa had never been within hundreds of miles of this spot, it was obvious that its selection as a site to build a fort (trading post) was based on information from Colter.

The group arrived at the chosen site in late October. On 21 November, they were still building the fort*—a main building for trading and to store goods, some cabins to live in, and a stockade. Sometime about this date, Lisa dispatched Colter with a pack of thirty pounds to "contact the Crow Nation and other tribes" to tell them of the post and Lisa's desire to trade with them for furs.

The wording of this part of Colter's instructions is most important to an understanding of his mission. He was *not* taking a walk, as has been implied. In that pack of thirty pounds were trade goods: vermillion, knives, mirrors, beads, perhaps a hatchet, and maybe a trade blanket. He was, in effect, a

---

*David Lavender says that Joseph Dixon told a preacher named Peter Cartwright that the three men quarrelled bitterly during the winter of 1806/07 and separated. Dixon gave no reason for the quarrel.

*Known variously as Fort Remon, Raymond, Lisa, or Manuel. Fort Raymond was most common. See Appendix A.

traveling salesman, going to display his wares and to urge the Indians to take furs to the post to trade.

In this guise, he would have traveled along the eastern edge of the Absaroka and Wind River ranges, going into the mouths of small canyons and gullies from which tributary creeks emerged, where he hoped to find Indian groups in their winter camps. Since he did not know the area, he could not have gone directly to Indian encampments. Instead, as he crossed each creek coming out of the foothills, he would have had to make a decision to turn either upstream or down to locate the Indians. He would have been faced with this decision more than forty times between the mouth of the Bighorn and the Wind River between present Riverton and Dubois, Wyoming. (The Bighorn and Wind River are the *same* stream. The name inexplicably changes from Wind River to Bighorn about halfway in its course.)

From late November until April, Colter would have been traveling in snow. Perhaps only a foot or two deep, it still would have slowed him down. Also, he would have been forced by Indian custom to stay a day and a night with each group he visited. One did not dash into an Indian encampment, make a hurried visit, and dash out. That would have been considered unfriendly. And to make friends was the purpose of Colter's trip. Therefore, it would have taken from thirty to fifty of the short winter days to reach either Togwotee Pass or Union Pass through the Wind River Range. These passes, 9,658 and 9,210 feet high respectively, would, at that time in winter have been choked with fifteen to thirty feet of snow. They were the lowest spots in either the Absaroka or Wind River ranges from Union Pass northward almost to where Colter began his trip.

Most of what we know of Colter's route comes from a map by William Clark on which the latter worked from 1806 to 1811. The manuscript map was then turned over to three men—a cartographer, an engraver, and a printer—but was not printed until 1814. The three were Samuel Harrison, John Vaughan, and Samuel Lewis, and one, or all, of them took great liberties with Clark's manuscript map, changing the direction of one river's flow, moving mountains and lakes around. These inaccuracies caused both Clark and Colter to be discredited since it was known that much of the information came from Colter. Not until Clark's manuscript map came to light, many, many years later, was it discovered that the errors were the fault of neither Clark nor Colter.

Clark's map is such small scale, a mile to a tiny fraction of an inch, that the route labeled "Colter's route in 1807" cannot be exactly placed throughout its length. The consensus of careful historians is that Colter went up the Bighorn to Pryor Creek, up that creek to its headwaters, and over the Divide into the valley of the Shoshone, striking that river somewhere east of the thermal features.

Colter then went up the Shoshone past the features labeled on the map as "Boiling spa"—or at least that's how the words appear—and this has puzzled all who have studied the map. Was Clark joking? He was not known to be witty or humorous. Also, there is some doubt that he would have heard of that small town in Belgium which has recently become a generic term for any natural hot water.

I've examined reproductions of both the printed map and Clark's manuscript map. The printed map does appear to say "spa." But, to me, the word on the manuscript map appears to be "spg," with the *g* written, as it often was then, as a smaller version of a capital *G*, which could be mistaken for a small *a* not closed up. What is important, however, is that there is no mention of sulphur or brimstone which would lead one to believe this was Colter's Hell, as so many later historians have claimed it was.

Colter's route then is shown turning southward along the foothills to the vicinity of Togwotee or Union Passes. These passes are about twenty airline miles apart. It is the consensus of historians that Colter turned and went across Togwotee Pass into Jackson's Hole. There is not much argument here. There is about *when* he made that part of his journey.

Those historians who maintain that he continued his journey in winter must not know what the terrain or the winters are like. He would have had to travel more than a hundred miles over severely rugged country where the snow ranged from six to forty feet deep. There would have been no game; the elk herds that now winter in Jackson's Hole are a modern invention. They are there in winter because they have been fed for over seventy-five years to keep them there. I cut and stacked hay to feed that herd in 1938. Jim Bridger, guiding an Army survey unit more than fifty years after Colter, said of crossing the area in winter that even a crow would have to carry its own rations to do so.

Further, we must consider *why* Colter wanted to cross to Pierre's Hole. He was *not* on an exploring trip, he was a traveling salesman making calls.

Colter must have learned that the area west of the Tetons was occupied by the Shoshone. Possibly he thought them to be the same Shoshone that he had encountered in Northern Idaho with Lewis and Clark. Those were Lemhi Shoshone, Sacajawea's tribe. The Snake River Plain Shoshone, though related, were not of that tribe.

Colter could have got his information from either the Crow or the Wind River Shoshone. The Wind River heads up near Togwotee Pass and runs southeast to about Riverton where it turns northward. The river in that section formed the boundary dividing the winter range of the Crow, on the north, from the Wind River Shoshone, on the south. No matter which tribe gave Colter his information, they would have known that the Snake River Plain Shoshone did not winter in Pierre's Hole but were some 200 miles southwest of there. All Indian tribes were acutely aware of the winter ranges of neighboring tribes. Such information was necessary to guard against attack on a group's horse herds because winter was when most horse stealing was done.

Anyone who knows the country and its winters would know that Colter wintered somewhere on the east slope of the Rockies, either with a group of Crow or Wind River Shoshone. To have attempted to cross the Wind River range, Jackson's Hole, and the Teton range in winter to contact Indians who were not there would have been both foolish and foolhardy. Colter was neither.

My belief, knowing what I do of Colter's natural curiosity, was that he would spend the winter with the Wind River Shoshone. Why?—to learn a new language, one he would need to communicate with the Snake River Plain Shoshone across the mountains to the west. There is no reason to believe he would have made the trip except to deal with this tribe. That would have been his purpose, and almost surely he would have known something of their language before he went, if it had been possible to do so.

However that may be, he crossed the Togwotee and Teton passes and came into Pierre's Hole sometime in 1808. The three things we can be positive about concerning his trip is that he left Fort Raymond sometime late November 1807, returned there before mid-July 1808, and was in Pierre's Hole in 1808.

We can be sure of the latter because in 1931, a man named William Beard and his son were plowing on their farm about 5½ miles east of Tetonia, Idaho, near the Idaho-Wyoming border, and they plowed up a stone. The stone, of rhyolite lava, was in the rough natural shape of a human head in profile. It was 13 by 8 inches and 4 inches thick. Carved on one side was the name, John Colter, on the other, the year 1808.*

Beard had never heard of John Colter, but kept the stone as a curiosity. Later, in 1933, a neighbor, Aubrey Lyon, who had heard of Colter, traded Beard a pair of used boots for it. Beard had no use for the stone, and he needed the boots.

Lyon took the stone into Jackson's Hole, to officials of the newly created (1929) Grand Teton National Park and offered it to them for their tiny museum.* The officials, suspecting a hoax, were dubious about accepting it. They did, however, submit the stone to exhaustive testing for authenticity.

First they talked to Beard. The fact clinching that Beard intended no hoax was that he had traded the stone for a pair of second-hand boots. Perpetrators of hoaxes, such as the Cardiff Giant and the Tuscan Statues, had done so to make fortunes. Scientists examined the stone and found it chemically identical to other rocks in the area and structurally similar. The erosion of the edges of the carved letters and figures, after 123 years, was consistent with weathering for such a period. All tests being positive—and with *no negative evidence*—the stone was declared authentic and was accepted by the museum, where it now resides. More recent testing has verified those earlier results.

So, we know that Colter was in Pierre's Hole sometime in the first six months of 1808. He was some 400 miles by any trail from Fort Raymond and traveling on foot. Clark's map shows that he recrossed the Tetons, skirted Jackson Lake on the west, entered Yellowstone Park somewhere near the

---

*Carving names on stones was old stuff to Colter. Some of Clark's group, traveling down the Yellowstone in 1806, had carved their names on Pompey's Pillar. Colter was with that group.

*I worked evenings in that museum in 1938.

center of its south border, and went north. Just where he turned east to once again strike the Shoshone is not known. However, near that point on the map route where he turned east, the words "Hot Spring Brimestone" appear. Since Clark turned his manuscript over to be printed in 1811, Colter had to be the source of that information. No one else, except Indians, had ever been there.

In Colter's time, and even into mine, the words *hell and brimstone* were constantly linked. I've heard my father use the terms together many times, and I've heard them used by circuit-riding preachers in their sermons. I've traced them back, in various writings and sermons, into the 1700s. Often, it was *hellfire and brimstone,* occasionally just *hell and brimstone,* but the terms were linked in common usage into the 1930s, at least in the Ozarks where I grew up.

This is almost positive proof that Yellowstone Park, and *not* the thermal features along the Shoshone River, was Colter's Hell, although some historians assert the opposite. None has even given a logical explanation for their choice—nor have I ever seen the word, *brimstone,* associated with the Shoshone features, and only rarely, the word, *sulphur.*

We know that Colter returned to Fort Raymond sometime before mid-July 1808 because Lisa departed for Saint Louis at that time and Colter returned before Lisa left.

Incidentally, in 1811, Lisa told Henry M. Brackenridge that there were thermal features along a river "about sixty miles south of here"* (the mouth of the Bighorn). Lisa did not mention sulphur, brimstone, or Colter's Hell. Nor did Brackenridge in *Views of Louisiana together with a Journal of a Voyage up the Missouri River in 1811.* This was three or four years *after* Colter made his trip but the term *Colter's Hell* was not then associated with the Shoshone River area. The term did not appear in print until after 1814, when Clark's map was published. Yet, those Shoshone River thermal features are mentioned several times before 1814, never as Colter's Hell. I can find nothing in all my research to indicate that the thermal features were known as Colter's Hell until fairly recently, and *no historian* who calls them that has made any kind of a reasonable case for doing so.

Lisa left Fort Raymond in July 1808 to take his furs downriver *and* to finance and organize the Saint Louis Missouri Fur Company, in partnership with Andrew Henry and Pierre Menard, among others.

In September, Colter went into the Gallatin Valley with several hundred Crow. The size of this group indicates a major fall hunt because such large groups formed almost always either for a major hunt or for war. In the Gallatin Valley, the Crow and Colter encountered a larger group of Blackfeet. They also were probably on a major fall hunt, gathering meat for the coming winter. The two groups clashed.

The reports say that Colter's efforts with his rifle were a major factor in

---

*This is an error on Lisa's part, the actual distance from Fort Raymond to the Cody area is more than twice 60 miles.

This sign, in Teton Basin beside State Highway 33, errs
on the distance to Fort Raymond and the location of Colter's Hell.
The information was taken from an early, local history.

the defeat of the Blackfeet, winning him the enmity of that tribe and the
loyalty of the Crow.

In the spring of 1809, Colter and John Potts went from Fort Raymond to
Three Forks on a *trapping* venture. It does not seem likely that that was the
real purpose. If beaver was their object, they needn't have gone 250 miles,
and into enemy territory, to find them. In view of later events, it's almost a
certainty that they were scouting the area for Andrew Henry and Pierre
Menard, who would be coming up from Saint Louis with a brigade of trappers later that year.

Potts and Colter were captured by Blackfeet. Potts was killed. Colter was
stripped naked and told to run for his life. He outran all but one of his
pursuers and managed to kill that one with his own spear. Then he made his
way back to Fort Raymond, naked.

After recovering and getting new clothing, he went down the Yellowstone
and the Missouri, to near Stanton, North Dakota, to meet Henry and Menard, coming up with keelboats loaded with men and supplies. This was in
October 1809. He guided Henry and some men on horseback to Fort Raymond while Menard brought up the keelboat. They wintered there (Fort
Raymond).

The following spring Colter guided Henry and Menard to Three Forks,
as related in the first chapter. But he may have done something else, even
more important.

No one has been able to find a reason for Henry's retreat up the
Madison. If escape from the attacks by the Blackfeet was the reason, he
could have more quickly and just as safely retreated up the Gallatin and back
to Fort Raymond.

But, suppose Colter, during the winter months of 1809/1810, whiling
away the winter hours at Fort Raymond, had told Henry of Pierre's Hole?
Henry was a businessman—a *gentleman*. He was no explorer, no adventurer.
But if Colter had told him of the beaver riches of the area west of the

Tetons, safely beyond—at that time—raids by the marauding Blackfeet, then Henry would have had ample reason to go south toward that area to conduct his trapping operations.

The beaver were there. When the next group of trappers came into the area, in 1819, they found plenty of beaver. Trapper's brigades of the North West Company and Hudson's Bay Company, led by Donald MacKenzie, Alexander Ross, and Michael Bourdon, reported taking 75,000 beaver from the area from 1819 to 1822. In 1820, MacKenzie wrote this about the area:

> Woods and valleys, rocks and plains, rivers and ravines alternately met us; but altogether it is a delightful country. There, animals of every class rove about undisturbed. Wherever there was a little plain, the red deer (elk) were seen grazing in herds about the rivers, and where there was a sapling, the ingenious and industrious beaver was at work. Otters sported in the eddies; the wolf and fox were seen sauntering in quest of prey; on the spreading branches of the stunted pines sat the raccoon secure. The badger sat quietly looking from his mound; and in numberless ravines, among bushes laden with fruit, the black, brown and grizzly bear were seen. The mountain sheep and goat, white as snow, browzed on the rocks and ridges, and the big horn species ran among the lofty cliffs. Eagles and vultures flew about the rivers.
>
> When we approached, most of these animals stood motionless. The report of a gun did not alarm them; they would give a frisk at each shot and stand again. Hordes of wild horses were likewise seen. They were the wildest of all the animals for none of them could be approached. One band contained more than two hundred.

This was the paradise that Colter would have told Henry about. I can think of no other reason for his trip up the Madison into the watershed of Henry's Fork. From Raynolds Pass, he would have seen the Tetons, and from Colter he would have known that the area he sought lay at their base. Traveling down a river—the one named for him—was at that time the normal practice of whites traveling in strange country. And of course, beaver were found nowhere else but along streams. We do not know why Henry and his men stopped in July where they did, with the Tetons in plain sight to the east, no more than forty miles away. But it is almost a certainty that he had heard of the area from Colter.

Colter left Henry's group at Three Forks, returned to Fort Raymond, and then went on to Saint Louis. There are reports that he was planning to return to the wilderness when he died of jaundice in 1813. He left behind men who, having traveled with him, learned from him and passed this knowledge on to others such as Jim Bridger, Thomas Fitzpatrick (Broken Hand), David Jackson (after whom Jackson's Hole is named), Jed and Thomas (Peg Leg) Smith, and William and Milton Sublette—all of whom left their mark on the area and all of whom learned of it from men who learned of it from Colter.

When Andrew Henry's group split up at Fort Henry in the spring of 1811, three men went east and south. The three—John Hoback, Jacob Reznor, and Edward Robinson—crossed Pierre's Hole to the Tetons, went along the base of the mountains to the Snake River, up to the junction of the Hoback River, and up that stream to the plateau at its headwaters. Here they turned northeast through Union Pass, crossed Wyoming in that direction, and reached the Missouri River near the North Dakota-South Dakota border. There they met Wilson Price Hunt, Astor's partner in the Pacific Fur Company. Hunt had started up the Missouri in 1810 and had talked to Colter in the fall of that year. Meeting three of his companions loaded with information about the area to the west was a happy accident.

Hunt's mission was to try to find an overland route from Saint Louis to the mouth of the Columbia. He was a businessman "first, last and always," but he was also a good leader of men. He was spoken of by his contemporaries as "able, courageous, amicable," though inexperienced in wilderness travel.

Hunt's party, in May 1811, obtained horses and started overland with Hoback and his companions as guides. They left two scientists, Thomas Nutall and John Bradbury, to continue on upriver with Lisa's group bound for Fort Raymond. Colter had advised Hunt to seek a route through Wyoming and southeast Idaho to avoid the dreaded Blackfeet on the northern route. Getting Hoback and the others to lead him was the only good luck Hunt had for the rest of his trip.

Hunt retraced the route over which Hoback had just come but, after crossing the Tetons, decided to try going down the Snake—known then as Mad River. Finding that too dangerous, they set out for Fort Henry. Hoback and his companions could not find the fort, but some friendly Shoshone Indians guided them to it. They arrived on 8 October 1811.

The placid appearance of the river at Fort Henry deceived them, and on the assumption that they could proceed to the Columbia by way of the river, they commenced to build canoes (dugouts) from cottonwood logs. It proved to be a terrible mistake.

Hunt had trapped and traded on this entire trip. He sent some or all of the furs he had obtained back overland along with some of his men. Then he and the rest set out downriver in fifteen dugout canoes, loaded with food, trade goods, and other supplies. They gave their horses to the Shoshones to

Fort Henry sign on Highway 191, now bypassed by a section of freeway.

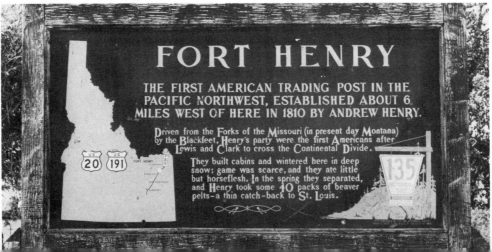

This little mound marks the site of Fort Henry, the first such
American construction west of the Rockies. Erected 1810.

mind until they returned. Hunt left behind a rock carved with the words
"Fort Henry 1811 by Cap Hunt." This stone was unearthed at the site in
1933.

Ten days down the river, rapids and falls on the main Snake brought
their river float to a halt. One man had been lost, along with considerable
quantities of supplies and goods. They went on by foot, cacheing the rest of
their goods and supplies, which were later found and taken by Indians.

Hunt took one group down the west side of the river. Donald MacKenzie
took several others down the east. This trek commenced about the first of
November. They reached the mouth of the Columbia on 15 February 1812.
In between, they nearly starved—and ate their dogs, moccasins, beaver skins,
and anything else they had that was edible. Even so, both groups were saved
from starving by friendly Nez Percé, Clatsop, and other Indians.

Hunt learned from his experiences, and those of Robert Stuart and others that he sent back to Saint Louis, across Pierre's Hole. Though Hunt's trip
was arduous and costly, it was, in the main, successful. He found the overland route that would become the Oregon Trail, over which thousands
would cross the west to settle in Oregon Territory.

It would be some years before that would take place. In the meantime, in
the War of 1812 with Britain, Astor and Hunt lost Astoria, and this war and
the following financial depression put the American fur trade into oblivion
until the 1820s. The Blackfeet inadvertently helped the cause of the British
by pushing American trappers out of Montana.

Donald MacKenzie, who had nearly lost his life and those of his men
while with Hunt, joined the North West Company and became a brigade
leader. He made several sallies from the area of the mouth of the Clearwater
into the area from the mouth of Henry's Fork southward, reaching Bear
Lake in 1819. It was on this trek that one of his trappers, an Iroquois Indian
named Pierre Tevanitagon, was alleged to have discovered Pierre's Hole,
hence the name.

Fort Henry Marker on farm road about 300 yards northwest
of the actual fort site.

Some historians say that Old Pierre, as he was known, actually did not
enter Pierre's Hole until 1820, but that is generally regarded as the time
MacKenzie first saw the area. What these people all ignore is that Colter and
several other American trappers had been there years before. Of course, the
Shoshone had been there for centuries.

No group of trappers—or Indians—ever wintered in the Hole. The trappers usually chose the areas of Cache Valley, Bear Lake, or even the mouth
of Bear River (Great Salt Lake) for wintering.

In 1822, William Ashley and Andrew Henry and the Rocky Mountain
Fur Company tried once more to trap and trade in Montana. They had
troubles enough to cause Ashley to give up the idea of fixed location posts
for trading and commence the *rendezvous* system—where goods and trappers, white and Indian, met at a predetermined place to trade. The area of
the Green River in Wyoming saw most of these but in 1829 and 1832, these
meetings were held in Pierre's Hole. (There were two held in 1829, one on
Wind River* and one in Pierre's Hole.)

The 1832 rendezvous in Pierre's Hole is famous for the battle between
the Blackfeet and the trappers and their Indian allies. Some historians have
accepted the trappers' version that the Indians they fought against were
Gros Ventres of the Prairie (Atsina), but this is careless research. They were

---

*Some sources put one 1829 rendezvous on the Popo Agie.

Sisika (Blackfeet). (See Appendix A, A Confusion of Names.) What made this particular fight famous was not that the trappers had strong Indian allies, Nez Percé and Flathead, but the number of men there who would later become famous in the fur trade. These included Jim Bridger, Kit Carson, the Sublettes, Jed Smith, Thomas Fitzpatrick (Broken Hand), Nathaniel Wyeth, and others.

The battle took place about three miles south of Driggs, Idaho (in what is Section 15, Township 4 north, Range 45 east). The Blackfeet did not start the fight, it started when a French trapper, Auguste Godin, treacherously murdered the Blackfeet leader. The battle lasted all day, with the Blackfeet forted up behind logs in heavy brush. They slipped away during the night. An estimated twenty-six to thirty Blackfeet were killed, as were three whites and ten of their Indian allies. There were no lasting effects. The claim that this battle put an end to use of Pierre's Hole for a rendezvous place ignores the facts: the Hole was simply too difficult to reach with loaded packtrains and the wagons that soon replaced them.

The fur trade was already slipping, the beaver hat of fashion had been replaced by the high silk hat. Though trappers continued to trap in the area, most of this later trapping was in the Gray's and Portneuf river areas. The British and the Americans had pretty well stripped Pierre's Hole of beaver.

In 1840, 1,600 Salish (Flathead) from northwestern Montana trekked out to meet the missionary Father Pierre Jean De Smet in Pierre's Hole, then crossed back into Montana. They camped at Henry's Lake where De Smet left a rock, later found, on which was carved "July 23, 1840 De Smet." He was also in the Henry's Fork area in 1841. At that time he visited Fort Hall and purchased bags of pemmican from the Hudson's Bay Company which then owned the post. De Smet called pemmican "Toro" and said he paid a dollar a bag for it. He didn't say how large the bags were.

From this time until 1860, occasional bands of trappers used the place as a starting point at which to gather before going to trap somewhere else. In 1860 Beaver Dick Leigh settled here with his wife Jenny, daughter of Chief

The Battle of Pierre's Hole was between trappers and Blackfeet—
not Gros Ventres (Atsina) who lived near the Blackfeet but were unrelated.

This marker along State 33 south of Driggs, Idaho, further perpetuates
the mistake about who the trappers fought.

Washakie of the Wind River Shoshone. Leigh was thus a brother-in-law of
Jim Bridger who also had married one of Washakie's daughters.

In the 1880s homesteaders were plagued by a band of ingenious and
brassy horse thieves. These brigands would steal horses in Pierre's Hole,
which the settlers now called Teton Basin, sell them in southern Wyoming,
steal horses in northern Wyoming, sell those in Montana, and then steal
horses in southwest Montana to sell in Teton Basin. In a few years the settlers found themselves buying back horses stolen from them some years earlier.

In 1879 a prairie fire started close to present Rexburg near the mouth of
Henry's Fork. Pushed by a sixty-mile-an-hour wind, the fire raced into Teton
Basin and the Island Park area. In forty-eight hours the fire had created a
wasteland of ashes over nearly all of Island Park and much of Teton Basin.
But both areas were only lightly settled, so there were no deaths or much
destruction of personal property.

As such places go, Teton Basin is still very lightly populated. Driggs, the
largest town in the basin, has about 700 people. That's more than twice the
total population of the other three villages in the Basin, and the total
number of people in Teton County is less than 3,000.

It is entirely farm-ranch country. Some coal was mined there about sixty
to seventy years ago, but not now. There is only light timber harvest; most of
the Basin is grassland. The north part is wheat country; the south part, grazing land. Agricultural practices have caused some silting of the Teton River
and its tributaries. This is slowly getting better as the farmers and ranchers,
with the urging of the county agents, are becoming aware that there is not an
unlimited amount of topsoil. As their fertilizer bills go up, they increasingly
seek better methods of holding onto what they have.

There does not, at present, appear to be any feasible industry, mining, or
other intense-usage practices to threaten the Basin. I hope that the environment will continue to improve and that the Teton Basin will still be one of
the most beautiful scenic areas in the world. To see it at its most glorious,
visit it in the fall.

11

TRAPPERS, TRADERS, INDIANS, SPIES

From 1808 to the 1880s the only people to come into the Teton Basin, or elsewhere in the Henry's Fork watershed, were trappers, traders, Indians, and spies—or people accompanying them.

The first of the traders was Wilson Price Hunt, Astor's partner. Though Hunt did not remain in the area, he told Astor of its wonders, and Astor's trappers were there from the 1820s until the beaver trade died out. It was Astor's American Fur Company that eventually pushed out the British and took over a near monopoly of the fur trade in the Rocky Mountains, which, in those days, were known as the Stony Mountains, Shining Mountains, or the White Mountains.

I can find no record in any of the documents of the day of serious trapping in the upper Henry's Fork-Island Park areas. Trappers traveled across the area, on their way from Pierre's Hole or Fort Hall to Montana or the Yellowstone, but I find no mention of trapping there.

Manuel Alvarez, a trapper brigade leader who would later become U.S. Consul to Mexico at Santa Fe, led a band of trappers from Fort Hall up Henry's Fork to the Firehole Geyser Basins in 1833. This was recorded by another trapper, Warren A. Ferris, in *Life in the Rocky Mountains (1830–35)*. But neither Ferris nor Osborne Russell (*Journal of a Trapper [1834–1843]*), make any mention of trapping anywhere on Henry's Fork.

The first serious trader to come with ideas of permanence was Nathaniel J. Wyeth. In 1832, Wyeth, son of a wealthy Boston hotel owner, gave up the management of a prosperous ice-shipping company to explore the possibilities of trading in the Rocky Mountains. He organized a group of other well-to-do young men to go into business with him and to accompany him west.

To prepare for the trip, he and his young partners camped and *roughed it,* on an island in Boston harbor for ten days before starting on their trip.

They left by ship for Baltimore on 11 March 1832, took the nation's first railroad from there to the foot of the Alleghenies, then went by steamboat down the Ohio, and up the Mississippi and Missouri to Independence. There they were able to hook up with the traders traveling to the rendezvous at Pierre's Hole.*

This was fortunate because one historian wrote this about Wyeth and his men: "A more naive group never essayed the trail west than the score who set out with Nathaniel Wyeth on his first venture in 1832." (Harriet D. Munnick, *Solomon Howard Smith, in The Mountain Men and the Fur Trade of the Far West.*)

Wyeth arrived in Pierre's Hole in time to be involved in the battle there, and he described the scene before the battle, giving us the best record of who was involved. There were, he said, 120 lodges (tepees) of Nez Percé, 80 lodges of Flathead (Salish), and 190 brigade trappers of the American and Rocky Mountain fur companies, plus a number of free trappers. He mentions Bridger, Carson, the Sublettes, and Fitzpatrick, plus many others who would become well known in the fur trade.

Wyeth proceeded on to the mouth of the Columbia to await the arrival of the brig, *Sultana,* with a load of trade goods previously shipped from Boston. But the brig had been sunk in a storm. Wyeth spent the winter at Fort Vancouver as a guest of The Hudson's Bay Company.

He left in February 1833 with two other men, struggled back across Idaho and the West to Saint Louis, and then went on to Boston. He arrived there in November 1833, having made some business deals on the way.

He had contracted with Milton Sublette to furnish supplies for the Rocky Mountain Fur Company at the 1834 Green River rendezvous at prices somewhat under those of other traders. It may be interesting, in this day of high prices, to look at some of that day's prices. Gunpowder was $1.50 a pound; lead, $1; shot, $1.25; blankets, $9 to $11; scarlet cloth (the Indian's favorite color) was $6 a yard! Tea kettles were $2; three-gallon iron kettles, $2.25; axes, $1; coffee, $1.25 a pound; flannel and calico, $1–$2 a yard; beads, except red ones, $2.50 a pound; vermillion (the favorite paint of all Indians), $3 a gallon; tobacco, $1.25 a pound; soap, $1.25 a pound. All goods were packed from Saint Louis to wherever the rendezvous had been decided on the previous year.

Traders advanced trappers up to $400 in goods, at 600 percent over Saint Louis prices. Two hundred per cent of this was interest. By this practice the traders kept the trappers constantly in debt and literally bound to deliver their furs to the trader they owed.

Milton Sublette was unable to go with Wyeth to the rendezvous because of a seriously diseased leg. When Wyeth arrived with his goods, he found that William Sublette, Milton's brother, had already forced the trappers to trade for *his* goods by foreclosing notes owed him. Wyeth received a $500

*Sublette, MacKenzie, *et al.*

guarantee but found himself with several thousand dollars in goods with no one to sell them to.

Wyeth proceeded on to the Snake River between the Blackfoot and Portneuf rivers and there built Fort Hall as a trading post on what was becoming the Oregon Trail. The post was completed by 4 August 1834, and it was a proper fort with a stockade, around the inside of which was an elevated walkway on which twelve men kept guard, having constantly at hand 100 loaded rifles.

Wyeth kept excellent records, his invoices have given us a clear picture of the commerce carried on here by his Columbia River Fishing and Trading Company. He recorded not only the first fishhooks west of the Rockies but the first mention of catching trout on hook and line, which occurred in the Snake River near Fort Hall.

He proceeded on to the mouth of the Columbia, arriving there September 1834, to begin trading for furs and salmon and to try to establish a trade in the latter. Some salmon did get back to Boston, but the venture was never a success.

An interesting sidelight to Wyeth's 1834 cross-continent jaunt is that he was accompanied by two to-be-famous scientists. One was John K. Townsend, an English naturalist only twenty-five years old. The other was Thomas Nuttall who had gone up the Missouri with Hunt and Lisa in 1811 to do research on birds and plants.

Nuttall had been curator of Harvard University's departments of Botany and Ornithology since 1822. This adventurous scientist was forty-eight years old when he accompanied Wyeth clear across the continent in 1834. But that was only the first step of a remarkable journey by this unique man.

After arriving at Fort Vancouver, having collected specimens of plants and identified birds all the way, Nuttall then began to *hitchhike* by sailing vessels down the West Coast of America, doing more collecting. In California, young Townsend took a ship to Hawaii to do more scientific work there. Nuttall continued down to San Diego, arriving in May 1836. Here occurred a remarkable coincidence that, to my knowledge, has never been commented on by any historian.

Nuttall had left Boston on his overland trip in February 1834. In August of that year, a young Harvard student had departed Boston as an ordinary seaman on the brig, *Pilgrim,* bound around the Horn to California. There he had engaged in the hide trade, and was set to return as a seaman, to Boston on the ship, *Alert,* loaded with hides, when Nuttall showed up with his crates and bags of specimens to take passage home on the same ship. These two, one a Harvard official, the other a student, had taken vastly different roads to arrive at the same place at the same time, each not knowing the other was there until they met. Nuttall had travelled 3,500 miles overland, then 1,400 miles by ship to arrive at San Diego. Richard Henry Dana had traveled over 14,000 miles by sea around the Horn to arrive at the same spot.

Both wrote important and famous books about their journeys. Nuttall's was *North American Sylva.* He acknowledges Wyeth's help by naming our two earliest large spring flowers: *Wyethia helianthoides* and *Wyethia amplexicaulis.* We call them white and yellow mule ears. Dana's, of course, was one of the greatest sea books of all time, *Two Years Before the Mast.*

Wyeth's trading company never was a great success and in 1837 he sold Fort Hall to the Hudson's Bay Company which operated it for years. Wyeth himself returned to Boston to the ice and hotel business. In his writings, he praised the Flathead and Nez Percé as devout, brave, and honest and deplored the Blackfeet as the worst desperadoes among Plains Indians. Others, including Bonneville, have confirmed his judgment.

Benjamin Louis Eulalie DeBonneville has caused historians some problems. Was he a military officer, a fur trader, a spy, or all three?

A West Point graduate, in 1831 Bonneville was a captain, with some experience in frontier posts. At this time he requested, and was granted, a leave of absence from August 1831 to October 1833, to engage in the fur trade. This kind of thing, though extremely unusual, was not completely unknown for a regular officer. But, in most cases, such absences were granted for the purpose of allowing the officer to take care of affairs; a family business, or something similar, due to the death of a parent or other relative. Allowing such an absence for the purpose of *commencing* a profit-making business was rare to unheard of.

Bonneville organized a group of trappers and moved west in 1832. He brought wagons and goods, was organized well, and reached Pierre's Hole in September of that year. He examined the battle site there with a professional eye and moved on. He wintered with the Nez Percé on the Salmon River in northern Idaho.

He would later praise these Indians as "pious, generous, industrious, more like a nation of saints than a horde of savages."

Bonneville trapped around the mouth of Henry's Fork and the south-central Idaho in 1833, wintering near the mouth of Portneuf River. But some of his men were ranging widely across the West, into northern California and Oregon. By the time Bonneville had finished his operations and returned east in the fall of 1835, his men had been in Utah, California, Oregon, Washington, most of Idaho, and nearly all of southern Wyoming. Many of them had roamed over arid areas of the Great Basin that never saw a beaver.

Bonneville was dismissed from the service for having overstayed his leave, but a few letters to the right people not only got him reinstated, but got all the back pay due him.

To one who knows the military and its way of doing things, it seems obvious that this was a planned covert intelligence operation. The *Oregon question* was beginning to occupy both American and British military officials; in 1840 it would reach the point where the slogan, *Fifty-four-forty or fight,* was taken seriously. Both countries felt the need to know more about the area.

The Hudson's Bay Company was ranging widely over the northwest and had several posts in Washington. Its men were constantly in Idaho, northern Montana, northern Oregon, and, occasionally, farther south. There is no question their brigade leaders' reports were used by the British military. We had no one—our trappers would not have been considered trustworthy agents by the U.S. military, and with the delicate political situation, we could not send an overt military force into the area. So, a trained, experienced military officer went in the guise of a trader. It may not have fooled the British, but it allowed them no protest.

Bonneville's reports and maps were of great value, and when the first immigrants moved over the Oregon Trail in 1840, they knew exactly where to travel in order to avoid trouble. Though immigrants to other areas often suffered enormous hardships, by comparison the Oregon Trailers did not. Bonneville had done an excellent job, and for it he is remembered in the naming of Lake Bonneville, a 20,000 square mile lake once in northern Utah. Great Salt Lake is its remnant. Also, his name is commemorated in Bonneville Dam on the Columbia River and in a county in Idaho. If he had merely been a careless officer who had overstayed his leave while trying to get rich, his dismissal would have stood, and he would never have been heard of again.

A young man who came west with Wyeth in 1834 left one of the better records of the period and the area. Osborne Russell, in *Journal of a Trapper* (1834–1843) gives a more intimate peek into the life of trappers and the practices of the day. He also gives us a look at the diet of trapper in ordinary times. It was meat, mostly boiled, and sometimes unseasoned. But there were occasional feasts. There was one on the Fourth of July 1839. Russell and his companions were camped on Jackson Lake, having trekked through Pierre's Hole on their way from Fort Hall. A brigade of French trappers was camped nearby and Russell and his friends wished to show them how they celebrated their independence. They killed buffalo, elk, mountain sheep, caught twenty *salmon trout* (the second recorded instance of trout caught on hook and line) and served the *Frenchies* a meal of three kinds of meat, trout, biscuits, and coffee.

But this grand feed was exceeded by one Russell records for Christmas 1840. He and his friends were wintering at Great Salt Lake. Wagons had bought supplies into this and other areas, so there was more *imported* food. The meal was composed of two kinds of meat—elk and deer—a flour pudding laced with dried fruit and topped with a sauce of fruit, water and sugar, sweet cakes, and coffee. From Russell's writings one gets the feeling that the trappers' monotonous diet of meat was not always satisfactory.

Russell spoke often of the trappers going out of their way some distance to obtain wild plums, berries, and choke cherries. On occasion they got into trouble with Indians who would be there after the same patch of fruit. Also, different tribes of Indians would fight over rights to a plum or berry patch.

Mayne Reid, a British historical novelist, spent the 1840s in the western U.S. traveling with trappers and the army. Reid was a keen and accurate observer and an indefatigable recorder of details. His gift of description was exceptional, and though he wrote fiction, it was fiction strongly based on fact. He once wrote of three trappers who left their fall camp to go gathering plums—the trappers term for wild plums, wild cherries and choke cherries. The trappers went knowing full well that Indians would also be out gathering fruit.

The trappers reached the hillside where they knew from previous trips that they would find a large patch of fruit, tied up their horses, took leather bags and made their way into the fruit patch, leaving their rifles on their saddles. This in itself was not as dangerous as it seems. The Indians, if there, would also have left their weapons with their tied up horses.

Sometime during the afternoon, Indians and trappers came together. First there were cries of surprise, then anger. Then the fight started, Indians hitting the trappers with baskets laden with fruit, the trappers swinging their parfleches lustily. Everyone was yelling furiously, venting their anger on the other *thieves*. Then the yells of rage became terror-stricken. The milling trappers and Indians had encroached on two huge grizzly bears who thought that they owned this patch of fruit. Trappers and Indians fled in terror, knocking each other down in their haste to get away from the deadliest threat in the Rocky Mountain West. The bears, who feared nothing, calmly returned to filling their stomachs.

Russell and others recorded the disappearance of the buffalo from the Snake River Plain between 1840 and 1843, and this, along with a scarcity of beaver, sent the trappers looking elsewhere. But it was a last hurrah. The fur trade was shrinking; trappers ventured to other places. It was a time of change. The last rendezvous was held in 1840.

The rendezvous was the only break in the trappers' year. "In effect the trappers worked eleven months for the sake of a debauch at rendezvous. Many of them thought it worth it. At the rendezvous they they found what they had yearned for all year: company, conversation, new clothes, dry shoes (sic), a variety of women, tobacco, and booze. For one glorious month they talked, bragged, fought, gambled, fornicated, and drank in a mighty exhibit of manliness before, broke and drained, they turned back into the mountains for another perilous year."—Bill Gilbert, *The Trail Blazers*.

Russell, Joe Meek (a trapper known for his exaggerated tales), and others went on to Oregon, the new frontier, where they became men of substance. But other trappers stayed on, willing to put up with diminishing financial returns for a life of untrammeled freedom.

12

THE INDIANS OF THE SNAKE RIVER PLAIN

UNTIL FAIRLY RECENTLY, THERE HAS BEEN LITTLE STUDY OF THE INDIANS of the Snake River Plain. Scientists and archaeologists have determined that forerunners of these people have lived on the Snake River Plain and in the Great Basin for 10,000 years, but we still know very little about them.

When the trappers first came into the area, the Plain was occupied by two related but different tribes. These were the Shoshone and the Bannock. Both were of the *Shoshonean* linguistic group, as were the other tribes of the Great Basin. These were the Ute, Commanche, and Paiute.

Shoshone (Sho-shown) is not a word of those tribes. It comes from the Lakotah Sioux word, *we-Chah-shah-nee,* meaning *unmanly people.* This is the plural; we spell it *Shoshoni.* The trappers corrupted the word to the present phonetic. The singular is *Shoshone,* and some writers use the plural, *Shoshones.* For want of a term, or name, from the tribes themselves, the Ute, Paiute, Commanche, Shoshoni (comprising several tribes), and Bannock are referred to as *Shoshoneans.* No one seems to know what the Shoshone called themselves; my letters to this tribe, now known as the Fort Hall Shoshone, or *Sho-Ban,* remain unanswered. The Sho-Ban designation refers to the fact that these two separate but related tribes, Shoshone and Bannock, share a reservation at Fort Hall, Idaho, on the Snake River.

This is not the original Fort Hall. There were several of them, built on different sites. The original site is considered to be either near the upper end of the American Falls Reservoir or, perhaps, under the waters of that lake.

It is interesting to note how the various Shoshonean tribes reacted to the obtaining of horses. The Commanche immediately adopted them—they obtained them about 1760—and became the most feared horsemen and war-riors of the southern Great Basin. The Paiute—also called Diggers, as were the Shoshoni—when they obtained horses, ate them.

The Bannock obtained horses in the mid-to late 1700s and immediately started the process of turning to a horse-buffalo culture, as had the Plains Indians east of the Rockies. By 1810 the Bannock were fully adapted to the horse-buffalo-tepee culture.

The Wind River Shoshone also got horses in the 1760-1780 period and at once immigrated to the more plentiful buffalo in the area along the base of the Wind River Range, and southward.

The Boise and Lemhi Shoshoni obtained horses from the Nez Percé, but these small northern Idaho tribes were not powerful enough to break out onto either the Snake River Plain, where the Bannock opposed them, or into Montana, where the rapacious Blackfeet held sway.

The Snake River Plain Shoshone were very late getting horses, about 1800 or a little later. Before, these people were rovers on foot across the upper Great Basin and Snake River Plain. They lived meagerly off whatever they could find: insects, roots, berries, seeds, fish, rodents, rabbits, and some larger game. Because of their relative inability to obtain enough of the latter, the Shoshone never were able to face a single year without having to travel widely and work continuously. They worked so hard and so many hours daily just to keep from starving that they had no time to develop a culture,* that is, a consistent style of living and rituals that carried on from generation to generation.

Their possessions were meager, just what they could carry on their backs. They lived in temporary shelters of a few shrubs or small bushes pulled together, tied, and covered with thatching of grass. To the other Shoshonean speaking tribes, the Snake River Plain Shoshone were known as *grass-house people*. Their weapons were good, though primitive. They made excellent bows, and their arrow points, knives, and scrapers were of the best quality. This was largely because they had access to two sources of obsidian. One was in the Black Rock Desert of northwestern Nevada, at the extreme western edge of their range. The other was Obsidian Cliff in Yellowstone Park, near the eastern edge of their range. They did not have the axe until they obtained metal ones from traders.

Obsidian is the finest of rocks for making such tools and weapons. It fractures to an edge that is many times sharper than that of the finest modern surgical instruments. Currently, technicians are experimenting with methods of fastening obsidian blades to handles of steel or plastic to make better surgeon's scalpels. Some are already in use.**

---

*"Culture is that complex whole which includes knowledge, beliefs, art, law, morals, customs and any other capabilities and habits acquired by man as a member of society." Peter Farb, *Man's Rise to Civilization as shown by the Indians of North America*, quoting Edward Taylor.

**This research was originated by archaeologist Dan Crabtree in southeast Idaho, along the Snake River Plain, in the area occupied by the Shoshone. It was developed in classes in Idaho State University and was reported in *American Medical News* on 2 November 1984.

Obsidian Cliff in Yellowstone Park on The Great Bannock Trail.
Indians came here for tool-making materials for at least 10,000 years.
This monolith is solid obsidian.

The scraper was the most important tool for all primitive tribes. There were many kinds; stone artifacts called *knives* by whites were, for the most part, some kind or form of scraper. They were used to shape anything: wood, stone, shell, horn or antler, and to dress skins and leather.

The skin scrapers of most Indian tribes were similar in construction. A wooden handle, generally curved, had affixed to it in some way a wedge-shaped, sharp-edged blade. The skin scrapers of the Snake River Plain Shoshone were of the highest quality, in form and materials, and were much coveted by surrounding tribes, and therefore, invaluable as trade material.

Generally, this Shoshone skin scraper had a handle a foot or so long, in the shape of a modified capital *J*. The curved arm of the *J* was somewhat shortened, and the blade fastened to it with cutting edge out. They looked something like a tiny adze, or even, in some cases, a wee garden hoe.

The blade was fastened against the inside of the arm of the *J* with the thick, top edge against a shoulder in the wood that jutted out, and with a flat surface along the inside of the arm to support the blade. Glue or rawhide was generally the fastening material. A thin strip of rawhide, wet, stretched,

Obsidian rock. This material fractures to an edge many times
sharper than the finest surgical steel. It is an unequaled
natural tool-making material.

and wrapped around both blade and handle arm, would shrink mightily as it
dried and clamp the obsidian blade to the wood with such pressure that it
indented it somewhat. The dried rawhide was almost as hard and unyielding
as iron. This scraper was used in fleshing, cleaning, and de-hairing skins and
also in cleaning, scraping, and dressing leather for clothing and other items.
It was used by pressing the edge of the blade against the material and pull-
ing toward the user. It acted in the same way to smooth or remove material
that a carpenter's plane does, except that it was pulled instead of pushed.

The Snake River Plain Shoshone did not have many items of value to
other tribes; the various types of scrapers made from obsidian were readily
tradeable, as also was the excellent clothing that Shoshone women made. It
was this scarcity of trade items that caused this tribe to be so late getting
horses—they had little to trade that would equal the value of a horse. An
ordinary, run-of-the-mill horse would generally be valued at ten dressed buffalo sleeping robes or six complete sets of clothing. The Shoshone, in many
cases, would trade scrapers—how many is not known—for robes and then,
eventually, the accumulated robes for a horse.

Once the Shoshone acquired some horses, they were than able to capture
others from the wild herds roaming the Plain. But the procurement of
horses throughout the tribe was a long, slow process. In 1818 Alexander
Ross commented in one of his many reports that the Snake River Plain
Shoshone had few horses and almost no firearms. Other traders and some
historians have indicated that they had horses and arms earlier than this. But
research shows that these people did *not* distinguish between the various
Shoshone tribes—the Wind River, the Lemhi, and the Boise—and even the
Bannock were all lumped together by most writers. There were those who
included the Ute, Paiute, and Commanche in the group of Shoshone tribes.
(Ake Hultkranz, Frank Gilbert Roe, and other careful historians have corrected this information.)

The Shoshone had developed into horse-buffalo culture by 1830, although they did not adopt the tepee until about 1860. Ironically, it was their obtaining horses that was to make them poorer than they were before. It enabled the Shoshone to wipe out the buffalo just at the time when they became dependent upon them.

When the Shoshone had to stalk the buffalo afoot and had no work animals to move large weights of meat and hides, their impact on the rather minor buffalo herds of the Snake River Plain was minimal. The horse changed all that—and the prospering Shoshone became wasteful. By 1840, Osborne Russell, Joe Meek, and others were remarking that buffalo were scarce. By 1843–45, they were gone forever from the Snake River Plain-Great Basin area. The Shoshone and Bannock turned to the east, to the still plentiful buffalo in the eastern Montana-northern Wyoming area. This brought them into conflict with the Crow and Blackfeet.

The Shoshone had neither the weapons nor the organization to resist these larger, better-armed, and organized tribes, so their trips into their territories were furtive and quick. Unable to fight their stronger adversaries, they tried to avoid them or to hide or flee rather than fight. It had always been so with the Shoshone. It was the reason the Sioux gave them the name meaning unmanly people.

When John Colter came into Pierre's Hole in 1808, the range of the Snake River Plain Shoshone was from just east of southcentral Oregon and westcentral Nevada to the western edge of the Continental Divide and from central Idaho to just south of Great Salt Lake. Even then the mounted and better-armed tribes around them were squeezing them into a narrow crescent of land along the Snake River from south of Boise to Henry's Lake. In the center of this area the Bannock occupied the best wintering areas near Raft River and the Portneuf Mountains, with the Shoshone on all sides except the north.

The furtive, evasive nature of the Shoshone, forced on them by conditions over which they had little control, not only got them the name by which we know them but also the secondary designation of *Snakes*. This came about because the sign used by most other tribes to designate the Shoshone was a sinuous wriggle of the hand and forearm with the hand vertically on edge. White trappers read this as *snake*. The sign for snake would have had the hand flat, palm down. The sign used meant *devious-untrustworthy*, and all who knew Shoshone, white or Indian, agreed that they were.

It was the disappearance of the buffalo that caused an abrupt change in the habits of both the Shoshone and Bannock tribes. The Shoshone had been accustomed to ranging back and forth across the entire Snake River Plain according to the season. In early spring they ranged smaller creeks and spring areas, eating new greenery. By June they were in Camas Meadows to obtain one of their main food items, camas roots. This plant *(Camassia quamash)* was one of the most important food plants west of the Rockies, and many Indian conflicts were over territoral rights to areas where this plant grew. The Lewis and Clark journals noted that there were times when these roots were the only food the expedition was able to obtain.

Camas Prairie, some 200 miles west of Camas Meadows, was a larger area with more plentiful plants. But it was in the heart of Bannock territory and unapproachable by the weaker Shoshone.

During the summer, the Shoshone were spread over the entire Plain, eating a variety of plants, roots, insects, fish (which they trapped in wicker traps, in weirs and in woven grass nets), and rabbits, which they drove into large-winged corrals made of sticks and brush. This practice is carried on by whites today. There are annual jackrabbit drives in southeastern Idaho, involving hundreds of people driving rabbits into fence corners where they are clubbed to death by thousands.

In the fall, the Shoshone worked westward to obtain salmon in the Snake River in southwest Idaho and to kill marmots—yellow-bellied marmots (*Marmota flaviventris*)—in the present Twin Falls area.

For several years after I came upon the above information, I was puzzled. Why go to a particular area to hunt marmots? This creature, closely related to the eastern woodchuck or groundhog, is ubiquitous throughout the northern Rocky Mountain West. Around my home they sometimes become so plentiful as to almost take over. My neighbors, on occasion, have had to kill numbers of them because they were undermining their house foundations with their digging. So, what was significant about the Twin Falls area?

In 1983, at the International Fly Fishers Conclave, held in West Yellowstone—now the permanent home of the Federation of Fly Fishers—I got my answer. One of the booths selling fly-tying materials had for sale a marmot skin. It was so huge that only its color made it recognizable.

"Where on earth did you get a marmot that size?" I asked the salesman.

"Over by Twin Falls," he replied.

"I never saw one nearly that large," I said.

"They're all about that big over there," he replied casually.

Further questioning elicited the information that the Twin Falls area marmots were in the seventeen- to twenty-pound range—a startling figure, since all the large ones, thousands of them, that I had seen elsewhere, were in the four- to seven-pound range. I've not been able to find what it is that makes them so large in the Twin Falls area or if they are a subspecies. But now I know why the Shoshone trekked to that area to kill marmots in the fall. Their flesh is delicious, and their fat, exceptional.

By 1845, the Shoshone and Bannock were making regular hunting trips over what was to become known as the Great Bannock Trail, to hunt buffalo in northwest Wyoming and southcentral Montana. Although some writers act as though the trail came into being only after 1840, Wayne Replogle,* who wrote the definitive work on the Trail, notes that it was in use for centuries prior to 1840. (See Bibliography.)

It is ironic that it is called by the name Bannock. The Shoshone were in the area earlier than the Bannock and originated the trail on foot. Also, they

---

*Replogle walked nearly every yard of the trail on foot over the several years of his research. His book is exceptional in having been so researched.

used it in greater numbers than any of the other tribes that used it—Nez Percé and Flathead, as well as Lemhi and Wind River Shoshone. But their shy ways and evasive disposition robbed them of being noted for many accomplishments.

Regular Indian trails from all over southeastern Idaho joined up in the area of Camas Meadows about thirty miles north of the mouth of Henry's Fork to become the Bannock Trail. It crossed northeastward across Shotgun Valley, past the north edge of the Island Park Reservoir, went northward across the center of Henry's Lake Flat, up the north side of Targhee Creek, and across Targhee Pass.

The trail passed northeastward along the foothills of Madison Basin (within two or three miles of my home), crossed Madison's South Fork and the Madison itself to the base of Horse Butte. From there it went up the Madison to Cory Spring—now under Hebgen Lake—which was a favored camping spot. It followed up the Madison to Maple Creek (known mistakenly for over eighty years, until just recently, as Cougar Creek) and then went over the low pass of the Gallatin Range to Obsidian Cliff. This, in centuries past, had been the main objective of the trail.

From Obsidian Cliff the trail branched: one going through Gardner's Hole to Mammoth and down the Yellowstone River; the other going over Blacktail Deer Plateau to Tower Falls, then east into Wyoming.

One of the great advantages of this trail was that its route did not expose its users to easy ambush. This was always an important consideration to any Indian tribe, but especially so to the Snake River Plain Shoshone.

Whichever tribe used the trail, they traveled and stopped in the small family group or clan that was the basis of Western Indian organization. During the fall communal hunt, nearly the entire tribe might be strung out along the 200 or so miles of the Trail, but they were always separated into their regular groups, not mingled.

It is interesting to note that the objective of this trek, the buffalo, had the same kind of group organization as that of the western Indians. In 1871 Major Richard Irving Dodge* wrote of riding through a buffalo herd twenty-five miles across that he estimated at 2 million animals. From their own level, it appeared to be a single gigantic herd, but when viewed from the top of a hill in the midst of the animals it was seen that the larger herd was actually composed of innumerable smaller herds of from fifty to two hundred, each compactly grouped and separate from other groups. Wayne Gard in *The Great Buffalo Hunt,* the chronicle of the buffalo-hide hunters, records that this small herd group was the normal, year-round organization of buffalo herds except during calving and mating season.

Some writers have intimated that it was the acquiring of rifles that allowed the Shoshone and Bannock to exterminate the buffalo from the Snake River Plain—not so. The muzzle-loading rifle was an inefficient weapon for mass killing of moving animals, especially from horseback. The practice of

*For whom Fort Dodge and Dodge City were named.

running buff, treated so romantically by fiction writers, which created the image of Buffalo Bill, was a development of the 1866–1880 period and was made possible by the development of the breech-loading rifle using cartridges.

Reloading a muzzle-loading rifle from the back of a galloping horse was an enormously difficult—and wasteful—process. The charge could not be measured, the ball could not be patched, and how much powder was spilled and how much went down the bore was always guesswork. Some rifles exploded during such operations due to overloading, which usually happened only during running battles. Thomas Fitzpatrick was said to have had such an accident which shattered his wrist, leading to his sobriquet *Broken Hand.*

On the other hand—no pun intended—the short, powerful Western Indian bow was very efficient for killing buffalo from the back of a running horse. The arrow could be sent into the buffalo's lungs from a range of no more than five feet. At that range it was difficult to miss placing the arrow exactly behind the shoulder to drive down entirely through both lungs, causing enormous hemmorhages that dropped the animal in a matter of yards. While it was breathing its last, the skillful Indian bowmen could place equally accurate arrows into two more buffalo. Several Indians on horseback, closing in on a group of buffalo from all sides, could kill nearly all of the animals in a small herd in a matter of five minutes. It was the horse and not the muzzle-loading rifle that allowed the wipe-out of the buffalo of the Snake River Plain and sent the Indians of that region over The Great Bannock Trail seeking buffalo elsewhere. And, of course, the horse allowed the carrying away of the meat back to wherever the Indians needed to transport it. Prior to obtaining horses the Snake River Plain Shoshone had no way of coping with huge quantities of food, had they been able to obtain it.

The Shoshone caused little or no trouble for the trappers—in fact, little trouble for whites at any time. When trouble did come it repeated a pattern that forms a record of injustice unequaled in the United States. And it was instigated not by Indians but by whites.

A treaty with the Shoshone and Bannock in 1863 resulted in these two tribes being put on a reservation at Fort Hall in 1867. Then, the usual pattern of injustice began. Whites settling in the area noticed that some choice land along the Snake River had been included in the reservation. They moved in and squatted on the land. When the Indians complained, the settlers screamed for the Army. The Army came and removed the Indians from *that area of their own reservation* and turned the land over to the whites.

A further injustice was being practiced at the same time. The food, supplies, and cattle promised the Shoshone and Bannock were delivered to the Shoshone—the Wind River Shoshone—on their reservation 250 miles away. When the starving Fort Hall Indians complained, they were told to go pack their own food if they wanted it delivered to Fort Hall. It took five years to get this situation changed. When the government finally did agree to deliver the promised food and cattle to Fort Hall, the Indian agents and the Army managed, as usual, to siphon off a good percentage and sell it to the settlers.

But further indignities were forthcoming. A railroad commenced to extend its lines across the reservation without even approaching the Indians to ask for right-of-way. When the Indians complained, the Indian agent and the Army did the usual thing: they removed the Indians from the proposed and actual right-of-way, further reducing the size of the reservation. No compensation was offered. Then another railroad and more settlers moved in, again the government response was the same—move the Indians out of the way of *progress.*

At the same time the Indians were refused the right to hunt off the reservation, and when some did, the Army confiscated their weapons. This led to the *Bannock War of 1878* by the near-starving tribes. The Indians were quickly subdued and pushed back onto a steadily shrinking reservation. Only years later was compensation offered for the theft of their land, and that was a pittance. At no time did the U.S. government live up to the provisions of its treaty with the Shoshone and Bannock. And even today, whites are fighting to prevent the Indians from running their own affairs. The tribes wish to lease, on a royalty basis, the mineral rights to certain areas of the reservation. Whites insist that the area be sold outright and the Indians move out of the area. They offer the usual pittance in compensation.

The Shoshone, more so than the Bannock, utilized the watershed of Henry's Fork and its tributaries. They roved and hunted regularly through the area around the mouth of the river and in the Teton Basin and Falls River areas. The area of Henry's Fork upstream of Ashton all the way to the Continental Divide was an almost unbroken lodgepole pine forest, not good for hunting and difficult to travel through. The exception was the Camas Meadow area north of the river and a smaller meadow area around Henry's Lake.

That situation was drastically altered by the raging prairie and forest fire of 1879, which wiped out most of the pine forest and left the area more open and more usable by wildlife, and thus more livable for people. By then the Indians had literally become prisoners on their own reservation.

13

TO THE MOUTH
OF THE RIVER

THE AREA FROM THE MOUTH OF THE NORTH BRANCH OF THE TETON River on down to where Henry's Fork enters the main Snake was once described by Warren A. Ferris (*Life in the Rocky Mountains, 1830–1835*) as a barren plain. Bonneville referred to it as a desert, and Alexander Ross said that it was barren of anything but cactus, sagebrush, and jackrabbits.

It is much different now, because this was the first area of Henry's Fork watershed to become heavily settled, beginning in 1879.

The river, now, is hemmed in by farms raising potatoes and hay and is invaded by weirs and diversion dams. It does not look like a trout stream; it is true that coarse fish outnumber the trout. But the trout are still there and some exceed fifteen pounds. The very lower end of the river is surrounded by cutoffs, swamps, spring creeks, and irrigation canals and is extremely difficult of approach. It is mostly fished by boat and by bait or lure fishers. Some very large trout have been caught here on Rapala lures originally intended for muskie. Still, it is a better trout stream than many waters with a greater reputation. It has excellent late fall mayfly and caddis hatches.

Recovery from the devastation of the flood caused by the Teton Dam disaster in 1976 is slowly improving, but some areas still look like a moonscape. The banks and bed of the Teton River still show the damage more plainly than most of the land around the river. However, thousands of acres of once productive farmland still have tons of stones and coarse gravel spread over it. The disaster has caused a population shift that is yet to be fully assessed.

The towns damaged by the flood have almost entirely recovered. It is ironical that, in some cases, the restored buildings are an improvement over the ones destroyed; in fact, some of those destroyed had already been abandoned due to age, to being obsolete, or because of dwindling population.

The population shift, commencing many years before the dam was constructed, has been downstream. The towns, and even the rural areas in the upper reaches of all the tributary watersheds, have been losing population to the towns downstream. Of all the towns in the Falls and Teton watersheds, and even some of those along the Henry's Fork itself, only Saint Anthony and Rexburg, both in the watershed of the main river, have had an increase in population.

Throughout the watershed, farms have been becoming larger; the small family farms being gobbled up and consolidated into larger farms and into agribusiness holdings. Good highways have aided the cause of relocation; farmers can reach the larger towns in an hour and thus take advantage of better prices and larger inventories. This, and the lack of industry, has tolled the knell of the smaller towns. Some, once with a population of several hundred, now have fewer than one hundred people. The shift has not only been downstream, but it has been away from the area. The total population of the entire watershed of Henry's Fork and its tributaries is somewhat less than it was ten years ago, and all indications are that the trend will continue.

What this means is that, in many cases, sewage problems caused by population growth, which is going on all over the country, is not happening in most of the Henry's Fork watershed. It *is* in the Last Chance area, as mentioned earlier.

The problem there is being addressed, although at present, the solution is not in sight.

The present areawide trend bodes well for improvement of conditions along Henry's Fork. Pollution, that modern bugbear, is slowly decreasing. So is erosion as farmers belatedly come to terms with loss of topsoil and higher fertilizer bills. Somewhat to the surprise of most people, the greatest threat to the quality of life along the river comes from growing numbers of recreation-seeking people. Some upstream areas have grown too fast and the heavy usage of water and land resources have caused problems that are now just being recognized. Thus, while the threat of damage to the lower river is diminishing, that of the upper is increasing. But awareness of the threat is widespread, and steps to improve the situation are being taken.

What this means to the lower river is that improving conditions, less damage to soil and water, and a growing awareness of the cost of such damage, will result in the lower river slowly becoming a better trout stream as the area as a whole becomes a better environment for man. As we say in Montana: a livable environment for trout means a quality environment for man.

14

FISHING DOWN THE RIVER

WHEN A FISHERMAN GETS TO TALKING ABOUT FAVORITE WATERS, IT CAN become boring to another fisherman who prefers different kinds of waters. In writing about the Henry's Fork, there are so many places that I am extremely fond of that I find it difficult to restrain myself. I will be as reasonable as I can.

There is about a mile and a quarter of really excellent water between the dam at Henry's Lake and the highway bridge. This is lovely trout water—riffles, runs, and pools—crooked and winding, with willows crowding the banks here, grass or sagebrush there, and each bit of water looking lovelier and more promising than the last.

The fish average a fair size, about fourteen inches, in my experience. There are brooks, cutthroats, rainbows, and some hybrids. They are usually in splendid condition.*

I have never seen anything like a major hatch (emergence) of mayflies on this stretch of river. Caddis are more numerous, and one will often find them fluttering around above the stream and alighting in the willows. But

---

*In 1984 two friends of mine who fish this stretch regularly reported to me on separate occasions that a large fish kill had occurred here. Some twenty or thirty dead fish had been seen by them, all upwards of a pound. They wanted to know if I had any information on the situation. I hadn't.

I called the biologists at the Henry's Lake hatchery and reported the kill. It happened that the kill had occurred during a drive by Fish and Wildlife agents against poachers on the lake and below the dam. Whether or not the fish kill was part of this the Fish and Game people couldn't say. They would investigate. My last call elicited the information that they were baffled. They could find no cause of death in fish analyzed by the laboratory. The investigation is continuing but with little hope of finding the cause. Apparently there are *natural* fish kills. There was one involving several hundred trout on the Madison in Bear Trap Canyon several years ago, and no cause was ever found.

134

A typical stretch of the Outlet—riffles leading into corner pools.
Lovely water to fish.

I've never seen any evidence of a *major* feeding period caused by these hatches.

Most of the time, especially in the fore part of the season, I find that the grouse-hackle wet flies that so fascinate Sylvester Nemes—he calls them soft hackles—are the best day-in, day-out medicine. His way of fishing them, the greased-line method, while often successful, is not the only useful method here. Dry-fly tackle *is* all that one needs. The size of this tackle is strictly a matter of choice. The stream is seldom more than twenty-five feet across, long casts almost never needed. So, a number 4 or 5 line will work as well as a heavier one. Strong winds will occasionally make heavier lines necessary.

Most fishermen I encounter here make a common mistake. They use leaders too long for best, accurate work on this often-confining small stream. You *do not* need a nine-and-a-half-foot leader here; seven feet is plenty, and five or six feet is usually better.

Consider: if you are using an eight-foot rod with a seven-foot leader and are casting twenty-five feet, you only have ten feet, just the tapered end, of fly line out. Shorten the leader, and you'll find you have better control of the cast. How fine the tip is, is up to the individual. I usually use 4X, not for invisibility, which concerns me not at all, but for flexibility, the far more important leader factor whether fishing wet or dry.

What about flies? Well, smaller is better than too large. In the grouse-hackle wets, 12s and 14s seem better most of the time than either larger or

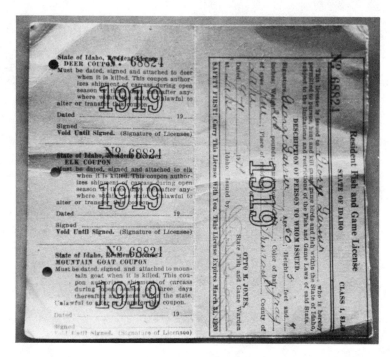

George Garner of Lake (Henry's Lake) Idaho, got a real bargain
for his $1.50 in 1919—permits for deer, elk, and mountain sheep, plus the
usual small game and fish.

tan, and grey bodies are all useful, as is a primrose yellow if you can find that
color in the shops. Of course, if you tie your own, it's no problem.

Several methods of fishing the fly are useful. Syl's up and across cast with
a long downstream float, mending the line as needed to eliminate drag, is a
good one. The same cast with a hand-twist retrieve works equally well most
times. And the rising-to-the-surface method will sometimes work when all
else fails. In this method, the rod is slowly raised and lowered throughout
the drift; slack is recovered each time the rod tip is lowered. And for spot
locations—deep holes of small area, dropoffs under willows, undercut banks,
and drifts—the Leisenring Lift is the deadliest method of all.

The water is varied. Riffles are usually easily read and easily fished. And
in this stretch, one can now and then see the trout in riffles, which greatly
simplifies things. Runs, deeper than riffles but with a broken surface, are
more difficult to read. Since the stream is small, the answer there is to be
thorough: cover the water. Pools are very difficult; there is often a bloom in
the water, a duskiness of dissolved organic material and/or algae that make
them impossible to read. Add to this the fact that, because of unseen bottom
irregularities, currents are quite contrary, and you have a most difficult situation. However, almost always, the larger fish, and sometimes the largest, will
be in these pools. The answer, for me at least, in fishing these particular
pools, is persistence. I just keep working the fly in the pool, varying the

Note the slogan at
the top of George Garner's 1927
Montana nonresident
fishing license.
And we thought this was a recent idea.

methods, being careful not to rip the water when I lift the fly to recast, and changing position each few minutes. A half hour to work a pool no more than twenty feet across and four feet deep is not too long.

Sometimes, in riffle, run, or pool, a nymph will work when the soft-hackle wets fail. General nymphs seem to work better more of the time than specific imitations. Trueblood's Otter Nymph in sizes 10 and 12 is good. The old Grey Nymph, sometimes called the Muskrat nymph, in the same sizes, also works. For a darker nymph, the Prince, Martinez Black, Zug Bug, or Pheasant Tail in sizes 12 and 14 are among the best. Dragonfly and damselfly nymphs are less effective. And, of course, don't forget the old reliable Wooly Worm with black, brown, or olive bodies, sizes 10 or 12, on 2XL hooks.

Leeches and streamers are a hit-and-miss proposition. But colorful streamers such as Mickey Finn or Spruce, sizes 6 or 8, long-shanked, occasionally produce a sizeable fish and seem the best bets to take a larger than average brook trout.

How about dry flies? If you include terrestrials—crickets, beetles, hoppers, ants, and such—they are the very best after late June. One includes here the general dry flies. My next-door neighbor, Charlie Van Tress, spends a lot of time on this stretch. He is a very good fisherman, and an intensely practical man. He is also almost a one-fly man—and that fly is the Humpy or Goofus Bug. Charlie probably has more success than anyone who fishes here regularly. Partly that's because he's a damn good fisherman, and partly it's because his chosen fly covers a lot of different possibilities. I'm sure it is often taken for an adult caddis; in the smaller sizes it works even during egg-laying flights of this ubiquitous insect. It may, in darker body colors, be taken for a beetle or cricket—in more neutral colors, for a hopper—and a lot of times, it is taken because it just looks buggy and alive. I'll go with Charlie and say that it's the best *shotgun* dry fly for this stream. Have it in a variety of sizes—10, 12, 14, and 16—and in several underbody colors, and in summer and fall you'll seldom be skunked—even if you're not the fisherman that Charlie is.

As indicated earlier, match-the-hatch flies and methods are seldom needed. But careful stalking, easy delivery of the fly, and persistence are. The fish are very wary, and while not unduly selective to pattern, they are to size and presentation. So, use some thought and care when fishing this stretch of lovely water. It is not the easy-fishing proposition that it appears.

Below the highway bridge, the river changes. The gradient flattens, the current becomes slower, and the river meanders. The first quarter mile downstream is considerably larger water than above the bridge, with wider, deeper pools and sweeping curves. I've never caught a fish larger than eight inches here except in the pools. Also, this stretch, next to the highway and with good parking spots, is much fished by bait fishermen and families with children. For the experienced fly fisher, it can produce two or three quite good fish, but most give it a pass.

The next four miles is more like the stretch just below the Henry's Lake dam, yet somewhat different. It is a bit slower most places and less crowded by willows, which soon peter out out almost entirely. It is more easily fished—the currents not so contrary and the water more easily read. The same flies and methods are needed, but the fishing is not so difficult.

One soon learns that the larger fish are located on the outside of bends, where the water is deeper and food is continually brought to trout holding here. Occasionally there will be small amounts of debris collected in these curves or there will be a patch of foam. Both signal that these are good holding and feeding spots.

Sometimes it pays to simply drop the fly into the foam or amongst the debris rather than letting it drift naturally into such spots. This is true with both wet and dry fly. I've dropped grouse-hackle wets *onto* such places. The flies were refused while they stayed afloat, only to be taken instantly when they sank. For some reason that I am totally at loss to explain, I find this very satisfying.

Crickets are more readily taken here than elsewhere on this stream, with the possible exception of Railroad Ranch, and ants are excellent most any time, in both wet and dry versions. I've found that a sandy red-brown pattern and a black pattern in sizes 14 and 16 is all that's needed.

From late June through September, most years, a hopper pattern is the one best fly. And here, I use a variety of sizes that I find largely unnecessary elsewhere. I start with size 10, 2XL in spring and work up in sizes to a size 6, 3XL by mid-September. Color changes as well as size changes are going on:

in spring the hoppers are grass green; by fall there are some grey and some brown ones, both mottled. The underbodies will be beige or pale yellow. The fish here, apparently because hoppers are a large part of their summer diet, are selective to both size and color. They will come to invesigate any lure that drops onto the water with a splat!—but they will turn away if the fly is not the right size and color.

The land is pasture for both cattle and sheep. As of 1984 it was not posted but that could change. Most of the landowners are aware of the fact that fishermen bring economic benefits to the area and that they also eat steak and hamburgers and wear woolen shirts. In other words, the fishermen are customers for the rancher's products. So, unless the fisherman foul up things by being uncouth slobs, I do not expect this area to be posted in the near future.

But one must be aware of the fact that range cattle *can* be dangerous. Cows are rarely so, but bulls are apt to be any time. Two summers ago, while fishing the middle of this section, I spent a good deal of my time avoiding a huge black bull with a decidedly grumpy disposition. It is not generally known but domestic bulls kill and injure more people each year in this country than any other animal. So go warily out there, but don't let yourself be deterred. Just avoid getting too close to *any* cattle and especially bulls. If necessary, cross the stream and put it between yourself and any suspiciously acting cattle.

You'd best wear boots or waders to fish this area. The stream can be covered easily from each bank, but it fishes better from one bank at times than from the other. Also, there are hundreds of springs, rivulets, branches, small creeks, little sloughs, cutoffs, and a canal or two, and much of the area is marshy. You *can* navigate dry-shod but you'll end up walking what seems like forever in order to get to spots on the river just a couple hundred yards away.

During the middle of the summer—late June to mid-August—one can have a gloriously lazy day just loafing slowly and steadily up this stream using a size-12 Goofus or Royal Wulff, drifting the fly down the main current. You'll miss some good spots, but you'll cover enough water—and you can do the whole thing with your mind in idle. It's one of the most relaxing and pleasant ways to fish, and it gives one time to absorb the unbelievable beauty that lies all around. I do this when I've become fatigued with my more or less constant research and just want to take a day off. I call such times my *postman's holidays*. But such days can become addictive. It's that pleasant.

At the lower end of this four-mile meadow stretch, near the south edge of Henry's Lake Flat, the land becomes very marshy and crowded with masses of intertwined willows. There are cutoffs and channels; the stream becomes what hydrologists call braided. There is about three miles of this kind of water, above and below the little wooden bridge located on the gravel road that leaves the highway at Island Park Lodge and runs to Big Springs. This *moose marsh* does contain moose and also quite a few larger-than-average trout. But fishing this stretch is an exercise in massive frustration.

I do not fish this marsh section often but each time I do, I remember a story that Ted Trueblood wrote about fishing such a place. He and some friends had been fishing it for a couple of years, with bait. Ted became interested in seeing if it could also be fished with flies.

He used the same gear that he had used fishing bait. This was an old nine foot True Temper steel rod equipped with a size G hard finish fly line that we called *enameled* back in the 1930s. As well as having a highly polished finish, these lines were stiff and slid easily through the guides.

He would tie a double-ended, two-foot leader to the line with a smooth knot. On the end of one leader was a small dipsey sinker; on the other, the chosen fly. He would reel up until both sinker and fly were against the rod tip, work the tip through openings in the willows until it was over open water, then feed the line out slowly through the guides until the fly and sinker were in the water. The sinker, of course, would sink almost straight down, but the fly, wet or dry, would drift downstream a bit. Then Trueblood would manipulate the rod tip to give the desired action. If the spot had been chosen correctly, a unsuspecting trout would take the fly almost at once, even if it was acting unnaturally. Then came the problem of trying to get the trout out of the water, up to the rod tip, and then through the opening in the willow mass.

I have done the same thing, using an old Heddon glass rod with oversize guides. I hooked fish almost every time I tried it. But the difficulty of getting the fly to the water was child's play compared to trying to work a vigorously struggling two-pound trout back through an opening in a tangled mass of willows. Nine times out of ten the trout escaped. Why go to such trouble to hook trout that were almost sure to get off? Simply to see if one could be landed, I suppose. I really don't know why I do it.

If this method does not appeal to you, and I'll bet it doesn't, there are a couple of others. But if one of the pleasures of fly fishing for you is in the rhythm of casting, you'd better look elsewhere. You don't cast at all on this stretch of Henry's Fork. Even if you could fight your way into the stream, you'll find that (1) you can't cast because the willows almost meet over your head, and (2) you can't wade because the water's too deep or the bottom too silty.

The only method that has worked for me is to work into the stream—this can take fifteen or twenty minutes—and if I've found a pace not too deep, I stand in the center and drift a fly straight downstream by feeding out line. I use big bivisible dries or Wooly Buggers. The advantage of this method is that the trout can *sometimes* be landed. But they can also become so entangled in the tree limbs above or the roots below that you not only lose the trout but the fly and leader as well.

Why do we do it? The fish are good size—two to two-and-a-half pounds, with larger ones a possibility. Then there's the challenge of difficult fishing for its own sake. And, one other thing: you won't find anyone else there.

Some people sneer at fishing a dry fly straight downstream as is necessary here. I wonder about anyone with such elite ideas. I do it in places where one doesn't have to sometimes, just because it's very effective. If one can cast normally, I use the *haystack* or *pileup* method: throwing out a lot of line, then jerking back on the rod to pile up a bunch of line that pays out slowly. This requires accurate adjustment to have your fly come over the fish just as you begin to run out of slack.

Here, in these confined waters, I peel off a good many yards of line from the rod tip and just drop this mess on the water in front of me with the fly downstream of the coiled-up line. This drifts off, and one hopes no strike will come when you still have thirty feet of coils on the water. After it straightens out, I lean the rod to one side or other, low under any limbs, and jerk the line back upstream, redumping the mess in a new spot for a new drift.

The major difficulty is in hooking the fish that takes the fly. Timing as well as length and strength of the strike can only be learned by practice. Sometimes I miss nine fish out of every ten that hit. I yell a lot when I miss, and I get frustrated when I miss six or eight in a row. But, Lord, it's fun and exciting and makes the old corpuscles gallop through your side streets.

Another method, not usable every place along the river here, but allowable in some areas, is to roll cast. This is possible in places where any kind of normal cast wouldn't be, but it, too, can be extremely frustrating; you will get hung up, you will lose flies and leaders. You'll also catch fish if you stay with it.

The water downstream of the little wooden bridge is easier of approach than that above and somewhat easier fished. The problems are exactly the same as above the bridge, but less severe. Sometimes, the trout are larger.

In the fall, September and October, there are run-up fish here, spawners from Island Park Reservoir. There are kokanee and coho salmon and some large rainbow trout. For those with the necessary strength and stubbornness, this can be an exciting time. It's much like steelhead fishing: bright flies, many—though not long—casts, and a few strikes. But a three to five pound, very strong fish in these confined waters will put your heart into your throat until you've got him safely in. Generally, you have to fish straight downstream and play the fly a long while before retrieving and casting again.

The end of this stretch comes where the outflow of Big Springs, a river in itself, joins the main river. There is a giant slow pool here, locally called the *Bathtub.* Just what are the boundaries of this pool is difficult to ascertain. The two streams approach each other almost at right angles. Then, just before they meet, they turn directly toward each other, with the combined waters, after mingling, moving away in about the same direction that the Big Springs outflow was moving before the two streams meet.

Why should this be a problem? Up until a few years ago, it wasn't. Until 1980 or 1981, the Big Springs Outlet—its official name—was open to fishing upstream from the juncture of the two streams to the Union Pacific Railroad trestle, three-quarters of a mile upstream from the Bathtub. But since then the entire Big Springs Outlet has been closed to fishing as a spawning-nursery-study stretch. Ok, fine, except now it may be illegal to fish certain portions of the Bathtub. But, if so, which portions? Actually, I doubt if the Fish and Game

Agents can themselves be sure where the closure begins, so it is unlikely one would be cited unless he was far enough up the Outlet so that it was clear that he was in violation of the closure. But one must be aware that this is an area where it is possible to unknowingly break the law while fishing.

Why not give the place a pass? Aha! that's the rub; this spot is absolutely loaded with trout, rainbows and brookies, and some of them are dandies. Because of the size of the pool, the contrariness of its currents, and its depth, the Bathtub is difficult to fish. But, I've seen rainbows above eight pounds here, and when a hatch comes on—not an infrequent occurrence here—I've seen the water literally covered with the rings of rising fish.

A lot of times the hatch (emergence) is midge, and how the fishermen curse when this is what the fish are taking. The problem is not only with the size of the insect—about size 20 or smaller—but with their numbers. They come on literally by the millions. The feeding seems to be a virtual frenzy, but just try to get the trout to take *your* fly.

I've mentioned that the fly called Peterson Palmer does great work here on these occasions. Its thin, peacock herl body and grizzly hackle simulate a hatching midge almost perfectly, but tiny wet flies sometimes work as well or better. Ray Bergman, in *With Fly, Plug and Bait,* wrote of fishing this spot, trying everything in his fly box before starting to take fish on a size-18 Blue Dun wet. Ray mentioned that the emerging naturals *were* midges, but the fish would have none of his match-the-hatch dries. When there is a saturation of midge on the water, my experience is that even the Peterson Palmer works better just under the surface than on it. Among the wet flies I've found that also work are the Blue Dun, Cahill, Grey Hackle Peacock, Grey Nymph, and a grouse-hackle wet with muskrat body. All must be size 18 or 20, and all must have thin bodies.

The North Fork Club stretch looking toward the Bathtub.

When the midge hatch is not on and there are no other flies in evidence, a leech or Wooly Bugger worked with six-inch strips of the line will produce, although not always. You'll not get many strikes to this method but the fish are nearly always upwards of two pounds.

Through the season, on the Bathtub one must try all kinds of flies and methods, but terrestrials are less successful than other flies, and wets or nymphs work more often than dries. When they are down, the fish are reluctant to come to the surface in this giant deep pool.

Downstream, there are deep, slow runs, some of which seem like pools. The area is marshy, and approach is difficult. There are many islands, and the stream on one side may be better, or more fishable, than that on the other. You have to explore and experiment. This stretch has been constantly stocked with hatchery catchables, and some seasons, this is all you'll catch.

Just downstream of the highway bridge at Mack's Inn the river moves out of its pool-and-deep-run appearance and starts to become riffles and runs. This continues all the way to the head of Coffee Pot Canyon, about 2½ miles downstream of the bridge. This is a most pleasant area to fish; the bottom is mostly bedrock or gravel over bedrock. Most of the fish will be those infernal hatchery catchables, but now and then, you'll stumble onto a pod of larger wild trout. But if pleasant, easy dry- or wet-fly fishing is what you're after, this is the place.

Upper Coffee Pot Rapids, the canyon, and Lower Coffee Pot Rapids are good to excellent fast-water fishing, except for a giant, deep, rock-bottomed pool in the canyon itself. There are more wild fish here than hatchery catchables.

Trying to find your way to the right place can be a nightmare. The area is laced with dirt roads; the ones that are marked do not go where the fisherman wishes. You can find Upper Coffee Pot Campground easily, but any spot in the canyon or even the lower rapids can elude you for hours. I know. Living about twenty miles away for twenty years, I come here frequently—and I am *never* sure I'll find the spot I'm looking for. A couple years ago Paul Collier and I spent four or five hours looking for the proper road into the heart of the canyon. It's only about two miles or so of river, but you cannot see either river or canyon until you're right on top of them. There are roads, roads, roads—one of which goes in a complete circle about a half mile long. You go in, at either end, headed toward where you know the river is, and come out at the same place five minutes later without having a clue as to where you turned.

What makes this worth while is that this section contains many run-up fish from Island Park Reservoir. The pocket-water fishing in the upper and lower rapids with the stonefly nymph is exciting and usually productive. And dry-fly fishing with a short leader to 2X and with large high-floating dries of size 8 or 10 can be even more so. Royal Wulff, Brown Bivisible, or Renegade are the favorites for this area and seem to work better than the Goofus Bug.

The deep, boulder-lined pools in the canyon are extremely difficult to fish. The canyon walls come right down to the water's edge. Your back cast—

Below Upper Coffee Pot Campground. The angler is in a choice location.

OPPOSITE PAGE: Coffee Pot Rapids. Good fishing—not difficult
to reach but not much fished.

unless you are Lefty Kreh—must be up or downstream. You *can* roll cast a
floating line *but* here, I've never known the trout here to come to the surface
for the fly. Favored flies are sculpin types, Matukas, leeches, large bucktails,
and the like. Roll casting one of these on a short, stout leader and Hi-D line
is like trying to distance cast a log chain.

Bob Jacklin, who has a fly shop in West Yellowstone, occasionally takes
one of these bottom-dwelling big rainbows. But Bob is an exceptional caster,
and one of the best with the streamer-bucktail lures favored here. I believe
his pet fly for this fishing is a yellow Muddler in large sizes: 4 or 2, 3XL.

The fine broken-topped run downstream of the lower rapids to about, or
even below, McCrea Bridge, is very, very good fly water. Alexander Mac-
Donald, in *On Becoming A Fly Fisherman,* touts it as perhaps the finest stretch
of the entire river with the exception of the Last Chance-Railroad Ranch
water. (See Bibliography.) He emphatically believes it to be the best piece of
water above Island Park Reservoir. There are about 2 to 2½ miles of this
water depending on the level of the reservoir. When the reservoir is low, one
can find excellent fishing as much as a mile downstream of McCrea Bridge.

There is a footbridge across the stream near Coffee Pot Lodge and another about a mile upstream. These two footbridges and McCrea Bridge give
the angler access to both banks of the stream in areas where it is sometimes
not possible to wade across. Also, large numbers of wild trout cruise up from
the reservoir into this stretch; some are more or less residents. All in all, this
is a truly fine piece of fly-fishing water and is a lovely section of the river. It
is more typically what most of us think of as a good trout stream than any
water above the canyon. It is a popular piece of water, yet most times, one
can have a quarter mile of one bank to himself, although not always the
exact stretch desired.

Since we will cover Island Park Reservoir and Henry's Lake elsewhere, it
is time to move on to one of my favorite stretches, Box Canyon. This is
arguably the finest piece of fast-water trout stream in the contiguous forty-
eight states.

It is *loaded* with wild trout* from fingerling size to over twenty pounds.
The fish are in better condition than those of any stream I know, not exclud-
ing the Bow River below Calgary, Alberta. I have fished over a dozen rainbow rivers in Alaska, and the fish in them are not equal in condition to Box
Canyon's mighty rainbows.

Condition in a fish is the ratio of girth to length. In some Box Canyon
rainbows it approaches 1:1. As related earlier Mike Lawson caught one here
on a salmon dry fly only twenty-two inches long that weighed 7½ pounds.
Koke Winter caught two that went 10 to 10½ pounds that were a scant
twenty-six inches long.

*There are only wild trout from Island Park Dam to Ashton Reservoir.

Around the curve to the left, the canyon narrows and grows steeper.
The giant pools there host rainbows to eight pounds.

Despite the powerful current surging through Box Canyon, the rubble-boulder river bed provides thousands upon thousands of current barriers, and these, in any fast stream, control the numbers of trout it can hold. Size of the barriers are, to some extent, indicators of the size of the fish. If the food is there, large barriers mean large fish. *And the food is there.*

There are at least five species of stonefly nymphs, including *Pteronarcys californica,* the salmonfly. There are a dozen species of mayfly, at least fifty species of caddis, tons of sculpins, and huge crayfish. (Crawfish, crawdad, ecrivisse, or whatever—crayfish is a corruption of the French *ecrivisse,* which is a corruption of the German *krebitz,* meaning crab.)

The nymphs of *Pteronarcys* are there in untold millions; these, sculpins, the smaller whitefish, crayfish and smaller members of its own kind are the grist upon which these giant rainbows feed. Thus, a lure resembling one of these is the best day-to-day fly to use. But, whichever of them one uses, it should be large. Nymph imitations of the *Pteronarcys,* Box Canyon Stone Nymph, for instance, are usually size 4, 4XL but are used up to size 2, 2XL. Sculpin patterns are used from 2, 4XL to 3/0, 2XL. Spruce steamers in sizes up to 2/0, 3XL, big Matukas, and huge brown bucktails are used to simulate the young whitefish. No one I know has a crayfish pattern,* but I found a

*After I wrote this I discovered Dick Nelson made a great crayfish imitation. He is also the originator of Aztec flies.

really great one on the floor of the West Yellowstone Convention Center during the 1984 Federation of Fly-Fishers (FFF) Conclave. My efforts to find the owner were fruitless, but whoever he or she is, I congratulate. This simple pattern, utilizing red-brown Furry Foam, is by far the best—and simplest—crayfish pattern I've ever seen (except for Dick Nelson's in the footnote below). The one I found was quite small, about size 8, 3XL. But its manner of tying is so simple and Furry Foam so versatile that it could easily be tied as large as 3/0, 3XL. And that would maybe be large enough to tempt a twenty pounder. I'll check it out and let you know.

The Box starts at the downstream side of Island Park Dam. The three-quarters of a mile of water between the dam and the mouth of the Buffalo is first-class fast-water fishing. It is not so fast as lower down the river, and the boulders on the bottom not so troublesome. It is much easier waded than the downstream section, the water is more easily read, and it has an abundance of trout. Unless the dam gates are wide open, one can reach just about any spot in this stretch comfortably.

Perhaps for this reason it is much favored by lady anglers. One sees them here more than any place on the river and they are all first-class fly fishers. But I do not know why they are here in such numbers. Last Chance Run and the upper Ranch water are easier to get to, easier waded, and pose fewer problems with current speed. A possible reason is that this is a place where one may expect to get into a very large fish. Women have caught rainbows here of fourteen pounds or more, and several have picked up trout in the six to eight-pound range.

I have been a fly fisher for over fifty years but I still get a chuckle out of our antics and actions. I sometimes come down to the boat landing here, the only access to this stretch, and stand on the bank to watch the people fishing. It is revealing although I'm not quite sure what it reveals. There will sometimes be as many as twenty people, men and women, fishing.

The river is about 150 feet wide, and twenty people scattered through its three-quarter-mile length do not crowd things. Each fisher will be in a different location and facing a different way than his or her neighbors. They will be using different flies and different methods. Sometimes nobody will be catching fish; sometimes everybody will.

It seems to me that the more I learn about fly fishing for trout, the less I know. When I see twenty people using different flies and different methods, all catching trout, I wonder if all the study I've done over the years was necessary. But when I see the same thing with no one catching anything, including me, I wonder if I've learned anything. It's a progressive puzzlement which can never be solved—and that's why we do it.

When the fish are on the feed here, they'll be taking match-the-hatch dries, soft-hackle wets, sunken nymph, emergent nymphs, attractor dries (Royal Wulff, *et al*) streamers, bucktails, Matukas, leeches, Wooly Buggers, Wooly Worms, hopper patterns, sculpin patterns, and lures that resemble nothing on earth. It's at times like this that I almost agree with Richard Muttkowski (*The Ecology of Trout Streams in Yellowstone Park*) when he quotes from his earlier collaboration with Robert Smith (*The Food of Trout Stream Insects in*

One can wade out from the bank in this stretch of upper Box Canyon;
farther down one can't except at very low water.

Yellowstone Park). He says, and *I* quote: "A fish is easily deceived, for he is not
very observant, his eyesight is poor and he recognizes things chiefly through
their movements. For instance, when an angler uses a fly, the fish is sup-
posedly deceived by three factors—form, pattern, and movement. In the
matter of form and pattern the fish's vision is too weak and nearsighted to
recognize the bait (sic) for what it is." These were trout he was writing about.

Unhappily for Muttkowski's wisdom, the above happens less often than
does the event of no one catching anything. I further researched Muttkowski
for an answer to that and found it. *The fish just weren't hungry,* he says.

As one moves deeper into the Canyon, his troubles multiply. The canyon
narrows with the walls moving in to the very edge of the water. Boulders in
the water get larger and more plentiful. Trees crowd the banks and hang out
over the water. The current speed increases, the water deepens. Why put up
with all this? The fish get larger and there are more of them. There are days
when one *can* catch a half dozen of four to six pounds. There are days when
one can also get skunked, but we don't talk about that.

Fast-water fishing has been my greatest and most enduring love in fly
fishing. I can no longer battle the streams on even terms, but if I have grown
older and weaker, I've also gotten foxier. I've learned to make conditions
work for me, instead of against me. In the Box this has resulted in using the
current to replace a backcast, by learning how to raise sunken line and fly
just close enough to the surface so that I can use the pull of the current to

load the rod, then pluck the fly from the water and swing it upstream and out with a tennis stroke. That is, a full-armed roundhouse swing with a stiff wrist. If you don't know the method, you'll find it in my *Nymph Fishing For Larger Trout.* (See Bibliography.)

One takes a position upstream of where one expects his fish to lie; then one casts upstream and out a bit. The rod tip is held pointing over the spot where the line enters the water and the tip swung downstream as fly and line move, keeping the tip pointing in the air above the point where the line enters. Slack is not retrieved, it is controlled by lifting the rod tip while still keeping it pointed in the direction of where the line enters the water. On longer casts one also raises the arms, so that at times, the rod tip and arms are as high as possible, straight up.

As the fly passes below straight across from where you're standing, the rod tip is lowered so as to keep only a slight droop in the line from tip to water. Always, one follows the drift of the fly by keeping the rod tip pointed in the direction of the line-water entry. Eventually, fly, line, and rod end up pointing straight downstream of the angler.

It is held there for ten or more seconds to allow the fly to lift off the bottom and come as near the surface as it will. Then one makes a powerful stiff-armed swing upstream with the rod parallel to the water, flinging line

In the heart of the Box. Here you can see some of the difficulties facing the wading fisher.

and fly up to a new starting point. This is a *sidearm* cast: the big weighted fly *never* comes over or near one's head if done properly.

The upstream cast is *only* to allow the fly to sink to the bottom by the time it drifts to a position straight across. From that point on, you are fishing the fly, trying to keep only that slight droop in the line, and feeling, or trying to feel, the fly bump along the bottom.

The strike will be a smash—a hard-jolting jerk. You must respond with equal vigor, a powerful lift upstream with the entire rod and a strong pull with the line hand. This is necessary to hook the fish and is why I never use leaders of less than ten-pound test when fishing this method. I first developed this method because I'm inherently lazy; later it came in handy as I became less strong.

It isn't only for the physically weak. I now and then encounter strong young men using it, having picked it up from my writings. Like the muscular young college giant I met on the lower Madison. This fellow had absolutely mastered the method and was hauling in sixteen to eighteen inch trout right along.

"Shucks," he said, when I had introduced myself and inquired why he was using the method, "it's not only that it's so successful but it's labor saving. I fish maybe fourteen hours a day, and fighting the current that long can wear you to a frazzle, even if you're not casting a heavy sinking line and weighted nymph. By using this method I can fish longer, better, and catch more big fish." And that's the name of that tune.

I find the big, weighted stonefly nymph the best day-in, day-out lure for these waters; some experts like Mike Lawson, Koke Winter, and Sheldon Jones do also. Others, Bob Jacklin for instance, favor the huge streamer-bucktail approach. The soft-hackle wets, and sometimes the high-riding dries, will often produce more fish. But never the largest ones.

Of course, salmonfly time is hatch-matching time. When the big, two-inch-long adults are flopping on the water regularly, it is useless to try anything else. On the Madison, during this period, one catches mostly sixteen-to twenty-two-inch trout. Here in the Box I've caught them from six inches to six pounds while standing in the same spot. How the small fish know that they can safely invade the lairs of the big fellows at this time baffles me. Any other time the little fellows would be gulped down at once.

The salmonfly hatch in the Box is of short duration, perhaps three to five days most years. It occurs *around* mid-June, some years, but a safer bet is the first week of that month. This hatch can be pandemonium time if you catch it on a good year.

A few years ago, I discovered an odd phenomenon during this hatch. I went over to fish it in Box Canyon and my wife asked me to bring home a couple of trout for her and her mother. So, I kept a couple in the twelve-inch range, since thirteen-inches is the upper limit for keepers here, except one a day of trophy size. When I gutted the two trout, as I always do immediately after catching them if I intend to keep any, I also opened their stomachs. Both stomachs contained only one thing: egg packets from adult female salmon flies. These packets are a dark-grey ball about the size of 00 buckshot, the individual eggs in a tightly packed cluster. Each trout had about twenty of these in its stomach.

I stopped fishing and picked a spot where I could see down into the water. Presently a female salmon fly came fluttering along—and plop!— dropped her egg packet just in front of me. A small trout flashed up and had it before it sank three inches. Through the rest of the day I saw this happen scores of times. I wondered if any packets ever got to the bottom. It emphasized the need for fecundity in these insects to insure their survival.

The nymph of *Pteronarcys californica* is in the stream three or four years. The variance is due to factors in the water: temperature, dissolved oxygen, amount of calcium carbonates, and perhaps other factors. By seining the nymphs just before hatch time, I've discovered four-year classes in some streams and only three-year classes in others. So, trout have at least three years to feed on the developing nymphs; they eat the adults by millions; and now, we find, they also swallow the egg packets. How do *any* survive? Only by producing more offspring than the trout, predacious insects, birds (eating adults), and other creatures can eat. I now wonder about something else.

While observing the egg-laying females, I saw three different methods of getting eggs into the stream. Some females flew over the water from one to ten feet above it and dropped packets. Others swooped down and dipped the tip of the abdomen into the water. Both of these type layers then flew blithely on about their business. Others flopped down onto the water, dropped their packets, and never rose again.

Now, I wonder, do the females lay or deposit more than one packet? If so, do they have to mate again? How many times can or do they mate? How many egg packets do they deposit? None of the scientific literature I've read deals at all with this. Nor do my friends, Bob Boyle and Eric Leiser, in *Stoneflies for the Angler,* which contains the most complete listing of scientific works dealing with stoneflies that I'm aware of.

It is this kind of thing that is always cropping up in my life of fly fishing for trout and researching associated matters. At times like these I'm almost overcome by the immensity of the whole thing; a many-headed hydra impossible to slay. The answer to one problem raises a multitude of questions. I shall never be done with it—and I think that's wonderful.

Although many large trout are caught during salmon fly time, the largest fall to other methods: to the nymph imitation, to streamers, and to leeches, Matuka, and sculpin patterns. No *one* pattern has had a monopoly on taking very large trout—nor does any one method.

Where to fish, in the section below the mouth of the Buffalo to the mouth of Box Canyon, is by hunch. There literally is no way to pick one spot over another. Partly this is because the fish are distributed throughout the stretch, partly because the fish move about, in their never-ending search for better holding spots. Because of this, those spots somewhat easier to get to are just as apt to produce a trophy as are the most difficult. In the old days, I'd tackle the most difficult to get to and to fish. Lately, I look for the easiest. I find *no* difference in sizes and numbers of trout over a period of time. You can plant your feet solidly on the bottom anywhere in Box Canyon, look around and say with satisfaction: *this is the place!*

As reported earlier, getting into and out of Box Canyon can be difficult. Some approaches are a bit easier than others and since, once in the river, one spot is apt to produce as well as another, I choose the easiest approach. You might think that everyone would and thus the easier spots to reach might be overcrowded. Not so. Fly fishers are an individualistic lot, and there are many who think, as I did in my youth, that the more difficult the approach, the better the fishing. In most places, this is true—but not in Box Canyon. The answer as to why is rather simple. The entire stretch is almost equally good in those things the trout requires: plenty of food, plenty of current barriers to form holding spots, a broken surface hiding the fish from view from above, and plenty of running room.

So, when you go to the Box, do not spend a lot of time agonizing over where to fish. Just get into the river and have at it.

Anywhere below Island Park Dam one is at the mercy of the dam keeper who controls the flow from here to below the confluence with Warm River. This dam keeper has absolutely no concern for the welfare of anything or anyone but the farmers and ranchers downstream, and the dam gates are operated with only that in mind. Water is held back or released with no consultation with any agency other than the one operating the dam and controlling the water rights. When I inquired about this, I was told that this organization owned the water and would do as it pleased with it. The attitude of the persons I dealt with was one of ill-concealed hostility and suspicion. Nor, at present, can anything be done to change this.

So, the quality of the fishing in this stretch, more than thirty miles of the best trout fishing anywhere, is dependent on water levels and flows. The trout are always there; the insects, also. The fluctuation of the water probably does not bother the trout overmuch, but it does bother the fishermen. In 1984 when the Island Park Reservoir was drained to allow checking of the dam for leaks and safety, the water ran high most of the summer and into September: it was difficult or dangerous to wade some places, and fishing generally was well below par. High-water levels break off and tear out weeds and send them floating down the river. Trout feed lustily during this kind of activity but the floating, drifting weeds play havoc with line and leader.

Of course, weeds are not much of a problem in Box Canyon—but high water is. It is difficult enough to wade here in low or normal flows. High flows make it almost impossible.

Some take to floating at this time. Floating regulations have undergone changes in recent years; once it was illegal to fish *while* floating, one had to get out of the craft to fish. Now, one can fish while floating, and most do. But it is not the best way, the old way of using the boat or raft to get to the chosen spot, then leaving it to fish, is a better method.

There is much recreational floating by people using boats, rafts, inflated innertubes, and what have you. As of now, it does not cause much of a problem to fishermen. In this kind of fast water, trout are not disturbed by passing watercraft unless they float right over them. I've spent a number of hours on the bottom in such places and not much frightens the trout there. It's incredibly noisy down there, rocks clicking and shifting, water slushing and thrashing, and there's a constant drift of organic material—leaves, limbs, grass, vines, etc.—and the fish do not pay much attention to either sound or movement. One can wade within four or five feet of them without causing the trout to move or take notice. In shallower water or slower currents, boats or other floating devices can be a problem, as on Michigan's Au Sable or Montana's Madison. But, unless a regular regatta is held in Box Canyon, it shouldn't bother either fish or fishermen.

From the mouth of the Canyon to the upper end of Railroad Ranch is a mile and a half of truly excellent trout fishing water. The bottom is gravel, or occasionally rubble, and the current and depth, most times, wadeable. There are weeds and boulders and shallow potholes, occasionally logs and drifts, and just about everything needed to make a trout happy. Insects are more than plentiful.

Among the mayflies are *Drunella grandis,* the Western Green Drake; *Ephemerella lacustris, inermis,* and *infrequens,* Pale Morning Duns; *Drunella flavilinea,* Slate Wing Olive; a dozen species of *Baetis,* including *tricaudatus,* Blue-Winged Olives; *Rhithrogena hageni,* Olive Dun (also called Pale Brown Dun); *Ephemera simulans,* Brown Drake; two species of *Epeorus;* two of *Callibaetis,* Speckled Duns or Spinners; *Heptagena elegantula,* Grey Dun; *Siphlonurus occidentalis,* Grey Drake; *Ironopsis grandis,* Red Quill; and *Tricorythodes minutus,* White-Winged Black (sometimes called *Caenis*). There are other mayflies, the only really important ones to the fly fisher are *Paraleptophlebia heteronea,* Black (or Dark Blue) Quill, and *P. bicornuta,* Mahogany Dun. Then there is the enormous numbers of the tiny *Pseudocloeon edmundsi,* Tiny Blue-Winged Olive, size 22–24, which blanket the lower end of Last Chance Run and upper Harriman State Park through summer and into fall. This is a most difficult hatch to fish with success, the flies so thick on the water that if your imitation is taken, it's more due to chance than skill. (See Appendix B for hatch times and locations.)

Caddis are perhaps more numerous than mayflies, there may be thirty to forty species of *Brachycentrus* and fifteen to twenty species of *Ryacophila* in this stretch. A variety of grouse-hackled wets with bodies of grey, tan, brown, and several shades of green will handle the pupal drift (pre-emergence) of these, and any caddis dry-fly pattern in grey or brown with bodies of grey, brown, yellow, or green, will take care of the hatch and egg-laying periods. Here the Elk Hair Caddis created by Al Troth is the number one choice for a dry, but Colorado King, Henryville, Katterman Special, Goddard, or King's River Caddis all work well in proper sizes—12 through 18—and at proper times. Caddis within a genera *(Brachycentrus* and *Ryacophila* here) may vary in size or color but do not differ in habits and habitat. Thus these flies need not be identified at all, scientifically. Just match size and color, and have at it.

There are a few small stoneflies in this stretch, called Yellow Sally. When even a few are on the water, the artificial will be taken well. (See Appendix B for pattern.) Fish the dry dead drift with an occasional twitch, or even a slight skittering.

Green Drake Madness Time is truly that. It occurs about 12 to 15 June most years and lasts about ten days. There will be from 100 to 300 people per day fishing this hatch from Box Canyon mouth to Osborne Bridge during that period. This is about seven miles of water; the stream from 100 to 200 feet wide. That many people fishing this much water wouldn't crowd things, but some stretches will be jammed, others almost empty of fishers. One can choose either to join the crowd or fish alone. The fishing may not live up to advance billing; the weather has a large effect on this. I've had great days in pouring rain and fair days during snowstorms—and have gotten skunked on bright sunshiny days. I've seen almost ideal days when no one seemed to be doing much and terrible days, weatherwise, when everybody was busy with fish. You pays your money, and you takes your chances.

One will see every variety and kind of fly fisher here during this hatch. Some are first-timers; some, old-timers. There are spectacular casters shooting seventy feet of line with ease, and others who can barely get the fly out. Yet those with the least experience have a good chance of getting many strikes and, occasionally, a trophy fish.

In 1982 I was down during this hatch, taking pictures and observing. I was a dark drizzly day, which was fine for my purpose, since I wanted to show the kind of weather that often prevails at this time. A hundred or more fishers filled the river from the upper boundary of Railroad Ranch to Henry's Fork Village. Action was scattered and sporadic.

I was parked just off the river bank, and had just returned to my car to change cameras when a fellow just opposite my car, about twenty feet out from the bank, got into a good fish. I glanced at the stick-on digital clock on the car dash, curious to see how long it would take to land the trout. Henry's Fork trout are very strong for their size and put up a long struggle in the larger sizes, and this one was in the five-to six-pound category. I wanted to get a picture of it being landed. I didn't. The fisherman had a friend, apparently more experienced than he, and the friend stood by throughout the struggle, offering advice and holding a net that might have held a large guppy. What he expected to do with it, I never found out. After forty-five minutes, during which time the angler never put enough pressure on the trout to more than slightly bend the rod, I gave up and left. Later, at lunch across the highway from where this fiasco took place, I found myself sitting next to this timid pair. I asked about the outcome of the struggle I had witnessed. They had lost the trout after an hour or so of playing it. When I inquired why the angler hadn't forced the fight, the two told me, in a superior manner, that you didn't force a large trout on a 4X leader. I was instantly reminded of something that Theodore Gordon once wrote, that there is nothing so ridiculous as to see a fine, large man being played by a fish.

It may be worthwhile at this point to talk about playing large fish because, from Box Canyon on downriver, one can get into fish running from five to twenty pounds at any time. Handling such fish is not easy; I know of no trout anywhere that are stronger than these Henry's Fork bruisers.

I'm always amused at people who are positive about just how to handle a very large trout. I never know just what to do and am always wondering during the struggle if I'm playing the fish properly for best results.

By and large, I keep on as much strain as tackle will allow, try to keep downstream of my fish, and hold the rod tip to one side or other to put on strain at an angle to the line of the current. Most times, this works in the smoother stretches where one has mobility to keep on terms with his trout, even though fine leaders are the rule here.

In Box Canyon, where the fish are apt to run larger and mobility is reduced to zero, it is a much tougher situation. Even a ten-pound test leader is no assurance of victory if a fifteen-pound fish gets below you and is broadside in those raging currents. Sometimes slacking completely will cause the fish to stop and remain until you can move down slowly and regain some line and some control.

When that doesn't stop a strong downstream run, snatching off yards of line, working it through the rod tip, and letting the current carry it below the fish will sometimes fool him into believing you're downstream. With luck, the fish will reverse direction and move back towards you.

Then there are times when there is absolutely nothing you can do that is going to make one bit of difference. If a strong, wily, and determined trout gets below you, and continues on toward the Pacific, you simply have to try to slug it out with him. You can try praying, sobbing, and cursing. I've tried all of them and have found that none of them—or anything else—is of any help. But times like these are the ones you'll remember long after the rest of the trip is forgotten, and it is these memories that will keep bringing you back to try again.

Although Green Drake time brings out the most fly fishers, the regulars of the Last Chance-Railroad Ranch mostly give it a pass. Most favor the Pale Morning Dun hatch which is not so concentrated and which spreads over a longer period. Of course, these fishermen generally have more time to spend than the visitor on vacation and are able to use a more leisurely approach.

For best day-in, day-out results through the season, the *Baetis*—Blue Dun, Blue-Winged Olive—hatches are consistent and the hopper season—late June through September—produces extremely well.

More and more regulars are coming to use emergent nymphs instead of concentrating on the dry fly. I have found that before, and even during, the Green Drake hatch, the emergent version of my Ida May nymph is a more consistent producer than the dry. One uses the same outfit, down to and including the leader, for both emergent nymph or dry fly. The cast and no-drag drift are the same. Just the fly, slightly under the surface with the emerger, is different.

On second thought, there is one difference. When the emergent nymph reaches the end of the drift, straight downstream, leave it hang there for up to thirty seconds. Fully one-fifth of my strikes come then, *but* it is very difficult to hook a trout that takes at this time. The straight upstream strike tends to pull the nymph straight forward and out of the fish's mouth. Also, if the rod is downstream parallel to the water, you'll break off the fish on the strike sometimes. But it is exciting, and you'll get more action with the emerger than with the dry.

The reason is basic; there are far more nymphs *in the water* than there ever are dries on the surface. A large portion of the mature nymphs never make it to the surface before being taken by a trout. The emerger works better because it's where more of the action is.

It only takes about forty minutes for me to get to Last Chance from my home, and like all fishermen, I tend to be a little eager and arrive early, before the hatch is underway. If there is absolutely no sign of fish working—few or no insects in the air and no spinner fall—then I go to the regular, sinking nymph and my method of fishing it. That is, a weighted Ida May on a short 3X leader and sunken line, fished dead drift. But, since I've been using the emerger—about eight or nine years—I also let the deeply sunken nymph hang straight downstream at the end of the drift, sometimes as long as two minutes. The difficulty in hooking the fish is still there but oddly, I sometimes get several hits to the same deeply sunken nymph at this time.

In fact, most of the morning hours in June can be more profitably spent with the nymph rather than with the dry fly, and this is especially true if no major hatch is on. Because of this, the Henry's Fork regulars have developed into perhaps the best *group* of nymph fishers in the nation. Certainly I see more good, experienced nymph fishers here than on any other stream in my area.

Even when there is a hatch on, if it is one of the minor hatches, such as some of the *Baetis* and *Callibaetis,* or even *Rhithrogena* and *Epeorus,* the proper nymph will not only work more consistently throughout the day than a dry, it will often produce larger trout.

One day two friends, George Harvey and Ralph *Doc* Dougherty, were fishing the Last Chance section using dry flies. They kept pretty steadily busy through the day, but the fish were not large. In the afternoon, George put on a number-14 brown nymph to go after a fish feeding under an overhanging bush. The limbs of the bush touched the water out from the bank, making it almost impossible to drift a dry fly into the area next to the bank where the fish was feeding. But the sunken fly and leader did the trick and George netted an eight pounder.

The favored nymphs here are the Hendrickson, Pheasant Tail, a small Otter Nymph, Zug Bug, and a strange caddis-larva job called by some *Bass Ackward* because of its reverse tie, head to the bend of the hook. These nymph patterns run to smaller sizes—12 to 16. The Ida May is also used since it became commercially available.

Of course, others are used, visitors who nymph fish tend to use their own patterns. That most of them, in the proper size range, seem to work is not only due to the skill of the user but to the fact that these waters contain at least 150 species of underwater forms to perhaps twice that many.

Streamers and bucktails are less used here than elsewhere—Railroad

Ranch excepted. Just why this is, I don't know, but perhaps its because the water is so suitable for dry fly and nymph fishing that fishermen tend to reserve it for those methods.

I believe that this stretch, Last Chance Run, which properly extends from the mouth of Box Canyon to the upper boundary of Railroad Ranch, is perhaps the most prolific piece of water for fly fishers of all types and skills of any in the contiguous forty-eight states when size as well as numbers of trout risen are considered. Stretches of the Yellowstone in the Park may produce somewhat greater numbers of trout but it will not give up eight-to twelve-pound fish as this water will. And no piece of trout water anywhere is more accessible; you can literally step out of your car and into the stream.

When the river is at normal depth, not being affected by releases from the dam, it is wadable almost everywhere: it has no deep pools or dropoffs. Pools, such as those large, very deep ones in the Railroad Ranch water, are good holding places for trout—but as Ray Bergman once pointed out, they are also excellent sulking places. Trout in pools do not often feed there. They move into shallows at the edges or into riffles or runs above and below. Pools, by their very nature, hold less numbers and kinds of insects.

And that brings us to the Ranch water. At its upper boundary this stretch joins Last Chance Run; the water is similar, but it already is beginning to deepen, and the bottom becomes somewhat different. The depth carries closer to the banks, and some of these banks are undercut. Others have shrubs, bushes, and grasses overhanging them. The fishing is becoming subtly different. The upper Ranch water still has the ease of approach that Last Chance Run does, but it offers some kinds of spot fishing that the Run doesn't. It will pay the angler to study these small differences before plunging in to fish. Otherwise some very good spots will go unnoticed and unfished.

As one procedes downstream into the Ranch, one will begin to discover silt in places along the bottom. This silt harbors a different kind of insect than does gravel. Oddly, it harbors few or no middle-sized mayfly types but does hold very large ones and very small ones. The larger ones are not numerous enough to cause any problem; not so with the smaller ones. Here *Tricorythodes minutus,* the Tiny White-Winged Black, formerly called *Caenis,* will at times hatch in veritable clouds. *Baetis propinqus,* Tiny Blue Quill, will show up. And *Pseudocloeon edmundsi,* Tiny Blue-Winged Olive, will literally blanket the water in September, although there are hatches of this tiny troublemaker from July to October. All three of these flies are in the 20–24 size range, with the last fly being the smallest. Its very numbers cause grief for the angler. With thousands upon thousands of the natural on the water, the angler's imitation has a small chance of being taken. All these blanket hatches of tiny flies go by the name of *Curse,* with some descriptive terms attached: for example, White Curse, Angler's Curse, and so forth. And cursing you will hear when these hatches are on, fish by the thousands feeding on them, and anglers by the score not catching anything.

From below the little low bridge crossing the river near the Ranch center, the water becomes wider and the bottom more silt covered. There are areas

Railroad Ranch water just below the old road bridge into the Ranch.
Acres of great trout water.

of shallow flats that are extensive. Mostly, these harbor small fish—but not always. As soon as you go plunging through them to get to a deeper channel beyond, you'll see the bow wave of a big rainbow surging ahead of you to deeper water. One can never take anything for granted on the Ranch.

Only long experience can tell you where and how to fish this water; the surface gives little clue as to where the fish might be lying. One old-timer told me that "you don't learn to fish the Ranch with your head, but with your feet." As a practical matter, this is true. Only after you have waded many times through this stretch from the bridge down to the deep pools opposite the Ranch buildings do you begin to learn how to fish the water.

Some fish it by simply covering the water thoroughly, so that no matter where the larger trout are, they have an opportunity to see the fly. The problem with this approach is that you often spook the small trout into alerting the larger ones and thus put them down.

Others fish only the banks, working upstream with dry fly, nymph, or terrestrial, spraying their casts in a fan shaped pattern twenty-five to thirty feet ahead of them: the first cast is dropped near the bank, the second out two feet, the third out six feet. Then the caster moves up five or ten feet and repeats the pattern. This is a good method but it covers only about one tenth of the available water.

Some of the old-timers use the above method and entirely ignore any ongoing hatch. They use general dry flies, general nymphs, and terrestrials—ants, hoppers, crickets, and beetles. By and large, this approach nets the bigger trout.

The great deep pools at the bend where the river swings away from the Ranch buildings and moves toward the highway, are a difficult proposition. I've never taken trout here unless some hatch was on. And I have better success with a nymph than with a dry. The Blue Dun or Hendrickson nymph, a Pheasant Tail, or an Otter Nymph in sizes 12 or 14 seem to work best. If the fish are working steadily on the current hatch, you'l need an emerger. I use my Natant Nylon Nymph in its dark phase for this condition.

Many good fly fishers believe that the water downstream of these great pools, on to the next fisherman's access, is the best of the Ranch water. They could be right.

It is more approachable throughout than some other stretches due to a narrowing of the stream, an improvement in bottom firmness, and the ability to wade closer to the area you are going to fish. Islands in the stream further help things by breaking the river into a series of channels which can be worked with shorter casts. There are not as many small fish to distract and interfere, but there are some quite large trout throughout this stretch.

The somewhat stronger current actually makes a drag-free float easier. The currents in the big pool areas are more subtle; false motion or drag is difficult to detect. But in their faster, more ripply currents, the defection is more quickly noticed and, thus, corrected.

One can spend an entire day on this stretch and, if one does his work well, still not cover more than one side of this mile stretch. Thurmon Creek comes out of the spillway of the dam forming Silver Lake and enters the river about the middle of this stretch. One can occasionally find a good pod of fish of one to two pounds milling around the area of the creek mouth; at other times the water will swarm with tiddlers. I don't yet know what causes this.

From the lower fisherman's access on down to Osborne Bridge, the river is shallower and swifter, and the fish generally smaller. It is seldom fished, and I've never seen anyone cover this piece of water thoroughly. Yet, it is a very pleasant stretch to fish with the grouse-hackled wet flies in sizes 12 and 14, using a greased-line, no-drag drift. Also, a method described by Larry Koller in *Taking Larger Trout* works very well with these same flies. In this method one casts straight across, holds the rod tip high, shaking it, and re-trieving rapidly with the line hand, causing the flies—Koller used two or three—to skip and skitter across the surface. This method brings a savage, slashing take and, now and then, a much larger trout than do other methods.

One can spend three weeks on the water from the mouth of Box Canyon to Osborne Bridge, and if he is thorough, never cover the same piece of water twice. As Howard Back said in *The Waters of Yellowstone with Rod and Fly*, "there is not an ell of this water one can afford to miss." I know of no other piece of any river anywhere that contains so many trout and of such size. And it is steadily improving as the Idaho Fish and Game Department continues its study of the area and applies the lessons learned.

15

ABOUT THOSE LAKES

It has often been stated that Henry's Lake is the best trout fishing lake anywhere in the United States. I believe that it is.

I've had the benefit of a varied and extensive fishing period in Alaska. During the two years I lived there, I roamed the entire northern section of that state (a territory then), covering it almost entirely except the Aleutian Chain and that portion of southeast Alaska extending down along Canada. I fished everywhere I went, and I asked about the fishing elsewhere. This was 1950–52. I do not believe that the noted fishing lakes of Alaska, such as Naknek and Iliamna, were as good then as Henry's Lake was, and as fly-fishing lakes, not nearly so.

As reported earlier herein, Henry's Lake suffered from drought during the 1967–79 period and its spawning streams were greatly affected. This inevitably led to a decline in the numbers of trout in the lake. However, nearly all lakes suffer such periodic declines due to natural factors. All well-nourished lakes, and Henry's is certainly that, rebound from such declines when conditions become more favorable. Unless the decline was caused by pollution, the recovery is usually rapid. Even when pollution was a severe and long-term problem, well-nourished lakes still recover when pollution is abated. Lake Erie is the best example of that.

So, Henry's Lake would have come back without help. But it got help in the form of two energetic and enthusiastic biologists and a large number of interested and determined people. Thus, its comeback has been more rapid than it would have been naturally. The fishing is now as good as it was twenty years ago and is improving every day.

The damming of the lake outlet in the mid-1920s improved the lake as a fishery by creating large shallow areas which are beneficial to more insect forms than are the deeper sections. It is the fertility of these flats that largely give the lake its overall richness. Also, the raising of the water level caused a number of springs to become incorporated in the lake bottom. Before the dam went in, Staley's Springs was a half mile back from the lake shore. (Incidentally, the resort now known as Staley's Springs was homesteaded by Sawtell in 1868, *but* his homestead did not include the springs themselves.

162

These were claimed by Ed Staley in the 1880s when he filed a homestead claim on the land surrounding the springs as well as taking over Sawtell's holdings.)

Staley's Springs and others covered by the raising of the lake level have been instrumental in keeping areas ice free in winter, thus minimizing, even preventing, winter kill of trout in the lake. They also have helped lower the temperature, which averaged 72° F. in summer prior to the dam being built. Thus, incorporating the springs in the lake bottom, along with the lake becoming deeper, has stabilized the lake temperature, making it cooler in summer but warmer in winter than formerly. Year-round growth of trout has been increased by this factor, and also by increasing the numbers and kinds of insects dwelling in the lake. All in all, the dam has been beneficial to the lake fishery.

This stabilization of temperature has allowed the scud (freshwater shrimp) to flourish. Year round, this one creature provides thirty-five percent of the trout's diet, and during certain periods the percentage is much higher. They are the single most important food for trout in the lake and, thus, for the fisherman to imitate.

An analyzation* of food items in the lake—available to the trout and utilized by them—shows that earthworms, caddis larvae and pupae, clams, damselfly nymphs, *Daphnia* (water fleas), dragonfly nymphs, leeches, mayfly nymphs, midge larvae, scuds, snails, water boatmen, water beetles and larvae, mites, sculpins, and terrestrial insects all form a portion of the diet. Some forms are seasonal: they will be a larger percentage of the diet at one time and be absent, or almost so, at another.

Trout in lakes—as well as streams—show a preference for certain food forms that become available certain times. Damselfly nymphs are present throughout the year *but* become very available only during the period when they are hatching into the adult form. They swim up to the surface and climb out onto weeds, grass, twigs, or the shore to split their nymphal shuck and become flying adults. This migration process makes them easily captured at this time, and the trouts' stomachs will show that damselfly nymphs form ninety percent of trout food during the emergence period. This happens *about* the last week of June and the first week of July.

Daphnia is actually the most prevalent food form for trout in the lake; it is present in far greater numbers than any other creature. But their tiny size make them almost impossible for the angler to imitate. At full growth, they reach a maximum of ³⁄₁₀ of a millimeter—about ⅛ of an inch—in length. Thus, although they *can* be imitated on a size-22 hook, it is rarely profitable to do so. These creatures exist by the hundreds of millions in Henry's Lake, the chance of *your* imitation being selected from those millions is about non-existent. *Daphnia* are prime food for fry and fingerlings.

*Conducted 1971–72 by the Idaho Fish and Game Department.

I've often stated my belief that a trout's selection of food items is based on three things: size, numbers, and availability. A fourth factor, ease of capture, is related to availability. And availability is often related to motion. A moving creature is more readily seen than motionless one of the same species. Some burrowing types of mayflies remain in their burrows most of the time. Thus, even though they might exist in great numbers and be of large size, their habits and habitat make them unavailable to the trout during most of the day or year. They become readily available *only* when they rise to the surface to undergo transformation into adults. Many lake mayflies are burrowers.

Sculpins move around, occupy the same habitat as the trout, and are large compared to any insect. They are thus a preferred food item by trout and rank third in importance among the trout foods of Henry's Lake.

Midges, in both larval and pupal forms, rank fourth on the list of creatures eaten by Henry's Lake trout. Here, numbers and availability are both factors causing them to be eaten. Midge larva are very active, moving to the surface and back throughout their larval life. Pupae are less active, some genera of midge pupa are almost dormant. At time of emergence, nearly all midge genera come into the surface film to make the transformation into the flying adult. And adult midges on the surface are greedily taken by trout. These insects in Henry's Lake will often cover the surface *if* the lake surface is smooth. The frequent winds of Henry's Lake often disperse the clouds of emerging midge adults.

All Henry's Lake midges, larva or adults, are relatively small. Generally a size 18 for the larvae is about right, and the adults range from that size to as small as 22. At present, I know of no commercial patterns for either locally available.

One of the most-favored artificials used at Henry's Lake is some pattern of leech. Thom Green was among the first of the regulars to use a leech pattern here. The Fish and Game study mentioned above shows that though leeches are minor in numbers compared to either scud or damselfly nymphs, their large size and method of movement make them one of the preferred trout foods. This is especially true of brook trout which spend more time in the shallows where leeches dwell than do either rainbow or cutthroat trout.

Leeches range through a great variety of sizes and colors; the ones in Henry's Lake are mostly pale olive or brown. At rest they may be no more than an inch long. But when they swim, with their up-and-down undulating motion, some stetch to almost six inches. Three to four inches is a better size for the artificial.

Various materials are used by fly tyers to make artificial leeches. I use car-washing shammy—the older and more used, the better. (See pattern in Appendix C.) Others use marabou or a combinatin of chenille and marabou. Some use a Wooly Bugger, and others olive or brown, narrow, long streamers.

Caddis form a good percentage of the diet of Henry's Lake trout. The larval forms are found more around bottom springs than elsewhere. The cased larvae are difficult to imitate in either appearance or motion. Still, *uncased* patterns imitating these larvae work, although I'm totally unable to explain why. There may be some *Rhyacophila* or *Goera* species in the lake; most of these do not make cases until time for pupation. All are some shade of green or, in some few, creamish yellow. Since the damselfly nymphs are also green, artificials of some shade of green are the best wet flies for Henry's Lake. In fact, the prevalent shrimp (scud) are a translucent green, also.

So, a green wet fly with a sparse hackle will work for several of the prevalent food forms in the lake. The wise angler would have several caddis larval imitations in various shades of green, some pupal patterns, also green, the green damselfly pattern, and a good scud or shrimp imitation in translucent green. (Bright green seal *hair* or dyed green polar bear underfur makes a good shrimp pattern.)

The shrimp would be my first choice. I have a good, easily tied shrimp pattern made with fluorescent green floss underbody, just covering the hook, then a body of bright green seal *hair*—not seal fur. Forming the rear tip, and over the back, a mallard or teal flank feather overwound with gold wire completes the pattern. (See Appendix C for how to tie some of these patterns.)

The shrimp will be found mostly around aquatic weed beds, although at times they will be in deep open water and occasionally in the grassy shallows.

Not much is known about the day-to-day habits of these *Gammaridae*. I am unable to find any study that delves deeply into their habitat selection. It may be that there are several species in the lake with different habitats. *Gammarus minus* and *Hyalella azteca* are both thought to be present; *Gammarus* is larger, more numerous, and the species most generally imitated. Patterns to imitate this species are the Werner Shrimp, Trueblood's Otter Shrimp (Nymph), Nyerges Nymph, Henry's Lake Nymph, and Yellow Scud. Although this creature does not make a pronounced metamorphosis, its size does change from smaller than a flea up to about three-quarters of an inch in length. It shape remains somewhat flealike. It is not, however, as curved or humpbacked in the water as most illustrations show it. In air, on any hard surface, or in the hand, shrimp curl, as do some stonefly nymphs. But in their natural habitat they are nearly straight—but humped—and are thicker in the middle.

(Ernie Schwiebert's *Nymphs* has paintings and descriptions of the freshwater shrimps. This book is a gold mine of information on underwater forms and one of three or four books having to do with fly fishing that I would not be without.)

I use my Shrimpy pattern in only two sizes, number 12 and number 10, both 1XL. Since there will be several sizes of these little animals in the water at any one time, I prefer to increase my chances by showing the fish the largest to be found. Females of *Gammarus* can produce ten or twelve broods of young during a single summer. The water can be loaded with the younger generations, but the larger sizes are more apt to catch the eye—and the trout.

The shrimp are active little creatures—darting, turning, rising and falling in the water—clambering around weeds and swimming rapidly in channels between weed beds.

One uses a line that will facilitate fishing the imitation at the desired depth. A floating line is used when the shrimp are active *over* the tops of weed beds. A sink-tip is most useful at moderate depths—one to two feet—and *around* weed beds. A Hi-D line is necessary when fishing three or more feet down. Don't destroy the efficiency of your sinking line by using too long a leader. Three or four feet is plenty, and half of that should be 4X tippet. You *don't need* a fancy tapered leader. I simply step down from my permanently attached leader butt of .018 inch in three steps: a piece of .014 inch and a piece of .010 inch, both one foot long, and a two foot tippet of .006 inch. Making this kind of a jump between sizes with a blood knot might cause problems. I only use one knot type, the Duncan Loop, for *all* fishing purposes. I can knot .020 to .004 with this knot and have a straight, smooth, trouble-free connection.

The method of fishing the shrimp varies with the water depth and the kinds or amounts of weeds. The deepwater method demands the least imagination. One simply casts out, lets the fly sink to the desired depth, and retrieves in short strips with pauses. Fishing the shallows requires the same presentation as with the floating line. In each case one varies the speed and length of the stripping action to obtain a scuttling motion. A steady retrieve is far less effective than a more erratic one.

Around the weed beds, the motion must be more varied. In addition to a scuttling motion, one wants to simulate the clambering and crawling of the natural by lifting and lowering the rod tip. This must be done slowly because the up-and-down movement of these creatures is much slower than their transverse movement. In the channels between weed beds, work the shrimp up and down with a varied motion: a lift, then allow the lure to settle a bit, lift again, and then lower the rod tip far down. In life these scuds do not sustain motion very long in any direction. The nearer one can come to simulating their actions, the more success one will have. Swing the rod slowly from far to one side to far to the other to obtain a change in lateral direction. Try to keep in mind what the fly is doing in response to your manipulations of rod tip and line. A bit of weight on the leader a foot ahead of the fly helps all presentations.

Because of the imagination required to handle the shrimp imitation, some fly fishers do not use it. Instead, they go with the leech or a sculpin imitation and a steady stripping retrieve. But with all three imitations, a more varied retrieve is better than a steady one.

Although I seldom see people fishing leech imitations in the shallows, that's where more leeches are found. However, the trout may not always be there. Leeches fished in the shallows seem to work better in dim light—

morning, evening, and overcast days. The amount of light also affects the depth other creatures will be found. Shrimp, especially, will be deeper on bright days.

Dry-fly fishing on Henry's Lake not only depends on hatches but on the lack of wind. Still days or days with a light breeze can provide excellent dry-fly fishing *if* they are accompanied by a good caddis hatch or egg-laying flight. Early morning and late afternoon/evening are usually the best times for dry-fly fishing. All in all, though, dry-fly fishing is a secondary method on Henry's Lake.

Streamers to imitate small trout and dace are used with some success. Again, more of the former will be found in the shallows, while dace, shiners, and sculpins will be deeper. More sculpins than dace and shiners are taken by trout, apparently because trout and sculpins share the same habitat. Yet the dace and shiner types of streamers, properly used, produce good results. If I were after a large brook trout, I'd use a number 2, 4XL Mickey Finn in the shallows during periods of dim light. A Spruce Streamer or a Trude Streamer might work also.

So, your best anytime bet on Henry's Lake is a shrimp pattern. This will probably get you the greatest amount of action. But for larger trout, the leech probably is the best bet. Fish it in the channels between the weed beds or over the tops of the weeds that lack a foot or so of reaching the surface. Six-inch strips of the line, with an occasional short pause, seem to work better than a steady or hand-twist retrieve. Fish it with the same motion in the shallows.

Sculpins are usually found deep; they are bottom dwellers by preference. Your chances are better with the imitation near the bottom whatever depth you are fishing. Fish it with an erratic, darting action, moving the rod the maximum distance right and left while stripping. Try to vary the action as much as possible and not have your fly going the same direction for more than a few seconds. Up-and-down motions of the rod tip of only a foot or so will also help. Let the fly pause and sink to the bottom every other cast. Use your imagination.

Just as I was finishing writing the above, I got in the mail a Christmas card from biologist Bob Rohrer with a message about the fishing and a newsletter from the Henry's Lake Foundation. The news was exciting and gratifying. First, in 1984, as compared to 1983, the catch rate was up 34 percent. The total catch was up 127 percent. Angler usage was up but 70 percent; therefore, more fish per angler was the rule. A total of 276,000 trout were landed, more than twice the 1983 catch. Foundation President John O'Neall who has fished the lake for twenty years says 1984 was the best year ever for numbers and trout of fifteen to seventeen inches.

Larger fish formed a lesser percentage than in 1983. This is a normal condition: when the numbers of trout in a lake increase dramatically, the size drops as a result of competition for food.

The favored rainbow-cutthroat hybrid catch was below normal, this due to unfavorable conditions in hatching and stocking in the 1979–81 period. That was the time when the biologists were having difficulty maintaining enough pure cutthroats for their crossbreeding purposes.

It is believed that Henry's Lake is now at saturation: carrying all the trout it can without the size dropping further. However, if there are fewer to three-pound trout in the catch, there are many more anglers catching and releasing fifty or more trout in a day. And the size will increase since younger fish do now make up a majority of those caught. The size and catch rate is expected to stabilize about 1986–87, with Henry's Lake not only producing large numbers for the anglers but, also, more of trophy size.

This rather startling quick comeback is due mainly to the efforts of the Idaho Fish and Game biologists—including Bob Rohrer, Bob Spateholtz, and fishery manager Steve Elle—the work of the Henry's Lake Foundation with its screening of irrigation canals which at times drained off ninety percent of newborn fry, and other steps to prevent spawning and nursery mortality.

Both the Fish and Game department and the Foundation will continue their efforts to raise the quality of the Henry's Lake fishery. As I said before, the future of the lake is in the best possible hands, and its future is bright, bright, bright.

The Fish and Game biologists are also working to improve the fishery in Island Park Reservoir. But, here, the solutions are far more complex because the reservoir is a more complex body of water than is Henry's Lake.

The spawning and nursery streams are longer and larger and, thus, are susceptible to more damage by overgrazing, breakdown of banks by cattle, and even drought. And less attention, research, and study has been done on these streams. When such study does start it will take longer simply because more miles of stream are involved. But be of good cheer, the Fish and Game people are working on the problem and they will get answers and results.

As mentioned earlier, this lake is somewhat different than other artificial impounds. Its greatest length does not lie up the river its dam contains. Only about three miles of lake stretch northwestward from the dam up Henry's Fork. Two miles reach eastward up Crow Creek, and more than seven miles stretch westward up the valley of Icehouse Creek. Thus, the greatest length of the lake, nearly ten miles, lies *across* the stem of the river itself. The Icehouse Creek branch and the Henry's Fork branch encircle a large island, I.P. Bills Island, in the area a mile and a half west of the dam. I.P. Bills was an entrepreneur in the area who purchased a lodge resort from A. S. Trude that Trude called Lock Leven Lodge. Bills operated it as the Lakeside Lodge. Before he sold the lodge in 1953, Bills had built a causeway across the Henry's Fork branch of the reservoir to his property on the island, which he developed into a very lovely, summer-home resort area. (I have been unable to find what the initials, I.P., in Bills' name stood for. I've been told that he called himself Island Park Bills.) Bills and the Trude family (the Trudes owned most of the property in this area), were ardent conservationists and took steps to protect the area from wanton spoliation. Both required restrictive covenants of the U.S. government before granting it easements to flood portions of their property. These covenants, to protect birds and wildlife in areas not flooded, are still in effect.

Island Park reservoir, and some of the streams running into it, have been stocked with rainbows for many years. George Rea, who had homesteaded the property later acquired by Trude, had a hatchery-trout farm on a spring feeder of either Icehouse or Sheridan Creeks in 1895. By 1899 he also was raising brook trout for sale.

Meanwhile, the state of Idaho had formed a fish and game department and issued word that the commercial sale of trout would be prohibited. The state's first game warden, a man named Charles Arbuckle, strongly opposed Rea's efforts to sell his trout. Rea's plea that his *domesticated* trout were no different as a commodity than chickens, pigs, or cows raised for human consumption fell on deaf ears. The Idaho legislature passed laws forbidding the selling or shipping of all trout—and other game. Rea went bankrupt as a result of these well-intentioned laws.

The whole thing was aimed at poachers in the Island Park-Henry's Lake area who were catching and selling about fifty tons a year of wild trout. They were also killing several hundred elk and buffalo in Yellowstone Park and shipping it as beef. Beaver Dick Leigh, shortly before his death, informed Arbuckle that several sled loads of elk and buffalo meat had been gathered from Yellowstone Park and shipped via the railroad at Monida as beef. Leigh pointed out that this was possible *only* with the connivance of Arbuckle's wardens, who were taking bribes to look the other way. In the process of controlling wholesale poaching, George Rea and his trout farming operation became a casualty. His holdings were then taken over by Trude.

Thus, latecomers to the scene have referred to the original rainbow stock in Henry's Fork as *Trude rainbows* but Trude himself had nothing to do with their being in the river, and of course, in Island Park Reservoir, after the dam was built.

Since the only rainbow hatchery operating *anywhere* when Rea commenced his operations was the U.S. hatchery on the McCloud River in northern California, that had to be the source of Rea's stock. It is now known that some of the eggs hatched in the early years of the McCloud River hatchery were taken from steelhead. There were no dams on the Sacramento River or the tributary McCloud in those days, and steelhead ran from the ocean all the way to the McCloud hadwaters to spawn. It was this that caused a fall run of spawning rainbows on Henry's Fork above the mouths of Icehouse and Sheridan creeks in the 1900–1935 period. After Island Park Dam was built, the *only* fall run of rainbow spawners was upstream of Island Park Reservoir. Since the river below Island Park Dam had been stocked from the early 1920s with rainbows that never ran in the fall, it seems obvious that the fall spawning rainbows could only have come from Rea's hatchery.

Old timers, among them Don Martinez, Vint Johnson, and others early in the fly shop business in West Yellowstone, used to hit this spawning run just above Coffee Pot Canyon in October. Letters from Martinez to Ray Bergman mention this run, saying that the fish *averaged* larger than some West Coast steelhead. Martinez said that these big, fall-running rainbows would go between five and seven pounds, with seldom a trout under three.

I have seen very large rainbows in Henry's Fork in mid-winter—December and January—as recently as five years ago. Whether or not this is a remainder of Rea's stock or big fish running down Big Springs Outlet from their usual spot near the springs, I don't know. But during the period 1970–79 that I made winter trips over to the section of the river between the Bathtub and the head of Coffee Pot Canyon, I never failed to see many large rainbows—some in the eight- to nine-pound class—and seldom did I see one less than three pounds.

I now wonder if there is still a fall run of rainbows out of Island Park Reservoir that for some reason is running later—November, perhaps. No one—biologists, or fishermen or local residents—have been able to give me an answer as to the origin of those big trout. But one year-round resident of the Big Springs-Mack's Inn area—the late Robert Wuthrich, who had lived there since the mid-1920s—told me that he saw numbers of larger rainbow trout in the river above Coffee Pot Canyon to the Bathtub every winter. Robert, an old friend, was a nature observer, a superb photographer, and a cross-country skier who knew more of what was going on in the Island Park area than anyone. His information led to my own investigations during which I also saw those big trout.

After much consideration, I have developed a theory. I believe the trout that Robert and I saw *were* remains of Rea's old stock. I believe that they are now running much later due to the fact that over many generations they have become accustomed to the shorter distance they need to go to spawn in late winter or very early spring. In the McCloud River, the rainbows had nearly 500 miles to travel from the ocean to reach their spawning grounds. Thus, they ran in September and October. When the eggs were transferred to Rea's hatchery, the trout continued to start their run at the same time their ancestors had. But over the years, any wild creature adapts to change—it is part of what Darwin called natural selection. There have been almost ninety generations of McCloud River rainbows running in Henry's Fork. That's enough generations for the trout to adapt to a later starting date, since they now run only about thirty miles to spawn.

I believe that one could prove this by fishing the run in late November, if regulations would permit. On the other hand, few fishermen would brave late-November cold and possible two feet of snow to fish this run. The visiting anglers would all be gone, and there is not a large enough group of resident fly fishers to make a change of regulations worthwhile. Still, I'm intrigued by the possibilities.

All this speculation points up the fact that Island Park Reservoir still hosts a sizeable number of very large trout. The reservoir has been treated with rotenone and other piscicides at least twice in the last twenty-five years to remove coarse fish. The results in that direction have been disappointing. But, both times, great numbers of rainbows above four pounds were found in the lake.

As far as I know, no really big trout, over twelve pounds, have turned up. This is in line with conditions in the lake. It is colder and less fertile than Henry's Lake. For years we've heard the old littany that trout are a cold-water fish. But that depends on the definition of cold.

It has been learned that trout grow best in waters of 62 to 67 degrees Fahrenheit, all other factors being favorable. In most cases, trout food also grows best at those temperatures. One occasionally hears of large trout coming from cold lakes. What is seldom stated is that (1) there are special conditions existing there, and (2) these trout are quite old by trout standards.

A fish will continue to grow throughout his life under favorable conditions. Brook trout, stunted from overpopulation in small streams, have been taken, scale read for age, and then planted in more favorable streams, where within a year they would sometimes go from six inches and two ounces to sixteen inches and two pounds. In some cases, the fish have doubled that growth.

One of the conditions that promotes a good growth rate is stability of temperature which stimulates year-round feeding. This is another factor that Henry's Lake has, that Island Park Reservoir does not.

Still, the reservoir holds a large head of fish, and a good percentage are over two pounds. Fly caught trout do not often exceed this figure; most of the larger trout caught in Island Park Reservoir are taken by trolling with Flatfish, spoons, and sometimes bait.

That's all right; it's a good lake for the bait fisher and troller—less good for the fly fisher. We fly fishers sometimes tend to think in exclusive terms, but there are more fishers who do not fly fish than there are that do. These people are entitled to an equal chance at their sport, and Island Park Reservoir gives them not only a beautiful lake in splendid surroundings but one particularly suited to their methods. Good for them.

One of the things that make it more difficult for the fly fisher is that there are forty to fifty miles of shoreline, much of which is only approachable by boat. There are several roads which approach the lake shore, but they do not, generally, flank it for any great distance. Fly fishing the center of the lake, or the open water, brings but small success with the fly. One must pursue the trout in the shallows, and this is especially true for the day fly fisher.

Mayfly hatches seem sporadic, and isolated. They do not happen, at least in my rather limited experience, in several areas at the same time. Nor have I ever seen what could be termed a blanket hatch with much of the water covered by floating naturals.

Caddis are somewhat the same, but emergences of this fly seem to last longer. This could be because caddis sometimes live for two or three weeks, and thus today's emergers may mingle with last week's egg layers.

The area around the shoreline of the tributary creek mouth seem to be more generally productive than other areas. And Island Park Reservoir is not subject to the same frequency and ferocity of winds as on Henry's Lake. This reservoir is not so closely clasped in the embrace of the surrounding mountains as is Henry's Lake. Much of the shoreline is guarded by the dense lodgepole forest which also buffers the winds.

There seems to be little or no friction between the many boaters and the shoreline fishers. Mainly, the boaters—trolling, water skiing, or pleasure cruising—stay in the open water. At present, there is more than enough room for everyone.

Although one does not often hear of large trout—ten pounds and up—being taken, every summer will produce catches of forty or fifty trout per day to the diligent fly fishers who are regulars here.

So, with Henry's Lake and Island Park Reservoir in rather close proximity, the fly fisher who likes lakes has a couple of beauties to fish. The lakes are about as different as lakes can be, and this, too, adds to the charm. All in all, the fisher who prefers lake fly fishing could not find more variety and such excellent fishing in so small an area. At least, not anywhere I ever heard about.

Ashton Reservoir is not a top flight lake for the fly fisher. Trollers and bait fishers do very well here, in what is actually but a wider, deeper section of river. The reservoir is two to three miles long, depending on water levels. It is seldom a quarter mile wide. I've never seen or heard of fly fishers fishing this lake. Its regulars are bait fishers, fishing for a trout dinner. There are some few trollers and spin casters.

The Idaho Fish and Game 1981–85 Fisheries Management Plan gives this section, from the dam to the Highway 191–20 bridge, a low priority. It notes that the catch rate is about .5 fish per hour, that catchables are stocked, and that some kokanee exist. This stretch, 4.2 miles of water, is treated as a subsistence fishery. It does not get much use otherwise. However, it does hold a good pod of large trout that run up as far as the mouth of Warm River, or perhaps further, during spawning season. Some of these fish might be caught in the very latter part of the regular season, and some large trout do remain in the river after spawning. By and large, this lake has a very low impact on the river above or on fishing pressure.

Ashton Reservoir does, however, have a marked effect on the river below the dam, about forty-three miles of water. It cools the water and adds oxyen; it improves the trout-holding capability and thus, the fishing, for about half of those miles. This, in my opinion is its major contribution to the Henry's Fork fishery—although the largest trout caught in this river was in the four miles of water between Ashton Dam and the Highway 191–20 bridge—a 24½ pound brown from a very old stocking.

There are four or five tributary creeks that run into the reservoir. On the north, Cedar Hollow, Rattlesnake, Kerr, Putney, and Willow creeks enter. Some join before they enter the river channel. In spring, the fishing around the mouths of these creeks, and a quarter mile or so upstream provides good fly fishing. On the south, a small creek enters opposite the mouth of Willow Creek. It is of good report in the spring. As to whether these creeks hold running spawners, I can find no information. This particular area is perhaps the least known of the entire river except to local people, and not many of those have any information about the trout. Since this section is easily reached by several roads and warms more quickly in spring than anywhere upstream, its a good place to open the season.

16

FISHING THE
LOWER RIVER

THE COOLER WATER COMING OUT OF THE ASHTON DAM TAILRACE BENE-
fits the trout for perhaps the next twenty miles, down to the mouth of the
North Fork of Teton River. The first seven miles, from Ashton Dam to the
mouth of Falls River, is excellent large-river fishing for strong, lusty rainbows.

There are *more* fish in this stretch; though the fish are fewer downstream
of the mouth of Falls River, they are larger. Some of five or more pounds are
caught regularly, and larger ones are reported taken every year. There is
good to excellent fishing right in the town of Saint Anthony. About a mile of
very good water runs through this lovely small town, and Mike Lawson's son,
Shaun, caught a twenty-six-inch, seven-pound trout near a wing dam at the
east edge of town when he was not yet six years old.

This town is famous along Henry's Fork for its annual Fisherman's
Breakfast which opens the trout season. Eight- to ten-thousand people, anglers and their families, attend each year. Mountains of flapjacks, eggs, sau-
sage, and potatoes and barrels of coffee are consumed before hitting the
stream for a day's fishing. Everything is free, furnished by local merchants
and boosters, who also do all the work. The event is regularly telecast by
Idaho Falls television stations and is an Henry's Fork institution.

Fly fishing is not practiced as much in this twenty-mile stretch as is bait
and lure fishing. Yet, there is excellent fly fishing all along here and plenty of
insects and good hatches. Bing Lempke, the only person I know who knows
the insects in the lower river as well as the upper, says there are excellent
late-season hatches here and good hatches all season long. There are several
large mayflies in the lower river that are not found above Ashton Dam.
Among these are *Ameletus oregonenus* and *spartasus, Stenonema terminatum,* two
Callibaetus, some *Ephemerella,* and *Ephoron album,* Snowflake Dun. The latter,
in late October, furnishes excellent dry-fly fishing for quite large trout.

There are numbers of forage fish and leeches, so the streamer fisherman also will have good fishing and may take the largest trout to fall to the fly. Caddis are not as prevalent here as farther upstream, but there are good hatches; some large caddis, size 10, hatch in summer. All in all, this is a very propitious area for those who can handle the long casts sometimes required. Of course, a boat or canoe can be used to drift the stream and put you closer to your fish. There are five bridges along this stretch where one can put in or take out a canoe or boat. Since a good bit of the river in these twenty miles is unwadable due to depth, drifting or float fishing is a good way to reach these waters.

The lesser numbers of trout in the lower fifteen miles of this stretch is not caused by the warming of the river, as most people think. It is caused by loss of fry, fingerling, and even larger fish into the diversion ditches and canals that abound here. (See next chapter for fuller discussion of this.) The river, at present, may lose as much as seventy percent of its fry and fingerlings into ditches and canals.

The stream is difficult to read because of depth and the amount of organic material in the water. This is largely caused by return irrigation water carrying debris from the fields of hay and potatoes growing along here. One is faced with having to cover rather large areas of water without much of a clue as to whether or not one is fishing over trout or barren water. For this reason, fly fishers tend to focus their attention on the banks. Since the river generally is deep enough right at the bank to hold even very large trout, and since there are usually willows, service berry, or other overhanging shrubs, fishing the shoreline produces very good results.

I like a two-fisherman approach. One can be using the dry fly as they work upstream. This will leave many areas unfished because the tips of many tree limbs lop over and touch or enter the water. The second fisherman uses a floating line also, *but* at the end of his leader will be a nymph, caddis pupal imitation, or soft-hackled wet fly. These, all unweighted, will usually get deep enough to avoid getting tangled in the overhanging limbs but not so deep that one is fishing blind. I've done this with a companion, in areas along here where one can wade, and the fishing was excellent by any standard. The fish we caught were not large, fourteen to about seventeen inches, but were all bright young fish in excellent condition.

It comes to me now that all the large fish I have seen, those running five to eight or more pounds, have all been in the middle area of the river. Also, for reasons unknown to me, these larger fish seem to band together, anywhere from four or five to more than a dozen in a group. The only place I have seen large trout singly along here was just off, and up in, the mouth of Falls River. I've seen some whoppers there.

I don't do streamer fishing much anymore, but I've seen others along here using them, and they are very successful. The Muddler, Olive Matukas, and brown or green Marabou Muddlers are used. Also, Zonkers, leeches, large Wooly Buggers, and big bucktails work well. Because of the light-diffracting quality of the organic material in the water, some fishers use streamers with tinsel garland bodies, or lots of silver mylar or pearlescent flashabou in their makeup. It's an old fly fisherman's maxim that the trout will not take your fly if he can't see it. So, here, use something big, flashy, and of a color easily seen in this darker water.

From just above Saint Anthony downstream, the river starts the process of becoming what hydrologists call braided. It starts with an island or two in the stream; these increase in both sizes and numbers as one moves downstream until just before it enters the Snake River, Henry's Fork is a many-channeled stream.

From Saint Anthony to the mouth of the Teton River's north fork, this is an aid to the fisher. It not only gives him a smaller stream to work, but the islands increase the number of banks to be fished. I like to fish this kind of water; it gives me a different feeling about a river and a great deal of satisfaction. I've talked to other men who feel the same way, and we agree that we can no more explain our feelings than we can give reasons for the partners we marry. One reason may be similar; one can get a greater feeling of intimacy in the smaller streams around the islands than out on the big, wide river.

For whatever reason, I enjoy fishing such areas. And it is invariably more productive. Since there are greater numbers of good holding areas due to there being more shoreline, and more bank cover, there are more trout there than in the same area of open river.

One of the less-desirable features along here is that areas of silt bottom increase in size and numbers. This cuts down on the kinds of insects and fish food present. And this means lesser numbers of trout in such areas. Also, silted areas are seldom good holding areas for trout. And they are difficult to wade. So, as one proceeds downstream, the need for a boat or canoe or some floating device becomes greater. Below the mouth of Teton's north fork, on to where the Henry's Fork enters the Snake, it is difficult to impossible to wade and fish, and even to approach the stream. Yet this is still a good trout-fishing area and not much fished. It is better in spring and fall than mid-summer.

There are three bridges crossing the river below Saint Anthony, and these divide the river neatly into stretches that make a good one-day float. Because these are farm roads across the bridges, and they lace throughout the area, one can conveniently get to both the put-in and take-out points without excessive driving. It requires, however, either two cars or three people. If there are three people, one drives the car from the put-in to the take-out point, and the other two float the river. One fishes, one works the boat, changing on an agreed on basis. The fellow who drove the car to the take-out point is, of course, restricted to fishing the areas he can wade around this lower bridge.

If this does not seem worth the trouble, let me point out that the fish average a very good size indeed, and you probably will be the only persons fishing the entire five to seven mile stretch of river. The slow current speed also makes for excellent coverage of the water. On a day where you want to try something different, and perhaps catch a very large trout, or even several, consider float fishing one of the three sections between the bridges here.

17

PROBLEMS: PAST, PRESENT, AND FUTURE

ALL WATERSHEDS HAVE PROBLEMS, SOME CAUSED BY MAN, SOME BY NATURE. Some of those problems, created in the past, often extend into the present or even the future. One past problem in Henry's Fork watershed would have undoubtedly extended itself for a very long time had it not been aborted *before* it became a real problem. The very fact, that except for some chance, unknown at this time, that it would have happened, is blood-chilling when its possible effects are considered.

In 1941, before we entered World War II, the U.S. Army proposed, and started to build, an enormous military complex on Henry's Lake Flat. It would have covered twenty-two square miles with over a hundred buildings, some the size of a football field.

It was to have been a post for training and testing men and weapons in severe winter conditions. More than 15,000 soldiers and more than 3000 officers and civilians were to have operated this complex. Tanks, trucks, amphibious vehicles, and other equipment were to be tested. Over a hundred miles of roads, blacktop, and gravel, would have been built. Great garages and maintenance shops would have covered the flat.

The most chilling thing, however, was the plan to use the area for testing heavy artillery in very cold weather. A firing range *across* Henry's Lake was planned. Big guns on the east edge of the flat would have hurled their missiles across the lake, on to the base of the Centennial Mountains—mainly Sawtell Peak and Red Rock Pass. The damage would have been monstrous. And, since the Army, once entrenched in an area, is almost impossible to dislodge, that very thing could have been going on for the past forty-five years. It frightens me just to think about it.

George Garner, circa 1930, with an afternoon's catch from Henry's Lake. Today's angler would not find such a catch exceptional or unusual for an afternoon's fishing—but he could not keep them all.

I have been unable to find what caused cancellation of the project. It was *not* a paper project: building had commenced. The first buildings, to house planning offices and to garage some vehicles, were completed. Their concrete foundations can still be seen today across the road from and a little east of Valley View Truck Stop. Those buildings mysteriously burned down, and later, the entire project was canceled. The why is still missing.

It was greatly favored by state, county, and city officials, who babbled happily about the number of jobs. No one, at least in the press, said anything negative about the project. No one mentioned the enormous environmental damage that would occur. In the tradition of the times and of the West: *never was heard a discouraging word.* But something happened. We may never know what caused the cancellation—but be eternally grateful for it. And be eternally vigilant; it can happen again. There is always someone, somewhere, who thinks any part of the country is wasted that is not covered with black-top, concrete, and buildings. And since *civilization* requires water, water, and more water, lakes and streams are high on planners' lists of places that must be developed.

Prior to the late 1800s, the Henry's Fork area was so lightly settled that little change took place except in the area around the mouth of the river. Growth and change was slow in the early 1900s. Then in 1919 came the first project that caused a considerable change.

In that year, a railroad tie-cutting* operation started in the Island Park

*These timbers under the rails are called *ties* because they *tie* the rails together.

area. It lasted until the Depression caused its demise. At its peak, 1500 people were cutting timber and making railroad ties, from Ashton Bench to Henry's Lake Flat. Most of the work was along the Union Pacific Railroad from just east of Last Chance to Big Springs. Along the railroad sidings in the areas of Trude, Guild, Island Park, and Big Springs, tie-cutting camps of several hundred people each sprang up.

It is estimated that tie-hack crews at the peak of production were cutting down and making into railroad ties some 12,000 trees per day, 72,000 trees per week, or 3,600,000 trees per year. And this rape of the timber went on for about fifteen years.

Since the work was all done by hand—falling and bucking the trees into lengths with a two-man crosscut saw, chopping, scoring, and hewing the ties to shape with chopping axe and broad axe—the damage did not proceed as fast as it would have today. And what stopped it was the economics of the Depression, not concern for the environment. It is still economics that keeps it from happening again.

The lodgepole pine, in the timber industry, is rated as a trash tree or weed tree. These designations mean that it has limited value and a very limited number of uses. It's low value yield, and nothing else, has saved the lodgepole forests from being decimated. True, the Forest Service has imposed some restrictions on all kinds of timbering operations. But until fairly recently, the Forest Service has acted as though its main purpose was to make the production of timber products easier and cheaper for those engaged in it.

In the Island Park area, it takes about eighty years for a lodgepole tree to reach useful size for lumbering purposes. This, too, has been of help in directing the timber industry's attention to more profitable areas, and away from Henry's Fork. But if the economic situation ever favors the harvesting of lodgepole pine, the cutters and slashers will be back. Depend on it.

However, there is hope that the fairly recent upsurge of concern for the environment will be strong enough and widespread enough to forestall the kind of outrages that have taken place in the past. The Forest Service, due to public awareness and pressure, has been moving more in the direction of *wiser* use, not *more* use. This will be a continuing thing as younger, better-educated, and more environmentally oriented people replace those whose only thought was to provide maximum help to the timber industry.

Actually, the tie-hacking of the 1920–35 era was not all bad. The trees had to be cut selectively. Only trees that would provide a tie with a face of eight inches could be used. Since felling a tree is the slowest and most back-breaking part of the work when a crosscut saw is the tool, workers fell only those trees that would make several ties of eight-foot length.

Had this been done with care, it would have been good for the forest, removing only mature trees, letting in sunlight, making things generally better for those trees left, as well as other plants, and even birds and animals. But speed was the watchword, not care. The tie-hacks were paid twenty-eight to thirty-six cents per tie. More ties meant more money. Thus, no attention was paid to damage to other trees or to the soil. Nor was any cleanup or restoration work even contemplated. The ties were skidded on sledges, hauled on wagons, and dragged singly or by bunches, tearing up the forest floor terribly. Only the fact that the workers mostly chose very flat surfaces to operate on saved the forest floor from being heavily damaged by erosion. The operation was terminated before the workers had to go onto the steep mountainsides to find mature trees.

From the mid-1930s to the early 1960s, overgrazing posed the greatest threat to the Henry's Fork watershed. At one time more than three million sheep and cattle grazed the watershed, and the newspapers and Forest Service releases talked happily of four million or more domestic animals to eventually be using public lands in the area. At this time, overgrazing was endemic in the west and it continued until much of the public land was in poor or unsatisfactory condition. 728 million acres of public land was overgrazed during the 1900–1960 period. But, slowly, the Forest Service and other government agencies began to recognize the problem as it took more and more acres to feed one animal. Discontent by the cattle and sheep raisers and public muttering which grew in amount and intensity forced changes and reductions in the number of animals grazing public land. Court cases brought by outraged environmentalists resulted in the federal courts ordering the various agencies not only to reduce the number of grazing animals per unit area but to study and commence the restoration of the worse-damaged areas.

At present, the Targhee National Forest and the Bureau of Land Management people are limiting the number of animals grazing public land, are continually examining for areas of abuse, and in general, are moving strongly to protect and preserve the lands under their control. The excesses of the past have been recognized and are now being guarded against. There has been much improvement, and that is continuing. The future of the watershed is much brighter than it was even twenty years ago.

The major problem—past, present and future—is irrigation. Even as the land was being settled, irrigation commenced, and it is now the dominant practice affecting the river, tributaries, and watershed.

Idaho is the most heavily irrigated state in the nation. Thirteenth in size, it is third in the number of irrigation dams and canals. It has *more* than 5,000 dams and *more* than 15,000 miles of canals for irrigation. It uses ten million acre-feet of water for irrigation each year. In gallons, that's 3,265,000,000,000—three trillion, two hundred sixty-five billion—gallons of water removed from rivers and spread on the land.*

In the Henry's Fork watershed there are five major irrigation dams and eighty or so diversions—forty canals and an equal number of ditches—draining water from Henry's Fork and its tributaries. This, if handled properly, and with consideration for other factors, would not, in itself, be a great problem. But it is handled with no consideration other than to get the

---

*That's enough water to cover the states of Connecticut and New Jersey one foot deep.

farmer and rancher his water wherever he wants it and whenever he wants it. Because water rights in Idaho are treated as an absolute right, at present there exists no way of checking abuses.

As of now there is no way of preventing an organized irrigation district from drying a stream up completely. About ten years ago, the Snake River below Palisades Dam was dried up for several miles when the dam gates were closed completely. The Henry's Fork, for years, was dried up from the Island Park Dam down to the entry of the Buffalo River every winter. All the irrigation district people I talked to rejected, some angrily, any thought of some form of control over their use of what is actually public water. Ninety-three percent of the water entering the Henry's Fork and its tributaries originates on public lands.

The eighty or so diversions leaving the Henry's Fork and its tributaries to carry irrigation water are all unscreened. *All of them.* How many fry, fingerlings, and larger trout are lost into these drains can only be conjectured. Where there has been some study, estimates range as high as seventy percent of fry and fingerlings. Larger fish are considered not to be so badly affected.

Fortunately, most of the canals and diversions are in the lower river. This localizes the problem where the fishery is less utilized. At present, there is no plan by anyone or any organization to screen the inlets and outlets of irrigation diversions except around Henry's Lake. It would not only be very expensive originally but would be a continuing expense unless the modern, but very costly, self-cleaning roller screens were installed. And no one in this irrigation system is going to bear that expense.

Expansion of recreation facilities and associated housing on the upper river—Last Chance, Island Park, and surrounding areas—is starting to show signs of being a problem. This is aggravated by a lack of zoning laws which can prevent abuses. There is enough land, and area, to handle any expected new building expansion. But the lack of zoning laws encourage builders to cut corners and to create problems that are then blithely handed over to the county (Fremont County) to take care of.

The situation with regards to the need of a proper sewage system at Last Chance is in need of immediate address. Already there are builders and developers panting to build condominiums and more condominiums right on the very banks of the river at Last Chance. The people there are attempting to get a moratorium on such building until an answer to the sewage problem is found. As usual, the builders are pressing to build now, before new regulations make it more expensive. The state of Idaho, and the various counties have shown reluctance to create laws that might inhibit growth and the creation of more jobs by making construction or development more expensive. Unscrupulous developers are quick to take advantage of the lack of laws protecting the public, and there have been *build and get out* projects which are now beginning to show signs of desertion.

The area of the Henry's Fork watershed, especially the Ashton Bench-Continental Divide area, is a most attractive place to either vacation or live. More and more people are coming in to build summer homes. The severe winters and lack of year round employment opportunities will always limit permanent full-time residency. But it is the full-time resident who will be stuck with any mess and the cost of fixing it up unless laws are soon passed to protect them. I don't expect this to happen.

I do expect, however, such wildcat building to be self limiting. It has been everywhere I've ever seen resort development. Usually, there is a spurt of overbuilding, values start to diminish, the population levels off, and the get-rich-quick types move on. Just how much damage will be done to the eco-system, especially the river and its underlying aquifer, is open to question. The Fremont County Health Department is seriously trying to prevent any more damage, but their efforts are being sandbagged by powerful officials who see no evil in unrestrained building and development. The next five years will probably see the matter resolved. Whether the public wins or loses is still very much undecided.

Overall, the picture is bright. The federal agencies are generally more progressive than in the past, the Bureau of Reclamation excepted. This organization is still largely staffed with people who believe their sole purpose is to aid the farmer and rancher in obtaining what they want, and who resent the attempts by the public to have some control over its land and waters. State agencies also are taking a better posture toward protection and conservation. Tourism is becoming one of Idaho's most profitable businesses and officials are beginning to realize that people do not come here looking for a Los Angeles or a Chicago.

There are clouds in this otherwise bright picture, the ones we have just covered. They will clear away. But not without public pressure.

In the long run, the public will, will prevail. Public awareness of its ability to influence or delay change is growing rapidly. I believe that the Henry's Fork will survive growth largely unharmed.

There is one other cloud hanging around in the background: drilling for oil and geothermal energy sources has been contemplated. Permits for oil drilling were granted many years ago. All test wells drilled in southeast Idaho and southwest Montana came up dry. Until the energy crunch came along in 1975, things had been quiet, no wells drilled for many years. There was no financial incentive to do so. But the government offered huge tax incentives for the production or *attempted* production of geothermal energy. So the company that owned the oil drilling permits applied for permits to drill for geothermal sources. The way this matter was handled shows how a clever corporation and a compliant or inept government agency can work together to get a project past an unknowing or unsuspecting public.

This kind of thing has been going on for years. An example: back in the seventies, the government and others wanted to build a dam on the Yellowstone River, the longest undammed river left in the continental U.S. The law said hearings must be held. So a hearing was held. In the valley of the Yellowstone or cities nearby? Ha! The hearing was held in a small town over 250 miles from the Yellowstone River. But people got wind of it, the duplicity angered people who really had no interest otherwise and such an outcry arose that the federal government adopted a law that said such hearings could not be held farther away from the contemplated project than seventy miles.

So, when the company asked for drilling permits, it did not go to the Gallatin National Forest which controls forest lands in the Madison Basin and along the Yellowstone Park boundary, the area where the most geothermal sources were known to be. Instead, it went to the Targhee National Forest headquarters in Saint Anthony. The supervisor there aquiesced, and set out to do a Draft Environmental Statement (DES), and to hold a hearing. Using the fiction that the drilling would mostly be in the Island Park area, the project was called the Island Park Geothermal project.

The hearing was held in the winter of 1980/81 when it was known that many people of both the Island Park and West Yellowstone areas—where almost all businesses are seasonal—would be elsewhere on winter vacations. Also, the hearing was not held in Island Park, West Yellowstone, or even Saint Anthony. It was held in Rexburg, seventy-five miles from West Yellowstone, and near the limit of distance imposed by law.

The people there neither knew or cared much about the project. There was little opposition.

But some people in West Yellowstone were alerted. I was notified in California where I have to winter for health reasons. Letters were written, phone calls made to the Secretary of the Interior, to congressmen, and to senators; the press was notified. Using the "threat to Old Faithful" as a rallying cry, we stirred up enough outcry to force a hearing to be held in West Yellowstone in summer.

At that hearing the DES was torn to shreds—it was a totally inadequate document. We were able to show that in the eight known world geothermal areas, drilling for energy sources had taken place in seven and that in all seven, geothermal activity had declined. In Iceland, the earliest such source developed, the Geysir* (Gusher), no longer geysed—or gushed. Nor did any other once known geysers still gush, *except* those in Yellowstone Park where no such drilling was allowed.

Further, evidence was produced from scientific sources that *all* these drillings had produced a poisonous gas, hydrogen sulfide. An inversion over such an area in Italy had trapped hydrogen sulfide in the geothermal area, it built up to lethal levels, and people died. And the Madison Basin, in which West Yellowstone lies, is subject to several such inversions a year.

The upshot was that the Secretary of the Interior—who must authorize all such projects—criticized the DES severely, and issued an order that *no* drilling was to take place unless it could be proven in advance that the thermal features in Yellowstone Park would not be affected. This effectively killed the project—a negative theory cannot be proven. That is, you cannot prove that something does not exist or cannot happen. Can you *prove* there is no such thing as a unicorn? Or flying saucers?

*This Icelandic word *geysir* (= *gusher*) is used worldwide for such features.

So, we've dodged that bullet. But such corporations have plenty of ammo and long memories. They'll be back to try again. If we expect to preserve the Henry's Fork—and all else that matters—it's up to us—you and me. No longer can we *let George do it* because George has probably been hired by the corporation. And if we expect to get a show of public concern from government officials, we have to let them know, loud and clear, that we care. If they don't hear from us, they'd assume we don't care. And they'd be right.

18

THE RIVER AND THE WATERSHED

THE WATERSHED OF HENRY'S FORK, WHICH INCLUDES ALL ITS TRIBUTARY streams, comprises some 4,000 square miles. That includes all the land that slopes toward the streams. It does not, as so many people think, mean just the valleys of those streams.

Hynes, wonderful man, wrote that the valley rules the river.* What he does not say is that without that river, there would be no valley. The first river in that valley may have been of ice, water in a different form, but a river nevertheless. It moved dowhill under the influence of gravity, cutting, shaping, making the valley conform to its will. With the warming of later years, the ice became water and a river as we think of it. It ran through the valley, shaping it as the ice had.

The valley may rule the river but it can never do so completely. It may influence the river, but that is all. No matter how hard the rock, the irresistible cutting force of the river will eventually remove it. It is only a matter of time and time means nothing to a river. The shape and condition of the valley will eventually be determined by the river that runs through it. That which moves will always, in time, have its way with that which does not. The hammer shapes the hot iron and not the reverse.

What Hynes meant when he said that the valley rules the river was that the valley conditions the river. Its rocks and minerals determines the availability of its ions, and eventually, its clay, soil, and the drainage slope. This soil, and the climate, determines what plants may grow in the valley, and these supply the stream's organic matter. The organic matter reacts with the soil to control the release of ions, and the ions, particularly nitrate and phosphate, control the decay of detritus, which becomes the base of the food-

*H. B. N. Hynes. *The Stream and Its Valley*. Edgardo Baldi Memorial Lecture. See Bibliography.

cycle pyramid. Since these items—rocks, minerals, climate, and the resulting plant life, are infinitely different for every watershed or valley—each stream is an individual, similar to, but different from any other. It is these differences which make it so difficult to classify streams. A chalk stream, for instance, merely means a stream that is rich in calcium bicarbonates. A one word description is pitifully inadequate to define the character and quality of a stream.

It is these complexities that help rivers gain such a hold on man and his imagination. One can never know a river completely; there is always a mystery there. That does not explain the complete attraction rivers have for us; some of it is undoubtedly primal. All life was originally born of water—our attachment is perhaps atavistic. It is deep within some people, closer to the surface in others. But it is always there.

Laurie Lee, writing of the Thames* and its hold upon the English people, wrote as follows:

> It seems impossible to write about a river without calling at times on terms of the simplest symbolism. For the river is an archetype covering much that is fundamental in human experience and aspiration. It is the flow of time, the stream of consciousness, the blood of earth, the milk of man, the very cycle of life in its endless motion between land, sea and sky. For hundreds of thousands of years the survival of man depended on the sweet waters of the river; it quenched his thirst, protected him from his enemies, cut him a pathway through the impenetrable forests, was the scene of his earliest settlements, was the fruitful and restless god that dominated his life. Even today there is still a profound magic and mystery about a river, for second only to the related sea it lies nearest to man's heart and imagination.

For some of us, it is not second, but first, and I am one of those.

The volcanic rock underlying Henry's Fork and all its tributaries has greatly influenced both the character and quality of the streams cutting through it. Volcanic outpourings are very rich in minerals, and these minerals come out mostly in a form that breaks down quickly into soil. Not all of it spews forth in the form of lava rock. Quantities of ash are found in nearly all volcanic areas; enormous amounts of ash at one time dammed Henry's Fork, and impeded glaciers in its watershed. In cold country, such as southeast Idaho, volcanic rock near the surface is broken down quickly by water seeping into billions of openings, freezing and fracturing the rock into volcanic dust.

Scientific evidence shows that for a 4,000-year period prior to 1870, southeast Idaho was much colder and wetter than it has been since 1870. This is borne out to some extent by the reports of whites early in the area. All comment on the severity of the winters. Osborne Russell noted often that

*Lee, Laurie. *The Thames*. (Portraits of Rivers) Ed. Eileen Molony. London: Dennis Dobson Ltd. No date.

the area from the mouth of the river to across Teton Basin was very cold in winter, and snows of two to five feet were common. Other comments reflect this: Henry's men in 1811 told of a very cold 1810–11 winter at Fort Henry, with deep snows.

Not all were so accurate in weather information as was Hudson's Bay Company's Alexander Ross. Ross carried an accurate thermometer and kept journals containing excellent weather records. On 16 June 1824, Ross recorded a foot of snow and a temperature of 15 degrees below zero Fahrenheit in the foothills just north of Fort Hall. The winter of 1822–23 around the mouth of Henry's Fork was written of as "bitter cold, with deep snow" by Michael Bourdon, Ross's predecessor with Hudson's Bay Company.

The significance of this is in the fact that major lava outpourings were going on in the Henry's Lake watershed as recently as 2,000 years ago. In most areas, it takes a thousand years to build an inch of topsoil. The U.S. Geological Survey notes that soil in the entire Henry's Fork-upper Snake River watershed is shallow, and in many places, nonexistent.

These are some of the factors making the Henry's Fork the kind of river it is. The shallow soil, if over impervious rock, such as the enormous beds of limestone that underlie the entire area, would not absorb enough water to prevent a constant cycle of floods and droughts. The porous lava rock absorbs the water and holds it, like a giant sponge. It gives it up slowly and keeps its temperature more constant. These factors, plus the minerals released into the river, are responsible for the Henry's Fork being the great trout stream that it is.

The natural conditions being what they are, the river will improve as a trout stream *if* it is left to nature. That is true even with the level of irrigation currently taking place. Damage by man's activities can cause short-term problems for the stream. How do we stand in that area?

It is a recorded fact that people take less care of public lands than of their own. But at present, the Targhee National Forest is in better shape than it was twenty years ago and indications are that it will gain, not lose, in the direction of better ecological protection. At present, the number of domestic animals grazing forest rangeland is below established grazing capacities. Cattle are at eighty-eight percent of authorized grazing capacity; sheep, those "cloven hoofed woolly locusts" as they have been described, are at only 56 percent of capacity. The amount of land involved is 1.8 million acres, or over half the entire watershed. However, Targhee National Forest is the most fragmented such piece of public land I've ever seen. It is not the great solid block that one thinks of when a national forest comes to mind. It is, instead, broken up into twenty odd separate and separated chunks, some many, many miles from others. This makes it very difficult to oversee and manage, as well as requiring more money and manpower than a contiguous block would. And the Targhee, like nearly all public land management areas, currently has budget restrictions that do not allow the Forest officials to do the job as well as they could.

The thing that the fisherman will most associate with the present Targhee

National Forest budget restrictions, is that miles and miles of roads (1,776 total miles) have deteriorated and some campgrounds, of sixteen in the Henry's Fork watershed, have not been properly maintained. With respect to Targhee's attitude in this matter, it is a question of priorities. My opinion is that the Forest is being pretty well operated considering its budget shortcomings. One might not agree with the priority ratings, but if the operations of this huge, fragmented area was thrust into *your* hands, could you do better and render just decisions in every case? Think it over before you come down on forest service personnel.

The appearance of much of the timber land of the Targhee is unsightly due to the enormous infestation by the pine bark beetle. But the thinning and clearing caused by the dead trees being harvested for firewood and other domestic uses is almost entirely beneficial. Because of this, large areas will now become covered with grass, flowers, vines and shrubs which will not only benefit animals and birds but the forest as a whole by improving the water-holding qualities of the soil.

Each inch of rain or the equivalent in snow puts 113 *tons* of moisture on each acre of land. Three things happen to the rainfall: it runs off, sinks in, or evaporates. Too much runoff not only causes erosion, but carries the water too quickly away from where it is needed. Evergreen forests, especially dense evergreen forests, increase evaporation by delaying the descent of moisture to the soil.

Sink-in, the most-desirable avenue for rainwater, lets the water percolate down through soil and rock, to eventually reach the water table or the stream. A water table which reaches the stream evens its flow, moderates its temperature fluctuation, and enriches it. A good watershed with varied ground cover is best to cause this latter, most-beneficial effect. As of right now, the lands under the control of Targhee National Forest are mostly in good to excellent condition to promote sink-in.

What about private lands? County agricultural agents tell me that things could be better. I'd agree with that. But I worked with Soil Conservation people and county agents for several years, and I make allowances. These people, among the most valuable in the services they perform, of all government employees, always think that watershed conditions could be improved. When I pressed the local county agents of Teton, Madison, and Fremont counties for specifics, they admitted that about eighty percent of private land was in good condition, about fifteen percent in fair condition, and only five percent in poor condition. And said they, things are slowly getting better in the areas of erosion control, rotative grazing and cropping, and more judicious agricultural practices. Too many people still plow and disc at the wrong time of year, when wind or rain carries away the freshly turned soil, and far too many till the soil right up to the edge of gullies and creeks. But the increasing cost of such practices, including fertilizer, is accomplishing what the county agents could not. It is causing more and more farmers to cease such practices and turn to ways to save their precious topsoil.

Of course, these counties are not alone in bad farming practices. Every year farmers in the U.S. lose about one cubic mile of topsoil into rivers and streams, and to wind. Since the only thing that will keep a farmer in business is topsoil, I cannot understand why they let this happen. It would be the equivalent of a truck line leaving its vehicles out in the rain with their hoods up, allowing engines to rust away. But still it happens.

Other people not directly involved in living off the land are much worse than farmers in their disregard of protecting it. I have never been able to understand this either, that people not only carelessly, but sometimes willfully destroy the only thing in the world that keeps the human race alive. Not only that, but these people strongly resist any effort to make them stop their destruction or to make repair. I find it all incomprehensible.

When you live in a house that is damaged, you make repairs or soon you will have no home. This earth is our home, the only one we will ever have. We have damaged it badly, and we have not yet seriously begun to halt that damage or to make significant repairs. How much more damage it can suffer without collapsing no one knows, but it is significantly less capable of being repaired now than it was when I was born.

We are seeing presently, in Africa, the cost of thousands of years of mis-use and neglect of the land. People, seeing the faces of the starving on television, say that the problem is drought. They do not seem to know or understand that stripping the land of its vegetable top cover over large areas for long periods will cause drought in that area. We saw an example of that in our own country.

It occurred in the 1930s and was known as the Dust Bowl. It was brought about by planting for wheat during the 1914–20 period when World War I caused a big demand for wheat. So wheat was planted on land that never should have had its top cover removed by the plow. It was not drought that caused the Dust Bowl—*it was the Dust Bowl that caused the drought.*

It is the memory of this and the fear that it could happen again or be more widespread that causes county agents to be so conservative. They also know that when things start to get better, as they have for the past several years, that people tend to believe that the problem is over and to relax the fight. On that basis, the agent's attitude is the correct one. They have to keep the pressure on, or we could backslide.

I've walked over and driven through some of the farms and ranches in the Henry's Fork watershed, chosen randomly. There are signs of past ero-sion. Great ditches, gullies, and ravines exist on most farms and ranches, *but* in many cases, these are not now eroding further. Deep sod and heavy grass cover exists on the bottom and sides; there are forbs, herbs, shrubs, and wildflowers along the banks, forming an undisturbed buffer zone.

Some ditches and gullies are still eroding but are healing. The farmers or ranchers have established buffer zones on the banks at the top of such ditches, and sod is forming down the sides. Only a very few ditches were still eroding without signs of change, except for the worse. It is these latter that trouble the county agents.

Why all this concern? Because every human on earth lives in a watershed, and the quality of life on this planet is directly related to the quality of its rivers, and they to the quality of the watersheds.

Look at the poorest nations. Almost without exception their rivers are muddy, wide, and shallow. They flood in rainy season and shrink in the dry season. Their watersheds are sparsely vegetated, or in some cases, no vegetation is left. Even in the tropics, where abundant rainfall, long-growing seasons, and lush growth occurs, many, many farms no longer will support crops and have been abandoned. The farmers—pursuing a cut, burn, plant, erode, move-on cycle—have destroyed the land they once farmed.

So the health of the Henry's Fork is dependent on the health of its watershed. By and large, that watershed is in good condition. I know of no severely damaged areas of significant size. In almost all areas there is improvement; the conditions are better than they were ten years ago. And there is recently a significant change in the attitude of the county and city governments that bodes very well for the future, not only for Henry's Fork, its tributaries and watershed, but for all southern Idaho.

It has come to light only recently that ground water throughout southern Idaho is more or less intimately connected throughout the entire area because of the nature of the Snake River Plain aquifer. What that means is that pollution of the ground water in one area will eventually show in many, many other areas miles away. There is, according to a recent statement by the state health department, no way to safeguard any single water supply. What endangers one endangers all. So, there is a move under way to establish laws declaring the entire Snake River Plain aquifer a single entity under the law. Anti-pollution controls and health measures will apply area-wide, not just in one community or county.

If this comes to pass, and I believe that it will, and relatively soon, it will be an enormous boon for not only Henry's Fork waters, but for all rivers, streams, ponds, lakes, and wells in southern Idaho—in fact, for all fresh water in the area. When this happens, the quality of life will improve. Both trout and humans—all life will benefit. A livable environment for trout really means a quality environment for all living creatures sharing that environment. That is why this book is as much about trout as it is anything else. If the trout vanish, everything else will soon follow. Not just here, but everywhere where the importance of rivers and watersheds is forgotten.

But the trout is more than the canary in the mine. Its pursuit brings enjoyment, relaxation, and economic benefits wherever it exists. It no longer does in many areas where it once did, and the quality of life there has deteriorated. People from those areas, having let their trout streams be destroyed, for whatever reason, now come here to Henry's Fork, to find what they once had but what is now lost. And they bring their hearts with them. As you may have guessed by now, mine is already here.

APPENDIX A:
A CONFUSION
IN NAMES

WHEN WHITE FUR TRADERS AND TRAPPERS BEGAN TO MOVE INTO THE area north of Saint Louis and west of the Missouri River, they began a naming of things which resulted in a confusion which exists to this day. There are a number of reasons for this.

The whites did not come in a steady flow, but instead, in a series of pulses. Thus one group would move in, name things, then move on. Later, another group would do the same, then another and another. But that was only part of the problem. Because they did not speak the language of the Indians of the areas and because of a poor comprehension of sign language by the whites, there were many misunderstandings.

It started with the names of the Indian tribes. Almost none of the Indian tribes of the Great Plains westward are known to us by the name they call themselves, or even by a reasonable translation of that name into English, or French. Then, translating French into English, or just the sound of a word into another language compounded the confusion. (For instance, there is a stream named *Purgatoire*, purgatory-hell. But American trappers rendered the name as *Picketwire*, a totally different meaning.)

Actually, confusion was already rampant when the first French fur traders came into the area of North Dakota in 1738.

These traders brought with them, as guides and trappers, Indians from the east: Cree, Iroquois, and Delaware. The name of this latter tribe came from Lord Thomas de la Warr, a British governor along the Atlantic coast. This name was applied to a bay, then to the river that ran into it, and then to the Indians who dwelt along its headwaters south of Lake Erie.

This tribe's name for itself was *Gendat* (island dwellers). The French rendered this *Houandate* (Hoo-wan-dot). From this sound, the American settlers evoked two names, *Huron*, from the first part of the word and *Wyandotte* from the entire word. Then, to help matters along, the settlers also called them *Eries* and *Delawares*.

Many Indian and place names will be popping up throughout this book. To avoid confusion (if possible) and to reduce repetition, I thought it wise to straighten out some names, of Indian tribes and of places, in this appendix.

First the Indians. Nearly all Indians of North America call themselves by a name which in their language means *people* or *the people*. Sometimes a descriptive word is added. When they named themselves, they knew nothing of other races. But most of the names we know Indian tribes by were given them by other Indian tribes whom whites encountered earlier. One of the tribes the trappers encountered very early in their westward trek was the Arapaho. This was not this tribe's name for itself; they called themselves *Inuna-ina* (our people). The practice of our calling an Indian tribe by the name given by another tribe is constant and pervasive, and this too, led to much confusion.

The tribe we call *Arikara* (Uh-rik-uh-ruh) were also called *Arikaree* and *Rees*. They called themselves *Tanish*, meaning *the people*. The Indians known today as *Crow* were called *raven* by the Dakotah branch of the Sioux. Early white trappers, unfamiliar with this western bird, rendered it *Crow*. But these Indians called themselves *Absaroka* (Ahb-sair-uh-kuh) meaning *hawk people*. The Lakotah Sioux were much closer with their naming of them, the Lakotah name, *Cetan Mani* (Chay-tahn Mah-nee), meant *hawk that walks*. (Incidentally, the trappers pronounced *Absaroka*: Absarkee, which some historians still insist is correct. It is not.)

The Atsina were called *Gros Ventres* (Groh vont—big bellies) by the French trappers, who mistook the Blackfeet sign for this tribe, which actually meant *always hungry*.

The Atsina (Gros Ventres) were a sub-tribe of the Arapaho that split with them about 1800, and took up residence in Canada in 1824 along the Milk River, north of the Montana border. They were located between the Blackfeet on the west and the Assinaboine on the east. Their proximity to the Blackfeet caused great confusion among trappers who called both tribes by each other's name. The best example of this is found in some reports of the Battle of Pierre's Hole in July 1832. Some, even most, trappers, said the fight was with the Gros Ventres, and careless historians have perpetuated this error. Actually, the Indians arrayed against the trappers and their allies in that affair were Blackfeet. I can find no authentic record of the Atsina being west of the Rockies in numbers at any time. They did encounter trappers and did have occasional run-ins with them east of the Rockies, mostly while in northern Wyoming visiting their relatives, the Northern Cheyenne. The Atsina, among more knowledgeable whites, were called *Gros Ventres of the Prairie*. The Hidatsa were known as *Gros Ventres of the Missouri*.

The Bannock of Idaho were the recipients of an English mispronunciation of their name *Pah ahnuk*, meaning *people from across the water*.

The Commanche called themselves *nemene*, meaning *people*. The Mandan were also known to the whites at times as Gros Ventres, as were the Hidatsa (Minnetaree) who lived near them. Today, the U.S. government, in its infinite wisdom, has officially declared that to be their name because these tribes now share a reservation.

This brings us to the Sioux, the first tribe encountered by trappers in the early 1800s as they moved up the Missouri River. It was from this tribe that the trappers learned the names of tribes, at least what the Sioux called them, that lived to the north and west. This is somewhat ironic. The name, *Sioux*, came from another tribe, the Ojibway (Chippewa) who called them *Nah-doh-wey-soo.* The French shortened it and changed the spelling to *Sioux.* But the tribes known collectively as the Sioux were known to themselves as *Dakotah* (eastern), *Nakotah* (northern) and *Lakotah* (western). The names are the way these tribes pronounced them, and all mean the same thing, friends or allies.

The name *Shoshoni* (Shoh-shoh-nee) comes from the Lakotah word for those tribes, *we-Chah-shah-nee,* meaning, literally, *unmanly.* The sign for this was a slow sinuous wiggle of the hand and forearm, with the hand vertically on edge. The trappers thought it meant *snake* and called them *Snake Indians.* Actually, the sign meant deceitful, devious, or untrustworthy, hence, unmanly.

The names *Shoshone, Shoshoni,* and *Shoshonean* also have caused confusion by the manner in which they were used. As nearly as I can make out from reliable and careful historians, the pronunciation and meaning of the words are as follows: *Shoshone* (Shoh-shohn) could mean one Indian or one band or one tribe of Shoshone Indians. *Shoshones* was plural for tribes or individuals (so written). *Shoshoni* (Shoh-shoh-nee) meant two or more tribes of Shoshone Indians. *Shoshonean* (Shoh-shoh-nee-an) meant any or all tribes that spoke the Shoshonean language. These were Bannock, Ute, Paiute, Commanche, and Shoshone and their sub-tribes. There were many sub-tribes of the Shoshone; the Snake River Plain Shoshone, the Boise River Shoshone, the Lemhi Shoshone, and the Eastern or Wind River Shoshone, perhaps others. All these were somewhat culturally different from each other. Originally, these tribes occupied the area of western Wyoming, central and southern Idaho, northeastern Nevada, and a bit of Utah west of Great Salt Lake. Stronger tribes pushed them into pockets of country of rather small area, except for the Snake River Plain Shoshone. The Bannock took the best of their country, leaving them the arid and inhospitable Snake River Plain. This group is presently known also as *Fort Hall Shoshone.*

Below are some western tribes' names as they called themselves, and what whites call them.

White Name	Tribal Name	What it Meant
Arapaho	Inuna-ina	our people
Arikara	Tanish	the people
Bannock	Pah'anuk	people from across the water
Blackfeet	Siksika	people
Commanche	Nemene	people
Crow	Absaroka	hawk people
Gros Ventres (Missouri)	Hidatsa	river people
	Minnetaree	

White Name	Tribal Name	What it Meant
Gros Ventres (Prairie)	Atsina	people
Mandan	Numakaki	people
Nez Percé	Nimipu	the people
Sioux	Dakotah	friends or allies
	Lakotah	
	Nakotah	

Several people—traders, a priest, some historians—tried to work out what the real name of the Shoshone (and Shoshoni) was, but were puzzled by the sign for that tribe, the slow, sinuous wiggle of hand and forearm with hand on edge. As seen above, the Sioux derivation was *unmanly.* Here are some others: Alexander Ross, who was among the Shoshone in the 1820s, called them *Snakes,* interpreting the sign to mean a quick, sliding motion when hiding from trouble.* Father De Smet, among them in the 1840s said they were so poor they ate food of snakes. Ake Hultkrantz thought the sign meant *grass weavers,* the Shoshone were known to other Shoshonean speaking members as *grass house people.* Robert G. Bailey believed they were *salmon people,* since salmon formed a major portion of their diet, and he thought the sign meant salmon swimming. But most experts in sign language agree that the sign did mean *devious or untrustworthy,* which all who knew them agreed that they were. Alexander Ross, Donald MacKenzie, Peter Skene Ogden—traders for the North West Company and later for the Hudson's Bay Company—all spent some years among the Shoshone and all referred to this trbe in writing as "devious."

When whites in numbers first came among the Shoshone in the 1820s, this tribe was poorly armed with inferior bows, flint-tipped arrows and lances, and stone knives, and had few horses. All tribes around them had already obtained horses and guns. The Shoshone were forced to deal with stronger, mounted, better-armed, and more agressive tribes diplomatically or be wiped out. Thus, the term *devious,* perhaps deserved, should carry no stigma. It was a matter of survival. The use of the name, Snake, for this tribe was also applied to the river. But that did not come until much later than 1820.

Lewis and Clark called the river *the Great South Branch of the Columbia.* In 1811, Wilson Price Hunt called it *Mad River.* Some traders referred to it as the *Lewis River,* or the Lewis Fork of the Columbia. French trappers with the Hudson's Bay Company named it *La Maudite Riviere Enragee* (Accursed Mad River).

---

*The sign for snake would have had the hand held flat, palm down; otherwise it was exactly the same as the sign for devious.

The various Indian tribes called it *Pohogawa, Saptin, Shahaptin, Sho-sho-nee-pah,* and *Piupa.* All these names in one manner or another referred to the tribes that dwelt along it.

How the name *Shoshone* came to be applied to that river in Wyoming is a complete puzzle. The Crow name for that stream, as mentioned earlier, meant *the river that runs by the stinking water,* and early trappers referred to it as the *Stinking Water.* I cannot find who first applied the name, *Shoshone,* nor the reasoning for it.

What we know now as the Teton River, tributary to Henry's Fork, was first called *Pierre's River,* and the basin, *Pierre's Hole,* as mentioned earlier. Other rivers also have been called by other names.

But it was in the naming of fur trading posts, especially along the Missouri River, that name confusion became rampant.

Manuel Lisa was the leader of the second white expedition up the Missouri in 1807. He began the practice of naming fur trading posts, although the first fort was established by Lewis and Clark near present Williston, North Dakota. It was named Fort Mandan, after the Indian tribe living there. But Lisa later established a fort called Mandan near the mouth of the Little Missouri River, many miles downstream. This fort was also known as Fort Manuel and Fort Lisa.

Lisa's first fort was Fort Raymond (also called Lisa, Manuel, and Remon) at the mouth of the Big Horn on the Yellowstone River. He also established a Fort Manuel on the Missouri at the mouth of Grand River, and Fort Lisa below the mouth of the Platte River (near Council Bluffs, Iowa).

The original Fort Henry was on Henry's Fork west of Saint Anthony, Idaho, but there was later a Fort Henry on the Missouri at the mouth of the Musselshell River, on the Missouri at the mouth of the Yellowstone River, and on the Yellowstone at the mouth of the Big Horn, near the original Fort Raymond.

There were a number of other forts: Fort Laramie at the junction of the North Platte and Laramie rivers, Fort Kiowa on the Missouri near present Brule, South Dakota, Fort Bridger in southwestern Wyoming—but the names of these forts were never confused by later names. The others caused enormous confusion because trappers would refer to the fort by the name that it had when they knew it. Historians, trying to piece information together, were sometimes unaware that the fort had other names in other periods or that forts by the same name had been located elsewhere.

If you don't think this is serious, consider the confusion of having three to five Jim Bridgers, not otherwise identified, operating in the Rocky Mountains over a forty-year period. People who make history are seldom concerned with recording it, and this is where confusion begins. Add to this the fact that trappers living for years in the wilderness sometimes lost track of what year it was, plus the fact that many trappers on whom historians later depended for information were undependable in their memories—and some were outright liars—then you can begin to perceive what an uncertain science the recording of history is.

APPENDIX B: NATURAL INSECTS AND ARTIFICIAL COUNTERPARTS

MAYFLIES

Dates of Emergence	Scientific Name	Common Name/ Hook Size	River Location

Dates of Emergence	Scientific Name	Common Name/ Hook Size	River Location

Dates of Emergence	Scientific Name	Common Name/ Hook Size	River Location
Mid-May	*Ameletus oregonensis*	Brown Dun (16)	Below Ashton Dam
Mid-June	*A. spartasus*	Brown Dun (16)	Below Ashton Dam
1 July through Mid-August	*Baetis bicaudatus*	Tiny Blue-Winged Olive (22)	Box Canyon to Riverside
Mid-July through late August	*B. insignificans*	Tiny Blue-Winged Olive(22–24)	Box Canyon to Riverside
15 July through Oct	*B. parvus*	Tiny Brown Dun (22)	Railroad Ranch
Late June through late July	*B. propinquis*	Tiny Blue Quill (22)	Box Canyon to Riverside
Entire season	*B. tricaudatus*	Blue-Winged Olive (16–18)	Box Canyon to Riverside
Mid-July through mid-August	*Callibaetis coloradensis*	Speckled Dun, Speckled Spinner (14)	Box Canyon to Riverside

August through Sept	C. nigritus	Speckled Spinner (16)	Box Canyon to Riverside
Mid-July	Cinygma dimicki	Light Cahill (12)	Mack's Inn to Osborne Bridge
August	Drunella coloradensis (formerly Ephemerella as were all Drunella genera below)	Slate Olive Dun (14)	Box Canyon to Riverside
15–30 June	Drunella flavilinea	Slate Wing Olive (16)	Entire river
Last half of June	D. grandis	Western Green Drake (10)	Box Canyon to Riverside
Late June through 10 July	Ephemera simulans	Brown Drake (10–12)	Box Canyon to Riverside
Late July	Epeorus longimanus	Brown Dun (14)	Box Canyon to Riverside
Late July	E. nitidus	Slate Maroon Drake (16)	Box Canyon to Riverside
10 June through August	Ephemerella inermis infrequens lacustris	Pale Morning Dun(16–18)	Entire river
Late Oct	Ephoron album	White May Dun, Snowflake Dun (12–14)	Below Ashton Dam
15–31 August	Heptagenia elegantula	Grey Dun (12–14)	Box Canyon to Riverside
July	Iron albertae (formerly Epeorus)	Slate Cream Dun (14)	Box Canyon to Riverside
Late August	Ironopsis grandis	Red Quill (14–16)	Box Canyon to Riverside
Late August through Sept	Paraleptophlebia bicornuta	Mahogany Dun (16–18)	Last Chance to Railroad Ranch
Mid-July through mid-August	P. heteronea	Black Quill (18)	Box Canyon to Riverside

15 July through Oct	*Pseudocloeon edmundsi*	Tiny Blue-Winged Olive (22–24)	Railroad Ranch
Early June	*Rhithrogena hageni*	Olive Dun (16–18)	Box Canyon to Riverside
Mid-late April	*R. morrisoni*	not known (14–16)	Box Canyon to Riverside
15 August through 1 Sept	*Siphlonurus occidentalis*	Grey Drake (8–10)	Box Canyon to Riverside
Early July through Sept	*Stenonema terminatum*	Light Cahill (14)	Box Canyon to Riverside
Month of August	*Tricorythodes minutus*	White Wing Black (22)	Box Canyon to Riverside

CADDISFLIES

The various caddis emerge all season, and it is not really necessary to identify them to species level; members of a genera may vary in size and color but not in habits or habitat. The most prevalent genera are *Brachycentrus* and *Rhyacophila*. For the dry version, Elk Hair Caddis or Colorado King in sizes 12 to 20 will be needed to cover all hatches, and one needs them with grey, brown, and green bodies. This will cover nearly 100 species of these two genera and some others as well. To fish the pupal imitation, grouse- or partridge-hackled wets in size 12 through 18 with yellow, brown, tan, gray, and green bodies serve well enough. Larval imitations in the same color scheme will work at times.

STONEFLIES

Except for the Salmon Fly (*Pteronarcys* and *Calineuria, californicas*), and the Yellow Sallys (*Isoperla*), dry stonefly patterns are generally not needed. (See Appendix C.)

Pteronarcys and *Calineuria* emerge (hatch) from mid-May on the lower river to mid-June on the upper river in all fast, rocky waters. Any of the big (size 4, 3XL or 4XL) black nymph patterns, of which there are more than twenty, will work for the underwater form of *Pteronarcys*. These include Bitch Creek Nymph, Box Canyon Stone, Montana Nymph, Montana Stone (my pattern), Black Stone, Troth's Terrible Stone, Black Nature Nymph, Girdle Bug, Kaufmann's Stone, Soufal, and the black Wooly Worm. There are others. *Calineuria, Doroneuria,* and *Hesperoperia* are represented by my Yellow Stone nymph pattern and by the Amber Stone and Golden Stone commercial nymph patterns in size 8, 2XL; size 6, 2XL; and size 4, 3XL.

Yellow Sally is actually not one species (there are over fifty species in the genus *Isoperla*). Several patterns above in the smallest size will work for this, but one needs the dry pattern in Appendix C.

APPENDIX C: ARTIFICIALS, PATTERNS, AND TYING INSTRUCTIONS

MOST USED FLIES (COMMERCIAL) OF THE AREA

Dry Flies

Name	Type	Size
Name	Type	Size
Adams	Mayfly-caddis	10–16
Blue Dun	Mayfly	16–18
Blue-Winged Olive	"	14–18
Light Cahill	"	14–16
Pale Morning Dun	"	16
Slate Wing Olive	"	14–16
Speckled Dun, Spinner	"	14–16
Tups Indispensable (Onc of the best light general dries.)	"	14–16
Western Green Drake	"	10
Western Quill Gordon	"	12–14
White Wing Black	"	20
White Wing Sulphur Dun	"	20–22
Colorado King	Caddis	12–18
Elk Hair Caddis	"	10–18
Goddard Caddis	"	10–14
Henryville Special	"	12–16

Kings River Caddis	"	12–16
Bucktail Caddis	"	6–12
Great Orange Sedge	"	8, 2XL
Bird's Stonefly	Stonefly	4–6, 3XL
Bucktail Caddis (yellow body)	"	6-8, 3XL
Henry's Fork Salmon Fly	"	4–6, 3XL
Parks' Salmon Fly	"	4–6, 3XL
Troth's Salmon Fly	"	4, 3XL
Sofa Pillow	"	4–6, 3XL

Not all these patterns will be found in any one shop, also, there are eight or ten other patterns of the salmon fly sold in this area.

Dave's Hopper	Grasshopper	6–10, all 3XL
Henry's Fork Hopper	"	"
Letort Hopper	"	"

Cricket, ant, and beetle patterns will be found in most shops, by those names only. A good selection is one of the most important additions to your dry fly arsenal.

Grey Fox Variant	General	10–12
Hair Wing Variant (House and Lot)	"	10–12
Grey Wulff	"	"
Renegade	"	10–14
Royal Wulff	"	10–14
Royal Trude	"	"
Bivisibles	"	"
Goofus Bug (Humpy)	"	10–16

Nymphs

Amber Stone	Stonefly	4, 3XL to 8, 2XL
Golden Stone	"	"
Yellow Stone (my pattern)	"	"
Martinez Black	Stonefly-Mayfly	10–14
Ida May	Mayfly	10–12
Pheasant Tail	General	8–16
Gray Nymph	"	8–10
Muskrat Nymph	"	8–10
Fledermaus	"	8–10
Casual Dress	"	8–10
Tellico (One of the best general nymphs)	"	10–14, all 1XL
Gold Ribbed Hare's Ear (the best general nymph)	"	8–16
Zug Bug	General	10–16

Wet Flies

Grouse and brown, green, grey, orange, tan, and yellow bodies	Caddis	8–14
Brown Hackle, peacock	General	10–12
Carey Special	"	4–12
Blue Dun	May	12–18
Mallard Quill	"	14–16
Wooly Worm, yellow, brown, and olive bodies	"	8, 3X to 4, 4XL

Miscellaneous

Leeches, Matukas, streamers, bucktails, Wooly Buggers, Zonkers, and Aztecs are used all up and down Henry's Fork and its tributaries. Most do not have recognizable commercial names. Most shops carry a good selection but no shop will have all these patterns.

Below are tying instructions for some patterns that are quite useful but which either are not tied commercially, or are available only from limited sources.

YELLOW SALLY (AMERICAN)

HOOK: 10, 1XL light wire

TAIL: None

BODY: Fur or synthetic dubbing. Rear third, crimson, front two thirds, yellow or gold.

HACKLE: Ginger or light cree. Proper size for hook.

WING: Pale yellow polypropylene

THREAD: 6/0 primrose yellow

With hook in vise, barb mashed down, attach thread at bend. Tie on hackle by tip at bend. Spin on crimson dubbing one third shank length. Spin on yellow dubbing *to eye*. Body should be thickness of large darning needle or bodkin. Wind hackle palmer to just back of eye, there wind three closely spaced turns. Tie off, clip excess feather. Clip hackle very close on top, to about one-eighth inch on bottom. Leave sides full length. One must use hackle of proper size for the hook. Select a clump of polypropylene size of kitchen match, one and a half inches long. Tie on just back of eye to lie flat on top. Clip front material and finish head. Then, clip wing at back straight across so that it is one-third hook length longer than the hook.

This fly, a yellow stone fly, is imitative of a group of small yellow stoneflies found throughout the northern Rockies, and in the northwest from about San Francisco to the Canadian border. There are several species called Yellow Sallys—there may even be two or three genera. This fly will work for all of them. They hatch from May through September in the different waters. Not much is known about them and entomologists have suggested that the yellow stoneflies of *Isoperla*, *Alloperla*, and perhaps even *Isogenus* are all called Yellow Sally. It is of no importance; if there is a small yellow stone fly adult on the water or in the air, this pattern will usually work for it.

IDA MAY NYMPH

Although this, the most commercialized of my original patterns, is a may-fly imitation—*Drunella grandis,* the Western Green Drake—it also works for other dark mayfly nymphs, and for the smaller black stonefly nymphs.

HOOK: 10, 1XL regular wire.
TAIL: Soft, webby grizzly hackle dyed dark green.
BODY: Black yarn or fur.
RIB: Peacock herl, bronze.
OVERRIB: Fine gold wire.
HACKLE: Soft, webby grizzly dyed dark green.
THREAD: 6/0 black.

With hook in vise, barb mashed down, attach thread at bend. Tie in tail, about six fibers two thirds length of hook shank. Tie on gold wire and body material. Wind or dub body, tapered bluntly; that is, rather full from just forward of tail to just back of eye, fuller at thorax. End up tying off at base of thorax. Tie in one good, full, bronze peacock herl. Spiral herl *back* to tail, catch with one wrap of gold wire right at base of tail. Spiral wire forward over peacock herl to base of thorax. Tie off, clip excess herl at rear and wire at thorax. Spiral thread to just back of eye, working it down into thorax material. Tie on hackle and wind one-and-one-half turns. Hackle should slope rearward. Tie off, clip, and finish head rather large. If desired, three or four turns of lead wire, .025 inches, can be wound at thorax position before fly is started.

EMERGER IDA MAY

This fly was developed after I found that I got many strikes when the nymph came to the surface straight down stream due to current action, at the end of the drift. That still happens with the regular Ida May, but when it does, I switch over to this emerger because I get more hits on a drift, can almost always see the swirl of the take, and thus better hook the fish.

HOOK: 10, 1XL light wire.
TAIL: Very webby grizzly dyed dark green.
RIB: Peacock herl.
OVERRIB: Fine gold wire.
BODY: Furry Foam, beige, split or separated.
HACKLES: Webby grizzly dyed dark green.
THREAD: 6/0 black.
Two Pantone Markers, numbers Black-M and Olive 399M.

With hook in vise, barb mashed down, attach thread at bend. Tie in tail, four to six fibers of very webby grizzly dyed dark green. Tail is short, about three-eighths inch. Tie in gold wire. Cut strip of Furry Foam one-quarter inch wide, four inches long. Separate (pull apart) the layers, so that you have two strips. One will have a crisscross grid of nylon reinforcement fibers. Lay this aside for other use. Tie on the other at bend. Wind body, tapered bluntly, with *full* thorax. You will find that by adjusting the strength of pull, you can thin out or thicken the Furry Foam. You wind it just to make the body thicker. Finish at base of thorax and tie off. Clip excess. Tie on one bronze peacock herl at base of thorax and spiral back to bend. Wind one full turn of gold wire at tail, spiral gold wire forward to base of thorax, and tie off. Clip excess wire at thorax and herl at tail. Wind thread forward in a spiral and sink the thread into the body material. Tie on hackle, wind one turn, tie off, clip excess. Finish head large.

With olive Pantone marker, color back and down sides of body about halfway. Make dark by going over several times. With black marker, color thorax black over olive already there.

After catching several fish with this emerger, it may *appear* to have lost its effectiveness. Simply squeeze it in a pad of tissue, toilet paper, or other absorbent material, and it will float higher and become effective again. Or, if it doesn't, it's time to switch to a dry Green Drake.

LAZY LEECH

HOOK: 6, 2XL

BODY: Lead wire on hook shank covered with beige floss.

LEECH: A 3½- to 4-inch strip of car washing shammy, ⅜ inch wide at front, tapering to ¼ inch at rear. Color with Pantone marker, olive or brown.

TAIL AND GILLS: Olive or brown marabou.

With hook in vise, barb mashed down, wind lead wire to one quarter inch back of eye. Cover with floss or other material, coat with cement. Remove from vise, insert a needle in vise and clamp. Attach winding thread to needle, then tie tail end of shammy strip *on top* of needle. Tie on short bunch of marabou of proper color. Make several half hitches, cut thread, cement bindings, let dry. Slip off needle, put hook back in vise, attach thread (color to match leech) and tie on shammy leech by head end. Pointing this end before tying on helps avoid bulk. Tie a short bunch of marabou, proper color, under the *chin,* finish head and cement.

One can vary the length of the *tail* and *gills* on this fly but about an inch seems best. Of course, leeches have no gills, the addition of the marabou is to provide better action. Do not use too bulky a bunch of marabou for either tail or gills.

BIBLIOGRAPHY

Beal, Merrill D. *A History of Southeastern Idaho.* Caldwell: The Caxton Printers, 1942.

Beal, Merrill D. *Intermountain Railroads: Standard and Narrow Gauge.* Caldwell: The Caxton Printers, 1962.

Beal, Merrill D. *I Will Fight No More Forever.* Seattle: The University of Washington Press, 1963.

Beal, Samuel. *The Snake River Fork Country.* Rexburg: The Rexburg Journal, 1935.

Bergman, Ray. *With Fly, Plug, and Bait.* New York: William Morrow and Co., 1947.

Berry, Don. *A Majority of Scoundrels.* New York: Harper and Brothers, 1961.

Boyle, Robert H., and Eric Leiser. *Stoneflies for the Angler.* New York: Alfred A. Knopf, 1982.

Blankinship, J. W. *The Native Economic Plants of Montana.* Bozeman: Montana College Agricultural Experiment Station, 1905.

Blevins, Winfred. *Give Your Heart to the Hawks.* New York: Avon Books, 1973.

Brackenridge, Henry M. *Views of Louisiana. Together with a Journal of a Voyage up the Missouri River in 1811.* Chicago: Kraus Publishers, 1815.

Bradbury, John. *Travel in the Interior of America in the years 1809, 1810, and 1811.* Liverpool: Sherwood, Neely and Jones, 1817.

Brown, Jennie Broughton. *Fort Hall on the Oregon Trail.* Caldwell: The Caxton Printers, 1932.

Clements, Louis J. *A Collection of Upper Snake River Valley History, and Biography of Andrew Henry.* Rexburg: Eastern Idaho Publishing Co., 1968.

Clements, Louis J., and Harold Forbush. *Pioneering the Snake River Fork Country.* Rexburg: Eastern Idaho Publishing Co., 1972.

Dana, Richard Henry. *Two Years Before the Mast.* New York: P. F. Collier and Son Corp., 1909, 1971.

Deloria, Vine, Jr. *God is Red.* New York: Grosset and Dunlap, 1973.

Driggs, B. W. *History of Teton Valley, Idaho.* Edited by Louis J. Clements and Harold Forbush. Rexburg: Eastern Idaho Publishing Co., 1970.

Farb, Peter. *Man's Rise to Civilization as Shown by the Indians of North America.* New York: E. P. Dutton Co., 1968.

Ferris, Warren A. *Life in the Rocky Mountains (1830–1835)*. Denver: The Old West Publishing Co., 1940.

Gard, Wayne. *The Great Buffalo Hunt*. New York: Alfred A. Knopf, 1960.

Gilbert, Bill. *The Trail Blazers*. New York: Time-Life Books, 1973.

Green, Dean H., and James L. Allison. *Idaho's Gateway to Yellowstone: The Island Park Story*. Mack's Inn: Island Park-Gateway Publishing Co., 1974.

Hafele, Rick, and Dave Hughes. *Western Hatches*. Portland: Frank Amato Publications, 1981.

Hafen, Leroy R., ed. *The Mountain Men and the Fur Trade of the Far West*. 10 vols. Glendale: The Arthur H. Clark Co., 1965–72.

Haines, Aubrey. *The Bannock Indian Trail*. Mammoth: The Yellowstone Library and Museum Association, 1964.

Haines, Francis. *Indians of the Great Basin and Plateau*. New York: G. P. Putnam's Sons, 1970.

Haines, Francis. *The Nez Percé*. Norman: The University of Oklahoma Press, 1955.

Haines, Francis. *The Plains Indians*. New York: Thomas Y. Crowell Co., 1976.

Hall, Leonard. *Stars Upstream*. Columbia: The University of Missouri Press, 1969.

Hanson, Charles E. Jr. *The Plains Rifle*. New York: Bramhall House, 1960.

Harris, Burton. *John Colter, His Years in the Rockies*. New York: Charles Scribner's Sons, 1952.

Hill, Ruth Beebe. *Manta Yo*. New York: Doubleday and Co., 1979.

Hodges, Frederick W. *Handbook of American Indians North of Mexico*. 2 vols. New York: Pageant Books, 1971.

Holt, Vincent M. *Why Not Eat Insects*. Hampton: E. W. Classey Ltd., 1885.

Hultkranz, Ake. *Shoshone Indians*. New York and London: Garland Publishers, 1974.

Hyde, George E. *Indians of the High Plains*. Norman: University of Oklahoma Press, 1959.

Hynes, H. B. N. *The River and Its Valley:* Edgardo Baldi Memorial Lecture. Stuttgart: Verh. International Verein, Limnologist. October, 1975.

Irving, Washington. *The Adventures of Captain Bonneville*. Edited and annotated by Edgeley W. Todd. Norman: University of Oklahoma Press, 1961.

James, Thomas. *Three Years Among the Indians and Mexicans*. Philadelphia and New York: J. B. Lippincott Co., 1962.

Jennings, Jesse D., ed. *Ancient Native Americans*. San Francisco: W. H. Freeman and Co., 1978.

Kroeber, Alfred. *Ethnology of the Gros Ventres*. Anthropological Paper of the American Museum of Natural History, vol. I, Part 4. New York: American Museum of Natural History, 1908.

Lavender, David. *The Rockies*. New York: Harper and Row, 1968.

Lee, Laurie. *The Thames*. Portraits of Rivers, edited by Eileen Malony. London: Dennis Dobson Ltd., no date.

Lovell, Edith Haroldsen. *Captain Bonneville's County*. Idaho Falls: The Eastern Idaho Farmer, 1963.

MacDonald, Alexander. *Design for Angling*. Boston: Houghton, Mifflin Co., 1947.

—————. *On Becoming A Fly Fisherman*. New York: David McKay Co., 1959.

Madsen, Brigham D. *The Bannock of Idaho*. Caldwell: The Caxton Printers, 1958.

—————. *The Northern Shoshoni*. Caldwell: The Caxton Printers Ltd., 1980.

McCafferty, W. Patrick. *Aquatic Entomology*. Boston: Science Books International, 1981.

Manfred, Frederick. *Lord Grizzly*. Lincoln: University of Nebraska, 1954.

Marker, Joe L. *Eagle Rock, U.S.A.* No publisher or date.

Myers, John Myers. *The Saga of Hugh Glass*. Boston: Little, Brown and Co., 1963.

Oglesby, Richard Edward. *Manuel Lisa and the Opening of the Missouri Fur Trade*. Norman: University of Oklahoma Press, 1963.

Quammen, David. "Living Water." *Montana Outdoors,* May/June 1981.

Replogle, Wayne F. *Yellowstone's Bannock Indian Trails*. Mammoth: The Yellowstone Library and Museum Association, 1956.

Robertson, Frank. *Fort Hall*. New York: Hastings House, 1963.

Roe, Frank Gilbert. *The Indians and the Horse*. Norman: University of Oklahoma Press, 1955.

Ross, Alexander. *The Fur Hunters of the Far West*. Chicago: R. R. Donnelley and Sons, 1924.

Russell, Osborne. *Journal of a Trapper (1834–1843)*. Edited by Aubrey L. Haines. Lincoln: University of Nebraska Press, 1955.

Ruxton, George F. *Life in the Far West*. Edited by Leroy Hafen. Norman: University of Oklahoma Press, 1959.

Schooling, Sir William, K.B.E. *The Hudson's Bay Company, 1670–1920*. London: Hudson's Bay House, 1920.

Schwiebert, Ernest. *Nymphs*. New York: Winchester Press, 1973.

Smith, Robert B., and Robert L. Christiansen. "Yellowstone Park as a Window on the Earth's Interior." *Scientific American,* February 1980.

Snake River Echoes. Rexburg: Upper Snake River Valley Historical Society. Volume 10, No. 3. No author or date.

Stearns, Harold T., Lynn Crandall, Willard G. Steward, *Geology and Ground Water Resources of the Snake River Plain in Southeastern Idaho*. Washington, D.C.: U.S. Government Printing Office, 1938.

Sterling, Matthew W. *Indians of the Americas*. Washington, D.C.: The National Geographic Society, 1955.

Swisher, Doug, and Carl Richards, *Selective Trout*. New York: Crown Publishers, 1971; Nick Lyons Books, 1983.

Terrell, John Upton. *American Indian Almanac*. New York and Cleveland: The World Publishing Co., 1971.

Thomas, Janet. *This Side of the Mountains*. Idaho Falls: Harris Publishing Inc., 1975.

Thomas, Janet, Bernice McCowin, Mary Tingey, and Margaret Thomas, eds. *That Day in June, Reflections on the Teton Dam Disaster*. Rexburg: Ricks College Press, 1977.

Van Wormer, Joe. *The World of the Moose*. New York: J. B. Lippincott Co., 1972.

Vinton, Stallo. *John Colter, Discoverer of Yellowstone Park*. New York: E. Eberstadt, 1926.

Williams, Kim. *Eating Wild Plants*. Missoula: Mountain Press Publishing Co., 1984.

Wissler, Clark. *North American Indians of the Plains*. New York: The Anthropological Handbook Fund, 1948.

INDEX

Index to Insects and Artificial Flies